# SACRED PLACES

## The Biblical Theology of Place, Exploring Its Central Importance in God's Creation and Mission

"An expository journey through place, from the Garden of Eden to the New Jerusalem. Discovering the pattern of placement, displacement and re-placement in life and faith"

## C.J. SCOTT

WESTBOW
PRESS®
A DIVISION OF THOMAS NELSON
& ZONDERVAN

In partnership with Worldwide Mission Fellowship.
www.wwmf.org

A Humble Majesty Publication. www.humblemajesty.com

WestBow Press books may be ordered through booksellers or by contacting:

WestBow Press
A Division of Thomas Nelson & Zondervan
1663 Liberty Drive
Bloomington, IN 47403
www.westbowpress.com
1 (866) 928-1240

ISBN: 978-1-5127-7634-8 (sc)
ISBN: 978-1-5127-7635-5 (hc)
ISBN: 978-1-5127-7633-1 (e)

Library of Congress Control Number: 2017903035

Print information available on the last page.

WestBow Press rev. date: 05/03/2017

DEDICATED TO

GOD, THE FIRST PLACE MAKER
AND TO ANITA (MOTHER) GREENIDGE,
WHO MADE A PLACE FOR US

# CONTENTS

## Section 4:   Narrative

## Section 5:   History

# Section 6:    Application

# Section 7:    Study

# LANGUAGE NOTES

## Bible Translation

Unless otherwise indicated, all Scripture quotations are from the ESV® Bible (The Holy Bible, English Standard Version®), copyright © 2001 by Crossway, a publishing ministry of Good News Publishers. Used by permission. All rights reserved.

In line with the English language and the tradition of the KJV and ESV, I use a lower case he or him to refer to God as a proper person rather than a capital He or Him as found in other translations like the NIV and NKJV.

## Abbreviations

OT: Old Testament
NT: New Testament
ANE: Ancient Near East
ESV: English Standard Version
KJV: King James Versions
NIV: New International Version
NKJV: New King James Version

## Common Terms

### Place

When I say "place," I mean a specific location. The particular use of the word in this book is in regard to a space that has been endowed with special significance and worth through the decree and presence of God, and is therefore known as a "sacred place." A space can in a lesser sense become a place through normal people or events that endow it with importance.

### Space

A specific or less specific area that has not been endowed with particular importance or worth by God, men, or events.

## God-man

The two distinct natures of Jesus the Christ, namely the 100 percent human nature and the 100 percent God nature, unified in one person. In his incarnation, Jesus the eternal Word, who is God became flesh, becoming fully man while remaining fully God.

## Holy love

When this term is used, I mean it in the sense used by John Stott in *The Cross of Christ* to explain that which had to be satisfied by the penal substitutionary sacrifice of Jesus on the cross.

P. T. Forsyth is quoted as being a strong proponent for speaking of God's holy love rather than his love or holiness in isolation, which can be open to gross misinterpretation. He said, "Without a holy God there would be no problem of atonement. It is the holiness of God's love that necessitates the atoning Cross."[1]

## Gnosticism

Gnosticism is a complex set of beliefs, but at its core it denounces the entire physical world as inherently evil, believing that the one who created it (our God, Yahweh) is really the devil for trapping pure spirits in a prison of flesh, while Satan, the serpent in the Garden, is really God, seeking to enlighten and free man.

## Dualism

This is a philosophical position that affirms—among other things—that good and evil, spiritual and physical, God and the devil are all equal opposites. We, as Bible-believing Christians firmly disagree with this view of reality, which is embraced by Gnosticism.

We also disagree with the dualism proposed by Plato and adapted by many after him, which sees the world as having two very distinct stories: the upper story of the spiritual, faith, and God versus the lower story of the physical, facts, and experience.

---

[1] Peter Taylor Forsyth, *The Work of Christ* (London; Toronto: Hodder and Stoughton; The Westminster Company, n.d.), 79–80.

## Singular Field of Knowledge

We affirm that God created all realms, both physical and spiritual, and so believe in a single rather than divided fields of knowledge. We call this unified or total truth affecting all of life.

## Theology

The study of God, his ways, and message as revealed in his word recorded in the Bible. Theology can be understood as a science; it was once called the queen of the sciences because it gave purpose and a narrative framework to the discoveries of the other major scientific disciplines.

With its focus on the objective truth of God's revelation in the Bible, it stands apart from mere social science or philosophy.

# PREFACE

*Sacred Places* is a book that looks at the biblical theology of place, exploring its central importance in God's creation and mission. It takes its readers on an expository journey through place, from the Garden of Eden to the New Jerusalem, discovering the pattern of placement, displacement, and re-placement in life and faith.

If you are a Christian seeking to understand the Bible's teaching on place and how that affects both our faith and lives in the world, then this book is for you. It will open your eyes to the central importance of place and give you direction on how you can apply a healthy understanding of place to your life as a disciple of Jesus Christ, making you a better place maker and dweller.

Even if you are not Christian, I pray this book will open your eyes to the importance of place and point you to the original place maker, God, and his Son, Jesus Christ, who has gone to prepare a place for all those who put their faith and trust in him.

# INTRODUCTION

*H*ave you ever taken the time to consider the importance of place(s) or, better still, the difference between a space and a place? If you have, how about mere place as opposed to a sacred place? If like me, you have grown up in the relative wealth of the West, then it is unlikely that you have thought deeply or even consciously about these questions.

The thesis of this book is that place is far more important than we ever could have imagined. I am specifically proposing that (1) places are sacred because of God's decree and personal presence, (2) place plays a major role in God's creative and redemptive purposes, and (3) God's people are called to be both place makers and dwellers.

This book will focus on why places are so important and will focus in particular on things like the theology of place in the Bible, the centrality of place to the human experience, the land of Israel, places of worship, the promise of place in the gospel, and defining "place making" in the Earth.

One aim will be to highlight the lack of importance we have toward place in regard to life and theology. This is partly due to our Puritan heritage as evangelical Christians, whose ancestors understandably reacted against the state church in their day that had such a distorted view of place that too much emphasis was put on buildings and aesthetics. Their reaction caused the Puritans to swing the pendulum too far in the other direction by neglecting the natural and biblical order for place in both faith and life.

We will be seeking the biblical perspective on the importance of not just places but sacred places.

I've been married to my wife, Michelle, since June 2006. We have two beautiful children: our seven-year-old daughter, Hope, and four-year-old son, Joshua. I fellowship and serve at our church—Worldwide Mission Fellowship in West Norwood, which is in the south of London—in a number of capacities, including teaching, youth, and media ministries.

I have had the great joy and privilege to study the Bible and write about what I find ever since I started to read the Bible seriously, just before my twenty-first birthday back in 1999. It was at that time that God graciously brought this prodigal son from death to life.

It was in recent years, after an unexpected commission from my friend and pastor, Dennis Greenidge, that my writing and teaching ministry went public, with quite basic daily notes and reflections for our church's Bible reading plan in 2014, which takes us through the entire Bible each year.

Prior to this, my writing has been private or for projects with our local church media team, like "The Gospel, what is it and how does it affect you" in 2012 © Worldwide Mission Fellowship, and the media tract "Heaven or Hell" in 2009.

One of my callings in the body of Christ is to teach, and it seems the Lord has led that writing should be one of the mediums of this call. This is a book among others I have considered, prayed about, and felt inspired to write.

This is quite a remarkable development in my life because I don't consider myself a good writer and did not grow up thinking *Hmm, I would love to write a book*. In college, I was diagnosed with quite severe dyslexia, one of the symptoms being that while reading for any period of time, my overly dominant eyes start to fight each other, which results in the words shifting on the page.

Even teaching is a surprising development in my life. Growing up, friends and family always said I should teach, but I was never convinced. Yet, events conspired in such a way that for the majority of my professional life I have been a trainer or teacher. This really is remarkable because as a child I had a persistent stuttering tongue; I could barely string a sentence together, and now I speak publicly in my career (I have a full-time secular job) and now in service to the church too.

It would seem, in my case, that God has seen fit to glorify his name in my weaknesses rather than natural or obvious strengths. Any ability or opportunity I have been afforded to teach and write is only by his grace and surely by his strength and Spirit because without him I honestly could not do this.

I scraped through my A Levels in college and later in life did a vocational certificate to teach in further education at Canterbury Christ Church University, but I do not have a university degree, any letters after my name, nor have I been to Bible college. All of those are good things and worthy of pursuing, but that has not been the journey of my life. All of this, like Paul's thorn in the flesh, makes me even more reliant on God's sufficient grace to accomplish the tasks he has laid before me, to the glory of his name and the joy of all peoples.

In any case, I compiled a short list in 2014 of potential volumes I would consider writing. These included:

- *365-Day Daily Devotional Bible Study:* Based on the work published via our website and app (this seemed like the most obvious choice as a first book).
- *Humble Majesty: Our Identity in Christ:* A title that will be focused on discipleship and Christian character.
- *The Christian and Color?:* Challenging the status quo with regard to the language we use to describe men from different tribes, people groups, and languages.
- *A Christian View of Black History:* There are a lot of lies circulating about so-called "black history," and at the same time legitimate issues in that history remain lacking in their treatment by the church. This book would take an evangelical, apologetic, and corrective approach to the issues.
- Apologetics book/blog: Since making this list, I wrote and delivered a six-week apologetics course to our church at the request of Rev. Taylor. The course was called "Hold and Advance, Christian Apologetic Essentials" which may one day become a book.
- Ephesians study: An exegetical Bible study of the book.
- John study: An exegetical Bible study of the book.
- Romans study: An exegetical Bible study of the book.
- *Defending the Bible in English:* A response to KJV-only advocates.

It was while sitting in a place called Succat Hallel, a twenty-four-hour prayer center in the ancient city of Jerusalem, in February 2015 that I felt the Lord leading my heart to write this book first. This happened as we looked out of the panoramic windows in the prayer room, which overlook Jerusalem. I considered why this place of all places was so hotly contested, fought over, and yet so loved and revered by the majority of the world's population. We will explore the answers to this and related questions throughout the book.

I first began to think about the theology of place after attending a seminar in March 2013 at Spring Harvest in the UK with my wife, Michelle, and our two children, Hope and Joshua. At the camp, Graham Cray and Ruth Valerio briefly mentioned in a morning session called "The Think Zone" the fact that place as a concept is important but has been somewhat neglected in Christian literature.

The seeds that seminar watered were planted over many years under the teaching and discipleship of my own pastor, Dennis Greenidge at WWMF. Pastor Dennis would always emphasize the importance of places in the Bible, the meaning behind the names of these places, and in particular the significance of the land of Israel itself.

He had specifically mentioned years before about God healing the land and how strong the spiritual connection is between the people and the land on which they live.

This was all underscored by years of discipleship, which has involved (1) retreats away to special places (Ashburnham Place and Bore Place are two examples) to be alone with God, pray, and be taught the Bible; (2) mission trips to some of the most remote places of the Earth, from the north of Norway to Rwanda; and (3) many pilgrimages, tours, and prayer trips to Israel.

It is important that I make my presuppositions or starting position clear. I am an evangelical Christian. I believe the Bible is the inspired and inerrant word of God and that, as a cannon, it is closed or complete and so cannot be added to as holy Scripture.

I believe that God created everything. In particular, I believe the Earth was created in six literal days just a few thousand years ago as recorded in the Book of Genesis.

I would classify my theology as distinctly reformed. My beliefs follow the trajectory of the Protestant Reformation and align to both the Apostles' Creed and Nicene Creed. These beliefs are summarized well in the founding documents of my home church, Worldwide Mission Fellowship, as follows:

> We believe that the **Scriptures** of the Old and New Testaments are divinely inspired and completely inerrant in the original writings and of supreme and final authority in all matters of faith and life.

*We believe in* **one sovereign God**, *existing in three persons: Father, Son, and Holy Spirit, perfect in holiness, infinite in wisdom, unbounded in power, and measureless in love; that God is the source of all creation and that through the immediate exercise of His power, all things came into being.*

*We believe that* **Jesus the Messiah** *was eternally pre-existent and is co-equal with God the Father; that He took on Himself the nature of man through the virgin birth so that He possesses both divine and human natures.*

*We believe in* **His sinless life** *and perfect obedience to the Father's will; in His atoning death, burial, bodily resurrection, ascension into heaven, high-priestly intercession and His personal return in power and glory to consummate the prophesied purposes concerning His kingdom.*

*We believe that the* **Holy Spirit** *is co-equal and co-eternal with the Father and the Son; that He was active in the creation of all things and continues to be so in providence; that He convicts the world of sin, righteousness, and judgment and that He regenerates, sanctifies, baptizes, indwells, seals, illumines, guides and bestows His gifts upon all believers.*

*We believe that* **God created man** *in His image; that because of the disobedience of our first parents at the Garden of Eden, they lost their innocence and both they and their descendants, separated from God, suffer physical and spiritual death and that all human beings, with the exception of Jesus the Messiah, are sinners by nature and practice.*

*We believe that Jesus the Messiah* **died for our sins**, *according to the Scriptures, as a representative and substitutionary sacrifice; that all who believe in Him are justified, not by any works of righteousness they have done, but by His perfect righteousness and atoning blood and that there is no other name under Heaven by which we must be saved.*

*We believe in the* **bodily resurrection** *of the just and the unjust, the everlasting blessedness of the saved and the everlasting conscious punishment of the lost.*

*We believe that* **Israel exists as a covenant people** *through whom God continues to accomplish His purposes and that* **the Church is an elect people** *in accordance with the New Covenant, comprising both Jews and Gentiles who acknowledge Jesus as Redeemer.[2]*

Join me in the following chapters as we explore the Theology of Place together.

---

[2] "Worldwide Mission Fellowship Declaration of Faith," accessed December 13, 2016, http://www.wwmf.org/faith/.

# BOOK STRUCTURE

*T*he book is divided into seven major sections. Each will look at place from a slightly different perspective, but all will be informed by the overarching Christian worldview and metanarrative of God's creation, the fall of man, and the redemption of God's creation as revealed in the Bible. The sections are as follows:

1. *Philosophy:* exploring the concept of place itself and its philosophical implications within the human experience.

2. *Theology:* exploring place as a subject of theology with a particular focus on the definition of a sacred place.

3. *Scripture:* exploring the Biblical Theology of Place as a major theme throughout Scripture.

4. *Narrative:* this section will seek to harmonize the Theology of Place alongside the other overarching themes of the Bible like God as King.

5. *History:* two routes of exploration are embarked on here. The first is the history of the land of Israel and the Jewish people. The second is the history of the Church. Both are reviewed through the lens of place.

6. *Application:* exploring the various ways that the biblical theme and understanding of place can impact our lives and help us to be good place makers and dwellers in God's creation.

7. *Study:* this is a supplementary section containing appendixes, suggested resources for further study, and a bibliography.

# SECTION 1

---

## PHILOSOPHY

# PLACE

*I*n the early 2000s, I worked with a homeless outreach ministry at our church. We regularly would drive down to Holborn in the city of London to spend time with homeless people. We came with practical help like food and clothing, but the most memorable part of that ministry was sitting with these people and listening to their stories about how they ended up on the streets of London with nowhere to live.

I'll never forget the one night when we met a very angry man who was a bit of a troublemaker. I felt the Lord tell me to stick it out with this man despite his aggression. I kept talking to him, hearing his story of time in the army and the difficulty he found readjusting to civilian life. As a result, he had lost his family and his home; eventually, he ended up on the streets as a drunk. That night he heard the gospel and received the help and advice he needed to address his immediate problem to support him in getting out of the displaced state in which he found himself.

Those experiences on the streets of Holborn with so many displaced, homeless men and women have given rise to the questions we rarely ask: why is place important to us as humans? Why do we feel a need to help people without a place of their own?

Philosophy is concerned with life's big questions: who are we, where are we, what time is it, what is wrong with the world, how can the world be fixed, and why are we here?

When asking these big questions, we quickly will see that the concept of place has an impact on each and is a core part of reality as we know it. We will find that place is so fundamental a concept that we can easily live life without thinking deeply about it, just as we don't often think about breathing or the law of gravity. We simply assume these realities and intrinsically expect them to be part of our experience.

One of my main purposes in this book is to open our eyes to the centrality of place in our lives and reality as we know it.

I will list five basic areas of life that all of us as human beings should be able to relate to on some level. These aspects of life show that place is a vital, central theme not only of our existence and a flourishing life but also of God's creation and redemptive purposes as revealed in his written word, the Bible.

These five areas will give us a brief introduction to the importance, centrality, and impact of place.

# WHO WE ARE

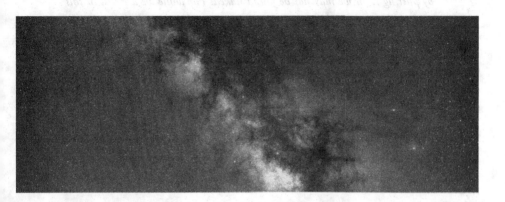

We are hardwired for place. It is literally a part of our makeup as human beings. God is our creator, and he has a place of his own—a home called heaven. We will explore its implications for us as his creatures later, but for now, it suffices to say that as our creator has a place, so do we creatures have a need and longing for place.

Without anyone teaching us, we form attachments to our home, family, community, and people group, and all this is centered on our need for placement in this life.

We, as physical, sentient creatures, need to be anchored in the here and now; we are bound by time and space. Thus, we are naturally drawn to the reality and necessity of place as a default position of our physical existence.

Physics reinforces the reality that we are beings that need a locale, a fixed area at any one time. We are not some ethereal gas or liquid; we are, in fact, highly complex beings. Each of us possesses our own body, which is bound by the simplest laws or limitations of the physical universe. Put simply, we can only be in one place at a time.

We are not disembodied spirits; we are spiritual beings housed in physical bodies. Our bodies are so crucial to our lives that if our spirit separates from our bodies, we experience death. So even our spirit has a place, the body, and even after death it longs for a new body, which we will receive at the resurrection.

Paul mentions the reality of our state in 2 Corinthians 5:1–4:

*For we know that if the tent that is our Earthly home is destroyed, we have a building from God, a house not made with hands, eternal in the heavens. For in this tent we groan, longing to put on our heavenly dwelling, if indeed by putting it on we may not be found naked. For while we are still in this tent, we groan, being burdened - not that we would be unclothed, but that we would be further clothed, so that what is mortal may be swallowed up by life.*

One of the most staggering realities found in God's Word is the way in which he chooses to create humankind. God created humankind's place—the earth—first and then created the first man from that material: the dust of the place.

This gives humans a vital connection to the place they were created to dwell in and rule over. We will look at this foundational truth in more detail later in this book.

# WHERE WE LIVE

*T*hink about where you live, where your parents and ancestors have lived. Consider your room, house, town, city, country, continent, and planet. If you really consider these things, you will begin to appreciate the importance and foundational centrality of place to the human experience.

The place in which we live can have a profound impact on our view of the world and our view of ourselves. Where we live can even mold our personality.

Sociologists have conducted numerous studies that demonstrate the powerful effect different areas and changes in environment can have on human beings.[3]

In addition, there are several trends in Western culture and pop culture that help make the case that the place in which we live is deeply important and central. The first is the trend to take out a twenty-five-year loan in order to own our own homes with a mortgage. Even for those of us who have not shackled ourselves to the debt incurred with a mortgage, rent remains one of the largest monthly bills. This is not something we question; we simply expect it to be so. This is in part because a home is so integral to our makeup that we subconsciously see the great worth in paying a heavy sum for a place to live.

The second is the popularity of house-hunting shows and home-improvement television shows. Again, this demonstrates that we have an appetite for place. We are drawn to it like a moth to a flame because we were created to be place dwellers and place makers.

---

[3] See the following link as one example http://soc.sagepub.com/content/37/1/13.full.pdf+html.

Below is a list of shows I remember seeing at least one episode of. There are of course many more that I have never seen, and it should be noted that the following list is largely from UK television:

1. DIY SOS
2. Escape to the Continent
3. Escape to the Country
4. Extreme Makeover: Home Edition
5. Homes under the Hammer
6. Location, Location, Location
7. Place In the Sun
8. Property Ladder
9. Relocation, Relocation
10. Room for Improvement
11. Secret Location
12. The House That £100k Built
13. The Home Show
14. Ugly House to Lovely House
15. Fixer Upper

There are even entire channels dedicated to the home. On Freeview in the UK, there is a channel called "Home," and I'm sure the USA has an equivalent.

There is nothing inherently wrong with this sort of media, and I mostly enjoy the format. These shows are only listed here to help point out the fact that as human beings we take very seriously the place we live.

There is a common saying that we should "make a house a home." The sentiment of that statement is that when a house is acquired, it is not yet a home. To transform it into a home, it will need to be decorated, furnished, lived in, and maintained. In other words, we strive to make a mere space into a place, endowed with a sense of worth, belonging, comfort, shelter, and style.

We endow the spaces in which we live with meaning by the care and attention we devote to them, the time we spend there, and the memories we attach to them—all serving to make the space a place.

# WHAT WE WORK FOR

We work to pay for a place to live—a place that is safe for us and our families. A place where children can be nourished and all members of the family can flourish.

Think about your own life; likely one of your major and most important investments is your mortgage so you can eventually own your own home. If not a mortgage, then the rent you pay for the place you are living in.

This point also covers what we study for, not that this is the only or even overriding motivation, but it is an underlying motivation for getting a good education and a fulfilling career.

Also the place we work in is important. Not all workplaces are the same; some places of work can be attractive because of the surrounding environment, working culture, and work-life balance opportunities.

# WHY WE FIGHT

F ight for territory is a common reason that humans go to war. We seek to expand the places that our nation, people, or movement can lay claim to. It has been claimed that most wars are motivated by religion, when in fact all wars are a striving for the expansion or protection of place as perceived by a people group.

As we look back over history, we can catalog the expansion efforts of the major conflicts from the most ancient civilization in Mesopotamia (Babylon) and Egypt, to the great empire-building land grabs of the Greeks and Romans, to the imperial expansion of China and European states.

Most recent in our collective memory will be the war for land waged by Germany in World War I and II and the defense of land by the United Kingdom and its allies on both sides of the Atlantic.

Even when we look at supposed religious or ideological wars like the one waged in Northern Ireland or in the Land of Israel and across the Middle East, the ultimate driving factor remains the expansion or retention of territory, of land, of space, ultimately of a place for a people. We will address this again in more detail when we conduct our case study on that most hotly contested place, the Land of Israel, in a later chapter.

Our desire to fight for our place is not only on the grand scale of international or civil war, it is even played out on our streets with rival gangs battling over "turf."

Place gives a sense of belonging, among many other things. It is, therefore, the prize in the battles that the disenfranchised, displaced youth in our inner cities wage among themselves. We will revisit this in more detail later on when we look at the social implications of place for our world today and our undeniable call to be place makers.

# WHAT WE BELIEVE IN

*T*he end of the gospel or good news we proclaim as evangelical Christians is that because of the life, death, resurrection, and ascension of Jesus, we can through faith by God's grace spend eternity in the place that Jesus has gone to prepare for us. The good news is that God wants to dwell with mankind and has made this possible through the cross.

We tell the good news that the King has been victorious, the kingdom of God has come, and heaven—the ultimate place—can be our home.

Jesus himself said in John 14:1–3:

> *Let not your hearts be troubled. Believe in God; believe also in me. In my Father's house are many rooms. If it were not so, would I have told you that I go to prepare a place for you? And if I go and prepare a place for you, I will come again and will take you to myself, that where I am you may be also.*

The author of Hebrews writes of believers who throughout redemptive history lived by faith in God, in part by fixing their hope on a place that God had built for them. We read this in Hebrews 11:10, "For he [Abraham, the father of faith] was looking forward to the city that has foundations, whose designer and builder is God."

The book of Hebrews goes on to describe the kingdom of heaven, the prize and promise of the gospel, as follows:

*But you have come to Mount Zion and to the city of the living God, the heavenly Jerusalem, and to innumerable angels in festal gathering, and to the assembly of the firstborn who are enrolled in heaven, and to God, the judge of all, and to the spirits of the righteous made perfect, and to Jesus, the mediator of a new covenant, and to the sprinkled blood that speaks a better word than the blood of Abel. (Hebrews 12:22–24)*

The Apostle Peter reminds us what we have been born again to in 1 Peter 1:3–5:

*Blessed be the God and Father of our Lord Jesus Christ! According to his great mercy, he has caused us to be born again to a living hope through the resurrection of Jesus Christ from the dead, to an inheritance that is imperishable, undefiled, and unfading, kept in heaven for you, who by God's power are being guarded through faith for a salvation ready to be revealed in the last time.*

This is not unique to the Christian faith. The majority of faiths have an end goal of a heavenly altered or exalted place of final or eternal dwelling.

Again, this is only a summary to give you context as you read this book. We will explore the centrality of place to the gospel in a later chapter.

*T*o finish this section, I want to give you a brief overview of our understanding of reality from a philosophical perspective. Our concern is that of epistemology, the study of knowledge or truth, exploring its nature, scope, and limits.

I covered this area in a short three-part course written for Worldwide Mission Fellowship while this book was going through the editing process. What follows are selected excerpts from the course.

## Key terms

**Philosophy:** The effort to think clearly and deeply about fundamental questions, including "What is knowledge?" (epistemology), "What is reality?" (metaphysics), and "What is good?" (ethics).

**Epistemology:** The branch of philosophy concerned with questions about knowledge and belief and related issues such as justification and truth.[4]

**Truth:** Truth is from a sense of being. Conformity to reality or actuality; often with the implication of dependability as opposed to what is false and wanting.

---

[4] C. Stephen Evans, *Pocket Dictionary of Apologetics & Philosophy of Religion* (2002), 39.

**Knowledge:** Knowledge is justified true belief. It can be propositional knowledge (knowing certain facts or states of affair) or experiential knowledge (knowing something because of direct personal experience).

**Worldview:** An articulation of the basic beliefs embedded in a shared grand story that are rooted in a faith commitment and that give shape and direction to the whole of our individual and corporate lives.[5]

A religious (all humans are religious) framework, which influences the way we interpret all reality and answer fundamental questions like "Where did we come from?"

**Upper story:** Term used to denote that which, in modern thinking, deals with significance or meaning, but which is not open to contact with verification by the world of facts that constitute the "lower story."[6]

**A closed system:** The way nature and natural laws are referred to by those who follow the presupposition of naturalism. The idea is that the laws of nature cannot be acted upon by an outside agent. The Bible teaches an open system in which God and other forces from the unseen/supernatural realm can interact with the natural realm, sometimes resulting in what we call miracles.

## God, the source of truth

In the Bible, God is described as a Rock who is firm and dependable and has the innate attribute of truth and faithfulness. He, therefore, exists as the very source of all that is real, even of reality itself; it all finds its origin in him and exists in context to him but remains distinct from him.

This state of God's being and the reality that he willfully created in relationship to himself, explains the nature of evil because evil is all that is not true, all that is perverted, against and diluted from the reality and truth of God's person and ways. This anti-truth is seen most clearly in the devil (see John 8:44).

God is both the moral lawgiver as the source of truth and judge of his creatures in correspondence to his own nature, which is pure truth or ultimate reality.

---

[5] Michael W. Goheen and Craig G. Bartholomew, *Living at the Crossroads: An Introduction to Christian Worldview* (Grand Rapids, MI: Baker Academic, 2008), 23.

[6] Francis A. Schaeffer, *The Complete Works of Francis A. Schaeffer: A Christian Worldview*, (Westchester, IL: Crossway Books, 1982), 1:202.

## Creation, fall, redemption

Taking the Bible as the ultimate authority for Christian thought, we can arrange our Christian worldview into three broad categories:

1. Creation > 2. Fall > 3. Redemption

The outline of creation, fall, and redemption defines the Bible's metanarrative, or big story of God, humanity, and the rest of creation. This is a real drama that encompasses all of reality. Nothing falls outside this framework except, of course, God himself in his holiness as both the ultimate essence and source of reality.

## A borrowed worldview

Naturalism, if consistent, only has a lower story; it has no purpose, meaning, or future, leading only to despair. In order to deal with this stark predicament, it needs to rely on the biblical worldview to lend meaning to life in an invented upper story to make everyone feel better about the pessimistic logical conclusion of this philosophy.

The naturalistic worldview is an impossible position because its own presupposition is that there is no rationality or meaning, which by definition refutes its own position and all views that attempt to say anything about anything.

All worldviews, even those (like postmodernism) that deny worldview or attainable knowledge do so with the currency of propositional and objective truth only produced from the biblical worldview, or the world as it really is.

## The supernatural universe

The fundamental nature of the universe is personal because it was designed and is maintained by God, who is a person, not a force.

It is natural because God has created nature with its corresponding laws. And it is supernatural because the unseen realm is part of the created sphere we call the universe or cosmos.

God is the only eternal one, not part of the creation. However, he transcends and so interacts with his creation within space-time.

# Unified truth

We reject the idea that all rational knowledge is restricted to scientific knowledge (lower story confinement). God is not just a force or idea but is a person who speaks and acts. God created everything; in particular, He created humans in His own image (Genesis 1:26). The universal, big questions of philosophy are the logical outcome of God's design.

This view tears down the firm walls erected by man, separating the lower story from the upper story. This view—known as a unified field of knowledge and truth—is the only satisfying, consistent, and logical model of reality as it really is rather than how men choose to perceive it.

## Key Scriptures dealing with "Truth"

The whole gospel of John, but in particular:

**John 14:6:** *Jesus said to him, "I am the way, and the truth, and the life. No one comes to the Father except through me."*

**John 17:3:** *"And this is eternal life, that they know you, the only true God, and Jesus Christ whom you have sent."*

**John 18:38:** *"Pilate said to him, 'What is truth?' After he had said this, he went back outside to the Jews and told them, "I find no guilt in him."*

**Acts 17:24–28:** *The God who made the world and everything in it, being Lord of heaven and earth, does not live in temples made by man, nor is he served by human hands, as though he needed anything, since he himself gives to all mankind life and breath and everything. And he made from one man every nation of mankind to live on all the face of the earth, having determined allotted periods and the boundaries of their dwelling place, that they should seek God, and perhaps feel their way toward him and find him. Yet he is actually not far from each one of us, for "'In him we live and move and have our being'; as even some of your own poets have said, "'For we are indeed his offspring.'"*

**Ephesians 4:21:** *"assuming that you have heard about him and were taught in him, as the truth is in Jesus."*

# SECTION 2

---

# THEOLOGY

# THE THEOLOGY OF PLACE

*J*ran a center for refugees and asylum seekers with a Christian Social Action Project called PECAN in Peckham, a deprived area of South London that, at the time, had high crime and unemployment rates. The center would offer free IT Training to refugees and asylum seekers who had been displaced from their own country.

I heard firsthand accounts of the atrocities they experienced in their homelands, which forced them to seek refuge in the UK. One particular account came from a doctor who had fled a North African county. Now as a displaced asylum seeker, his education and experience were of no use to him in the UK. The plight of such people reminds us again that place is no small thing. It is a crucial part of the human experience and of God's design for mankind and creation. In light of this, it is crucial that we understand the theological implications of place.

I use the phrase "theology of place" throughout this book. I do not claim to have coined this term; I'm sure someone used it before me. However, in this section, I will explain what I mean by this term, by looking at spaces, places, and sacred places. We will focus on the theological elements of place, which will lay the foundation for our next section, in which we will look at what the Bible has to say about place.

# WHAT IS THEOLOGY?

"Theology" is a compound of two words. The first is the Greek word *theos*, which means "god." The second word is *ology*, which comes from the Greek word *logos*, meaning "word, thought, or logic." Therefore, true theology is the study of the Word (*ology*/*logos*) of God (*theos*).

Theology is the study of God's written word, the Bible.

Dr. R.C. Sproul states that "theology is the word or logic of God Himself."[7] While M. J. Erickson defines theology as "the study or science of God."[8]

So when we speak of the "theology of place," we are talking about what the Bible teaches us about place. Later we will look in more detail at the theological method we will use. That is "Biblical theology," which we will use to trace the theme of place throughout the biblical text and reveal its lessons and message in the wider context of God's great story of redemption.

If you want to know more about theology, then see the suggested reading section for titles like *Everyone's a Theologian* by R.C. Sproul and *Christian Theology* by Millard J. Erickson.

---

[7] R.C. Sproul, *Everyone's a Theologian: An Introduction to Systematic Theology* (Orlando, FL: Reformation Trust, 2014), 4.

[8] Millard J. Erickson, *Christian Theology*, 3rd ed. (Grand Rapids, MI: Baker Academic, 2013), 8.

# SPACES VERSUS PLACES

One distinction we should make early on is the difference between spaces and places.

Simply put, I would describe a space as a naturally occurring or manmade physical area endowed with no particular or special importance, meaning, or purpose. On the other hand, I would describe a place as a physical area too, but one that is endowed with special importance, meaning, or purpose.

The worldview of naturalism—which gave birth to the origin narrative proposed by the Big Bang theory and evolutionary theory, coupled with the pragmatism of capitalism on one hand or communism on the other—has seen the triumph of space over place in both thought and practice.

In today's fast-paced world, place has been supplanted by space. Naturalism's story is of a purposeless existence by pure chance, which leads to a simple view of the intersection of time and space as a necessary function of being. This view has no special regard for one particular space over another; in turn, it has led in some ways to the death of our God-given sense of place in the world and the wider universe.

This current way of thinking has left humankind in a perpetual state of displacement. All the while, humans in their pride affirm that place no longer matters and that even space is just a by-product of existence.

The truth is that neither spaces nor places are accidental; they are each designed, and to neglect the necessity and importance of place will leave humanity in a constant state of unsettled conflict, discomfort, and general disorientation regarding their purpose in the wider context of God's creation, with particular regard to our responsibility to our fellow man.

# PLACES VERSUS SACRED PLACES

*T*here is a further distinction to be made between places and sacred places.

A single person or group can turn a space into a place by themselves, endowing the space with particular meaning and worth. This can often be a good thing, as when a house is made a home or a place of healing is built—a hospital, for example. This can also have a generally negative outcome when a place is made for the worship of false gods or in honor of something evil.

A truly sacred place, by contrast, is not made by men but God. It is by God's own decree and presence that a space becomes more than just a place but a sacred or holy place.

One of the clearest examples of this is in Scripture, where we observe the Holy Place in the tabernacle and temple, and more importantly the Holy of Holies with the Ark of the Covenant. The thing that made this place so special was God's manifest presence and his decree that it was in this sacred space that he would meet with the high priest and, by proxy, with his people. We will explore this in more detail in the chapter dedicated to a study of the tabernacle as "God's Tent."

# THE HISTORY OF PLACE
# IN THEOLOGY

*P*lace has been a neglected area in theology. This is partly due to a subtle dualism that exalts the spiritual over the material in a way that obscures the importance of God's purposes in the physical universe he has so skillfully created.

We must guard against subtle forms of Dualism and Gnosticism. Dualism essentially sees the universe as consisting of a balance of equal but opposite powers of evil versus good. Gnosticism developed this basic belief to oversimplify and corrupt the Christian understanding of the universe by stating that the spiritual realm is good and the physical or material world is evil. When this idea is stated in such vivid terms, we of course reject the assertion, but if we are not careful, subtle undertones of this belief system can undermine our appreciation of God's material creation, which he expressly said was good.

The reality is that Dualism is false because God is the only eternal being. Evil is not itself eternal but is in some ways a part of the creation that has its origin from the only eternal one, God.

Gnosticism inverts the truth by saying that YHWH—the God of the Bible—is evil, and Lucifer—the devil—is the good god who created the spirit of man (spirit is always good, remember) while the evil god (in their teaching this is the God of the

Bible) imprisoned the pure spirit of mankind in the physical universe, and physical bodies in particular. This is rank heresy.

The theology of place acts as a rebuke to the obvious heresy of Gnosticism and its subtle undertones that have crept into Christian thinking, especially regarding God and his creation.

The Gnostic teaching that the physical world is inherently evil can manifest itself in Christianity as an attitude or way of thinking that devalues and disregards the physical world. The theology of place acts as a corrective to this sort of thinking.

However, without using the term *theology of place*, Bible teachers, preachers, and theologians have studied and taught the truths highlighted in this book, which focuses on the importance of place in God's Word, creation, plans, and purposes.

The words and phrases below are themes used throughout theological history that point to the same truths we explore in this book without necessarily composing the ideas into a single coherent biblical theology.

## God's creation

All biblical teachers have always taught that God created the physical universe with a purpose in mind and that humans were created in the context of the wider universe to bring glory to God the Creator.

## The land of Israel

Many have taught on the importance of the Promised Land and how this helps to frame the narrative of the OT as God keeps covenant with the people of Israel.

## The gospel

Gospel preachers have pointed us to the importance of the Great Commission, where Jesus sends us out with the good news to everyone, everywhere (in every place). The teaching of the gospel also highlights the promise of our eternal home, which is in the place prepared for us.

## The new heaven and new earth

All teaching on the consummation speaks of the eternal place of the redeemed and the lost and the ultimate place, the new heaven and new earth joined in matrimony forever.

## Specialist "Place" Studies

This is by no means the first book on place from a Christian perspective. While searching through my library, I came across two others—Walter Brueggemann's *The Land: Place as Gift, Promise, and Challenge in Biblical Faith* and Craig G. Bartholomew's *Where Mortals Dwell: A Christian View of Place for Today.*

In writing this book, I made the decision not to engage with these works. I really wanted to make a fresh contribution without being influenced by these two works, which I'm sure are excellent. This way, in a later work I can genuinely cross-reference points of agreement and departure. Brueggemann and Bartholomew are both great teachers, and I'm sure they have much to contribute to this area of study. I look forward to reading both their writings on the subject in the near future.

Of course, there may be other books, journal articles, and works on the subject of place that I am not aware of. The point remains that, as a theological subject, place is a neglected area in comparison to other biblical studies. This book seeks to address that void by taking a fresh look at place and presenting the biblical theology in an approachable format for all Christians.

## Words pointing to the place theme in the Bible

As we survey the Bible, there are many words you can essentially substitute for space, place, or sacred place. These include but are not limited to:

- land, the land, or the Promised Land;

- Canaan, Jordan or beyond Jordan, Israel, Judah, Judea, and the many tribal area names like Benjamin, etc.;

- country, town, area, or mountain;

- altar, tabernacle, tent, house, palace, or temple;

- heaven, paradise, nations, and hades.

# SECTION 3

---

## SCRIPTURE

# PLACE IN THE BIBLE

My life as a Christian has been marked by the reading and study of God's Word. I have a journal from the earliest days of my walk, full of notes and reflections from Bible readings. This is not something unique to me, Christians from all walks of life and denominations center their lives around the study and application of God's written word found in the Bible.

As a community, we trust the Bible as the Word of God and look to it for revelation, inspiration, direction, training, and instruction. The nineteenth century preacher Charles Spurgeon said of the Bible in his sermon "The Bible, Tried and Proved:"

> *Does it not strike you as a marvel of condescension, that Jehovah, the infinite, should use words? He has arranged for us, in his wisdom, this way of communicating with one another; but as for himself, he is pure spirit and boundless: shall he contract his glorious thoughts into the narrow channel of sound, and ear, and nerve? Must the eternal mind use human words? The*

*glorious Jehovah spake worlds. The heavens and the earth were the utterances of his lips.*

*To him it seems more in accordance with his nature to speak tempests and thunders, than to stoop to the humble vowels and consonants of a creature of the dust. Will he in very deed communicate with man in man's own way? Yes, he stoops to speak to us by words. We bless the Lord for verbal inspiration, of which we can say, "I have esteemed the words of thy mouth more than my necessary food." I do not know of any other inspiration, neither am I able to conceive of any which can be of true service to us. We need a plain revelation upon which we can exercise faith ...*

*To us "every word of God is pure," and withal full of soul nutriment. "Man doth not live by bread only, but by every word that proceedeth out of the mouth of the Lord doth man live." We can heartily declare with the Psalmist, "Thou art my portion, O Lord: I have said that I would keep thy words."*[9]

Throughout Scripture, we see overarching themes of placement, displacement, and re-placement. This is by no means the only or even the central theme of biblical theology; however, it is a very important one and is a major part of the most central themes of Scripture like the Glory of God, love, and salvation.

The biblical theology of place has not received much attention in biblical studies, yet when we turn to the Scriptures with an awareness of the theme, it is everywhere.

This section will explore place in the Scriptures and define biblical theology, as we will use this approach to reveal the theology of place in the Bible.

[9] C. H. Spurgeon, The Metropolitan Tabernacle Pulpit Sermons. (London: Passmore & Alabaster, 1889), 35.

# THE BIBLE

efore we go any further we need to establish our presupposition or starting position regarding the Bible as Christians. In short, we believe the Bible is the Word God.

The following Scriptures are the Bible's commentary on itself:

> *2 Peter 1:19–21: "And we have the prophetic word more fully confirmed, to which you will do well to pay attention as to a lamp shining in a dark place, until the day dawns and the morning star rises in your hearts, knowing this first of all, that no prophecy of Scripture comes from someone's own interpretation. For no prophecy was ever produced by the will of man, but men spoke from God as they were carried along by the Holy Spirit."*

> *2 Timothy 3:16: "All Scripture is breathed out by God and profitable for teaching, for reproof, for correction, and for training in righteousness."*

> *Romans 15:4: "For whatever was written in former days was written for our instruction, that through endurance and through the encouragement of the Scriptures we might have hope."*

Think over the words you have just read and then consider what Jesus's view was on the origin and nature of the Scriptures by his statements (one from each gospel) in the following verses:

*Matthew 5:18: "For truly, I say to you, until heaven and earth pass away, not an iota, not a dot, will pass from the Law until all is accomplished."*

*Mark 14:49: "Day after day I was with you in the temple teaching, and you did not seize me. But let the Scriptures be fulfilled."*

*Luke 4:21: "And he began to say to them, 'Today this Scripture has been fulfilled in your hearing.'"*

*John 17:17: "Sanctify them in the truth; your word is truth."*

## Inspiration and authorship

As Christians, one of our core/essential beliefs that actually make us disciples of Jesus Christ is that God is the ultimate author of the Bible because he is the one who inspired the Bible's authors in their writings.

## Inerrancy and infallibility

Inerrancy means the Bible has no errors in its original autographs, while infallibility means the truth and claims of the Bible cannot fail.

## The canon

This refers to the collection of books included in the Bible and considered to be sacred Scripture. Each carries equal authority as God's revealed, written word.

When we talk about the canon, we are specifically talking about the thirty-nine books of the Old Testament and the twenty-seven books of the New Testament found in the Bible of evangelical Christians.

## Transmission and translation

The Bible was originally written thousands of years ago in the ancient languages of Hebrew, Aramaic, and Greek, yet the very words and message of the original writings have been transmitted through faithful translation of the Bible into English and many other languages.

There are many good essentially literal English translations of the sixty-six books of the Bible, including but not limited to the ESV, KJV, NKJV, HCSB, MEV, and NASB.

I have used the English Standard Version, which is a trustworthy modern English translation of the Bible. The ESV uses an essentially literal translation philosophy, which means it keeps the text true to the original words based on the most reliable documents and evangelical textual criticism while maintaining readability and literary flow.

Every word from the original languages, in the context of the passage, is translated into its nearest equivalent English word or phrase. However, it does not stop there, it attempts to express the finished result with ordinary word order and style, as far as possible without distorting the meaning of the text.[10]

---

[10] Wayne Grudem et al., *Translating Truth: The Case for Essentially Literal Bible Translation* (Wheaton: Crossway, 2005).

# BIBLICAL THEOLOGY

iblical theology is the endeavor to see the overarching theme(s) of the Bible that span both testaments. That is at least my short summary of it.

There are a few ways of thinking about biblical theology. It can be seen at the level of themes in one book or from one author; this is the classical approach. It can also be seen in terms of central themes and even a single or main theme of the entire Bible, as I mentioned above.

A more recent and quite helpful way of looking at biblical theology is to consider the unfolding biblical narrative or central story of the Bible and its related themes and message.

In this book we will be looking at place as a central biblical theme and its importance to the overall narrative of the Bible.

D. A. Carson[11] mentions a few things we ought to remember to help us do biblical theology well. I have used them as a guide to write the following list for us as we pursue a biblical theology of place:

1. **The Bible is a historical collection.** The Bible follows a real-life chronological order; it was not all written at the same time. We should pay

---

[11] D. A. Carson's list in the *NIV Zondervan Study Bible: Built on the Truth of Scripture and Centered on the Gospel Message* (Grand Rapids: Harper Collins, 2015).

attention to the sequence of events and the various levels of God's revelation as redemptive history unfolds.

2.  **The Bible's message is unified and coherent.** Approach the Bible with the belief (presupposition, perspective, or starting point) that the message of the Bible is unified and makes sense. This point is underpinned by a firm belief in God as the ultimate author of the Bible.

3.  **Stay true to the context of the Bible's text.** What is written actually meant something. This is where we must allow the text itself to inform our understanding, also known as inductive study. We must be dictated to by the text and try to leave as much of our own preconditions, worldviews, and traditions behind. We must put our faith in the integrity and intentional message of the text.

    This is where something called *hermeneutics* comes into play, which essentially means our method or rule for interpreting a passage. We must ensure we do not import our own meaning into the text but seek to extract the meaning, themes, and lessons native to the text itself.

4.  **Make connections throughout the Bible.** This is the overall aim of biblical theology—to identify theological connections, or themes, that run throughout the entire Bible. We will see in this work that one of the great themes of biblical theology is *place*.

5.  **State the obvious.** I have a philosophy that has always served me well when reading and studying the Bible: state the obvious. Sometimes as we read, we get lost in the "deep" and esoteric, when in fact by pausing, appreciating, and meditating on the blindingly obvious and apparently mediocre, we find the inherent truth, message, and power of God's Word.

    So join me on a journey through the Bible with your eyes wide open to the wonder of God's revelation to humankind.

We will be looking out for two thematic patterns in our overview of biblical theology in context to the theology of place; these are:

1.  The central theme and ultimate end of the Bible's narrative, which is *God and man, living together ... in one place*, which brings God glory and pleasure through his holy love while also bringing humans ultimate flourishing,

happiness, and satisfaction as we enjoy an eternal communal relationship with the Trinity.

In summary, *God, the victorious, glorious king, ruling his kingdom in the midst of his people for eternity in joy with holy love.*

2. The cyclical pattern of *placement, displacement, and re-placement* seen throughout redemptive history, which serves to underscore the importance of place in God's purposes in the natural and supernatural realms.

# 1. GOD AND MAN, LIVING TOGETHER ... IN ONE PLACE

One of the overarching themes of the Bible—seen clearly through Israel, redemptive history, the church, and the new heaven and earth—is God's desire to have his people live with him.

This is the ultimate direction of the biblical narrative from creation to consummation. In this story, place plays a significant and central role. We will explore the wonder of this truth in the chapter on God with His People later in the book (section four on narrative).

I see this as the main overarching theme of the Bible, or the single center and ultimate end of the Bible's narrative.

Allow me to map this out using a brief high-level eight-part summary:

1.  **God's Garden (Eden):** God created all things, including humankind. God lived in harmony and fellowship with humans before the fall, in the garden of Eden, the first sanctuary.

2.  **God's Mountain (Sinai):** God came down and met with his people on Mount Sinai in Horeb.

3.  **God's Tent (Tabernacle):** God comes closer than he did on the mountain through the tabernacle; he actually lives in the middle of his people.

4. **God's Land (Israel):** A home for God's covenant people, the Jews, where he would live and rule over them as their ultimate king.

5. **God's House (Temple):** The evolution of the traveling tent dwelling of God among his people through the tabernacle, the temple or house is a stationary home for God to dwell with his people.

6. **God Incarnate (Jesus):** Jesus is the second person of the Trinity, God of God, Light of Light. He became incarnate or, in other words, became human while remaining God, making him the one unique God-Man, 100 percent God while 100 percent man. Jesus is the highest expression of God's desire to live with his people; God became a man and lived in a body like us and with us.

7. **God's Body (Believers):** The Holy Spirit, the third person of the Trinity, now comes and actually lives inside believers in the same way that he once lived in the tabernacle or temple. We are individually and collectively the dwelling place of God on earth today.

8. **God's City (New Jerusalem):** In the consummation of all things, God's purpose in creation and redemption will be realized as he lives with us in the place Jesus went to prepare for us. God will live with us here on earth in the city he has built, the New Jerusalem.

# 2. PLACEMENT, DISPLACEMENT, AND RE-PLACEMENT

As we navigate our way through the Bible, highlighting the biblical theme of place, we notice it is broken into three major areas that are interrelated. These are: placement, displacement, and re-placement.

## Placement

Throughout the Bible—from the placement of creation, to the planting of a garden for man and woman, to the placement of Abraham and his decedents (Israel) in a specific land—placement is central and primary. Placement often points to God's original purpose or plan for an individual, nation, or thing. Placement then is an outworking or result of God's purposes and plans.

## Displacement

Displacement can come in a number of ways in the Bible. God can be the author of displacing a person or people as judgment for sin, as when humans were banished from the garden, or when Judah was taken captive to Babylon.

Displacement can also find its ultimate origin with the enemy of our soul, the devil, who schemes to see entire people groups as well as individuals displaced from God's plan and destiny for them through enticing man to sin and therefore suffer judicial and natural displacement.

# Re-Placement

We come full circle through re-placement. God is our savior and redeemer and seeks for humans to be re-placed according to his own redemptive purposes. Examples of this can be seen throughout redemptive history in God's dealings with Israel.

We see re-placement at work most clearly through the gospel, which seeks to reconcile mankind to God to live together forever in the place Jesus has prepared.

## A summary of the placement cycle

This is a high-level overview of placement, displacement, and re-placement in the Bible:

**Placement:** Creation and Eden.

**Displacement:** The fall and expulsion from Eden.

**Displacement:** Noah's flood.

**Re-placement:** Noah's covenant.

**Displacement:** Judgment at the Tower of Babel.

**Displacement:** Abraham's call.

**Placement:** Abraham's covenant.

**Displacement:** Israel in Egypt (time of Joseph).

**Displacement:** God judges Egypt.

**Re-Placement:** Joshua's conquest.

**Placement:** David's kingdom.

**Displacement:** Kingdom splits.

**Displacement:** Exile to Assyria and Babylon.

**Re-Placement:** The return to the land.

**Placement:** The first advent of the Messiah, Jesus the God-Man.

**Displacement:** The church disperses under persecution.

**Re-Placement:** Churches planted across the Earth.

**Re-Placement:** Final judgments and final dwelling place of the elect in the New Jerusalem with God.

This pattern is a part of our existence at its most basic level with regard to our birth, death, and resurrection.

Conception is our ultimate placement; at this point, we enter the world of space and time for the very first time. Death is our ultimate displacement with the separation of the spirit from the body. The coming resurrection, made possible through Jesus Christ, is the ultimate re-placement, when we will be clothed or housed again in our resurrection body, and our spirit will have found its eternal place in body as well as God's presence.

# BIBLICAL THEOLOGY:
## A PRIMER ON PLACE

*W*hat follows is in no way an exhaustive look at the role of "place" through the lens of placement, displacement, and re-placement throughout the Bible's narrative, central themes, and messages. It will look at selected highlights to give you a summary or primer to inspire further study and to open your eyes to reality as you read and meditate on the Scriptures yourself.

We will look at the following high points, meaning we will skip over large sections and often miss really important passages that also deal with the theology and centrality of place; however, an exhaustive exegetical study of this topic throughout the entire Bible would require a book dedicated to that end alone.

This will be a twelve-part whistle-stop tour, so buckle your seat belts and keep your eyes open for lessons along the way.

1.  **God's Garden: Eden**

    Here we will look at God's work and purpose in creation and, in particular, with man and the garden he made as a sacred place for man. We also see the first of the three great displacements as a result of the fall and the resulting judgment.

2. **God's Judgment: The Flood**

   The flood God sent in the days of Noah has implications for everything we understand about the world and place today. This is the second of the great displacements.

3. **God Displaces: Babel**

   Here there are implications for anthropology (the study of the origin and movement of humankind), culture, people groups, and languages. This is also the final of the great global displacements.

4. **God's Land: The Promised Land**

   The narrative-defining covenant that God made with Abraham regarding a land, people, and seed (Christ).

5. **God's Provision: Altars**

   We will look at one of Jacob's altars to explore this biblical and cultural concept with particular regard to place.

6. **God's Mountain: Sinai**

   The scene of the burning bush and the stage for God's great law covenant with Israel.

7. **God's Tent: The Tabernacle**

   We explore the sanctuary for which God gave instructions so he could dwell with his people in holiness.

8. **God's City: Jerusalem**

   A city so special that the "heaven" that will be on the earth in the end is called the New Jerusalem.

9. **God's House: The Temple**

   A study on the evolution of the tabernacle into a fixed structure referred to as the house of the Lord.

10. **God Incarnate: Jesus**

    The incarnation of Christ is the single most important event and person in the history of everything. In Jesus, we see God living in a body.

11. **God's Body: Believers and the Church**

    The Holy Spirit, God, living in believers as his representatives on the earth will be our focus here.

## 12. God's Glory and Presence: Heaven

A look at what the Bible says about heaven instead of what fictional books and movies say. This is also the conclusion to the Bible's narrative.

You will notice with each of these twelve areas we have kept God at the center, going from his garden, to his house, and finally to his glorious presence.

Redemptive history is not primarily about man and woman or even their relation to place but about God and his connection with place in light of his desire to dwell with human beings in an intimate, joy-filled relationship.

# GOD'S GARDEN: EDEN

*W*e begin by looking at creation and, in particular, God's purpose in creating the physical universe, preparing the Earth, and planting a garden in a specific place specially designed for man.

This lays the foundation for our understanding of place as an essential element of our existence, God's purposes, and redemptive history.

In today's world, it has become necessary to clearly define what we mean by creation. Our definition is simple and in accordance with the Bible's record as revealed in Genesis 1.

My own summary position on creation is that God created everything in all realms in accordance with the revealed historical and theological account recorded in the Bible.

See the suggested reading section for resources from Answers in Genesis, Day One Publishers, The Institute for Creation Research, and more.

## Placement in creation: Genesis 1:1

*In the beginning, God created the heavens and the earth.*

*—Genesis 1:1*

God's initial, intentional placement of the physical universe connects place to the very nature and fabric of reality.

Locality is an irrevocable constant of our plane of existence. At the root of creation is the creation of a vast space in a particular place known only by God.

The hand of the Creator in the open space of creation endows mere space with the import belonging to a place, which by his attention, decree, and Spirit more perfectly reflects the glory of his majesty.

The Copernican principle in science considers Earth's place in the wider cosmos, and when applied to the available data in honesty, points clearly to the hand of the God of the Bible, Yahweh, in the intricate design of the universe and the conscious placement of Earth in a compatible environment.

Michael Behe and James Golding's work on the privileged planet convincingly make the case for intelligent design based on Earth's placement in the solar system and the wider galaxy. In their work, they talk about the "galactic habitable zone," referring to the placement of Earth in the perfect galactic location for life to thrive and for humans to enjoy and explore the wonder of the surrounding cosmos.

## The first command, fill the earth: Genesis 1:28

*And God blessed them. And God said to them, "Be fruitful and multiply and fill the earth and subdue it, and have dominion over the fish of the sea and over the birds of the heavens and over every living thing that moves on the earth."*
—*Genesis 1:28*

The earth was created to be filled. This truth points to the importance of place in God's purposes for the earth. If the earth was not created to be filled, then it was created only as a space with no real meaning, it is the filling of the space of the earth that lends it significance.

Consider the other planets in our solar system; from what we understand, they are just vast spaces with minimal purpose.

God did not intend vast empty space. Although we must consider that it is against the backdrop of empty space that place finds its distinction as being more than just space.

We believe God created the entire creation (physical and spiritual) out of nothing or ex nihilo. There were no preexisting materials or structures used for the creation because God alone is eternal, and there is no evidence that this creation was formed from the ruins of another.

However, in the creation narrative, we are told that before God uttered a single word in regard to the physical creation, there was a great deep, and the Spirit of God moved over the face of the waters. That is all we are told; we are not given any more detail, and speculation is not helpful.

What we can derive from this record is that the deep and water were brought to order by the special creative act of God. From the seemingly unordered, purposeless, placeless deep, God supernaturally made a place over six successive twenty-four-hour days; that place was Earth.

## Made from the place itself: Genesis 2:7–8

*Then the LORD God formed the man of dust from the ground and breathed into his nostrils the breath of life, and the man became a living creature. And the LORD God planted a garden in Eden, in the east, and there he put the man whom he had formed.*

*—Genesis 2:7–8*

Man was formed from the place which he was created to inhabit, man has a special connection and kinship to place.

The creation narrative is the first really clear record of placement. God planted the garden and placed man there. Again we see the deliberate, purposeful, intentional action of God toward humans in regard to place.

The purposeful trajectory of this narrative does away with the shaky theories of theistic evolution and certainly leaves no room for naturalistic evolution.

The evolution narrative has no room for place, only accidental and purposeless space, which flies in the face of all we see and feel in the actual creation itself and the very nature of humankind.

## The displacement of creation: Genesis 3:17–19

*And to Adam he said, "Because you have listened to the voice of your wife and have eaten of the tree of which I commanded you, 'You shall not eat of it,' cursed is the ground because of you; in pain you shall eat of it all the days of your life; thorns and thistles it shall bring forth for you; and you shall eat the plants of the field. By the sweat of your face you shall eat bread, till you return to the ground, for out of it you were taken; for you are dust, and to dust you shall return."*

*—Genesis 3:17–19*

The judgment God gives to man is connected to the place where he placed man, namely the earth itself.

The very land in which the man lives and works becomes a reflection of the displacement of humankind.

Man is no longer in perfect harmony with the earth as God intended in creation. The earth fights man, and man has to fight against the earth rather than working with it in order to thrive.

Humans have been displaced as God's image bearers (we bore this image as God's council, government, or representatives in the place he had given to us, the earth) and so have lost command of the place created for them to live in and that God had given them dominion over.

## The displacement of man: Genesis 3:24

*He drove out the man, and at the east of the garden of Eden he placed the cherubim and a flaming sword that turned every way to guard the way to the tree of life.*

—*Genesis 3:24*

Man is physically displaced from the garden of Eden. In a sense, man is displaced from God's home because God walked with man in Eden, and the references to the garden, mountain, and the many waters of Eden point to this place being like a heaven on Earth, God's dwelling place among humankind. The ensuing biblical narrative will be a story of God's redemptive work to restore man and woman to Eden in the sense of God and humankind dwelling together in holy love and fellowship.

This displacement was very overt. Man was driven from the garden; it was not a natural displacement but one exacted as judgment. However, it is also the natural consequence of the change in relationship between God and humankind inaugurated by the fall.

The spiritual element to this displacement is that communion with God had changed too.

Placement is inextricably linked to relationship and fellowship. As we will see throughout the biblical narrative, humans are placed by God for relationship with

God. Displacement is a manifestation of the breakdown of that relationship at a fundamental level.

## The voice of the place: Genesis 4:10–12

*And the LORD said, "What have you done? The voice of your brother's blood is crying to me from the ground. And now you are cursed from the ground, which has opened its mouth to receive your brother's blood from your hand. When you work the ground, it shall no longer yield to you its strength. You shall be a fugitive and a wanderer on the earth."*

*—Genesis 4:10–12*

Places speak to God. I know that sounds a little out of left field, but it is true. Throughout Scripture, God tells us that the land has cried out to him just like the blood of Abel that the land received from the hand of Cain.

The earth received the innocent blood of Abel, and God heard the cry from the ground or place where he fell.

Part of Cain's judgment was that the ground he had desecrated by killing his own brother would curse or fight back at Cain. This theme of judgment coming from the land itself is picked up throughout Scripture where the land or place is desecrated by man's sin.

Cross-references for the voice of the land include:

1. Numbers 35:33
2. Deuteronomy 21:1–9
3. Job 16:18; 31:38
4. Psalm 106:38; Isaiah 24:5
5. Jeremiah 3:1–2, 9
6. Matthew 23:35
7. Hebrews 12:24

Being a fugitive with no fixed dwelling was the judgment given to Cain. God judged him with displacement.

This is an extension to the curse the fall of man has already brought to the earth. The crown of thorns endured by Jesus is really significant. It's a sign of the cursed earth and the truth that the Messiah will come to restore places for people to dwell in. This is noted in Isaiah 61 and claimed in part by Jesus in Luke 4, to be completed when he returns.

# GOD'S DISPLACEMENT: THE FLOOD

*J*he flood is simply the greatest ecological and penal event to happen since the creation of the world. Like the creation account, if the flood account is dismissed as myth then the foundation of our beliefs, the nature of our current reality, and even our understanding of the natural world has no true foundation.

As Psalm 11:3 says, "If the foundations are destroyed, what can the righteous do?"

## Displaced through judgment: Genesis 6:17

*For behold, I will bring a flood of waters upon the earth to destroy all flesh in which is the breath of life under heaven. Everything that is on the earth shall die.*

*—Genesis 6:17*

All living things are displaced in the greatest single judgment the world has ever seen in the global flood God sent in the days of Noah.

A flood, in particular, shines a light on displacement:

1. The great force of water literally moves things from one place to another.

2. Waters of a flood wash things away; therefore, it not only displaces but cleanses the defilement that contaminates the land.

3. It is generally agreed that the earth was once a single-mass continent, a single place, and that the breaking up of this supercontinent called Pangaea happened at Noah's flood. This is commonly referred to as the continental drift (although this was no drift, it was more like a catastrophic sprint).

This too has implications for place and displacement as a single place was broken into many, divided by oceans and seas. It is significant because, in the consummation of the age, there will be no sea. So the sea, which has become an instrument of displacement, is removed in the age to come, pointing to the perfection of place in the new heaven and earth.

"Then I saw a new heaven and a new earth, for the first heaven and the first earth had passed away, and the sea was no more" (Rev. 21:1).

## Re-placement through covenant: Genesis 6:18–19

*But I will establish my covenant with you, and you shall come into the ark, you, your sons, your wife, and your sons' wives with you. And of every living thing of all flesh, you shall bring two of every sort into the ark to keep them alive with you. They shall be male and female.*

—*Genesis 6:18–19*

The ark is God's instrument of re-placement for Noah, his family, and the animal kingdom.

The floodwaters also serve as a vehicle for re-placement, as the ark would float on the waves of the flood before settling in a new place.

Notice, God declares that he will establish his covenant with Noah before commanding Noah to enter the ark. The covenant serves as a foundation to the outworking of this re-placement in the earth for the elect family and creatures.

Throughout the Bible, we will see that covenant and places are very tightly linked. Some of the most important covenants in the Bible have place and dwelling with God as their ultimate aim or promise, pointing back to God's original plan in Eden.

## Creation suffers because of man's evil: Genesis 8:21

*And when the LORD smelled the pleasing aroma, the LORD said in his heart,*
*"I will never again curse the ground because of man, for the intention of man's*
*heart is evil from his youth. Neither will I ever again strike down every living*
*creature as I have done.*

*—Genesis 8:21*

Notice that the ground or place was cursed because of man's evil.

God makes a covenant with all humanity that the mass displacement of the global flood judgment, which was itself a curse from the ground (the great deep was broken up), would not happen again.

This shows God's commitment to re-placing humankind in the earth and his purposes in the earth in regard to place, which find their ultimate expression in the new heaven and earth, where God will restore Eden—where his place and our place were shared. God will be with us to dwell, and we will live with him forever.

This is the first part of the first "place covenant" God makes in the Bible.

## The original command, repeated: Genesis 9:1–2

*And God blessed Noah and his sons and said to them, "Be fruitful and*
*multiply and fill the earth. The fear of you and the dread of you shall be*
*upon every beast of the earth and upon every bird of the heavens, upon*
*everything that creeps on the ground and all the fish of the sea. Into your*
*hand they are delivered.*

*—Genesis 9:1–2*

Noah was blessed to be fruitful in the earth and to fill the earth, which reminds us of the decree God made to Adam to fill the open spaces, to be a place maker by filling the earth.

This is the latter half of the first place covenant in the Bible.

One of the core principles of the biblical understanding of place is that God intends for creation to be filled. God's creation is to be lived in and enjoyed by his creatures, which brings God glory and pleasure.

As stated in the first question in the Westminster Larger Catechism: "What is the chief and highest end of man? Man's chief and highest end is to glorify God, (Rom. 11:36, Cor. 10:31) and fully to enjoy him forever (Ps. 73:24–28, John 17:21–23)."[12]

John Piper modifies this slightly by stating the answer as follows: "The chief end of man is to glorify God by enjoying Him forever."[13]

Uninhabited creation is little more than empty space. A space becomes a place when it is endowed with import by God's presence, decree, or even his people.

As God's people, we are called to fill the earth with those who reflect God's glory and represent him before his creation.

We should fill the void, making spaces into places to the glory of God.

---

[12] *The Westminster Larger Catechism: With Scripture Proofs.* (Oak Harbor, WA: Logos Research Systems, Inc., 1996).

[13] John Piper, *Desiring God* (Sisters, OR: Multnomah Publishers, 2003), 18.

# GOD'S LAND:
# THE PROMISED LAND

$\mathcal{T}$he theology of place comes into central focus in the biblical narrative of redemptive history as God calls Abraham to live by faith, form a people, and makes a covenant to give them a place of their own.

## Cursed to be placeless: Genesis 9:25

*He said, "Cursed be Canaan; a servant of servants shall he be to his brothers."*
*—Genesis 9:25*

Canaan was cursed by losing the right to his own place and, instead, he became a servant to others whose place was secured. Notice that the Lord's blessing to the brothers also involved place; he mentions their tents, dwellings, and borders. Canaan, like his spiritual forefather Cain, is essentially cursed with placelessness.

*Placelessness* is a real problem in today's world. We have already mentioned that a desire for place, a sense of belonging, a home, an anchor, and a safe space is part and parcel of being human; our nature longs for it, and our mortal frame needs it.

The human soul is disrupted and distressed by placelessness. What is alarming in today's culture is our apparent apathy in the wake of the placeless epidemic.

Some of the causes for this include the prevailing worldview of naturalistic evolution, which exalts meaningless space, chance, and pragmatism and does not recognize the design, necessity, or centrality of place in the world, similar to their disdain for anything that points to the transcendent creator, God, and of course their animosity to God himself.

A catalyst for placelessness nuanced in our day is the exchanging of the spaces and places of the real world for the relative placelessness of life online. Although it must be said that even this can be redeemed to some degree to help fight the battle against placelessness and restore a biblical understand and application of place for all peoples.

A major concern from a Christian worldview is that the placelessness imposed on Canaan as a curse is now being embraced as a way of life and a philosophy of thought. This is a self-destructive trend.

At the same time, we must remain aware of the placelessness inflicted on many around the world through exploitation, slavery, and war. This is brought into vivid focus for those of us living in Europe now in 2016, where the Syrian refugee crisis has seen thousands of displaced people pouring in through our borders to escape the conflict.

We must seek to stem the epidemic tide of placelessness, whether it exists as a result of the fall, is self-imposed, or is imposed by others.

## Man, defined by place: Genesis 10:31

*These are the sons of Shem, by their clans, their languages, their lands, and their nations.*

—*Genesis 10:31*

People are defined by the place (land) in which they live. Today the enemy would like people to be defined by the color of their skin rather than their attachment to a place.

This is one of the devil's tactics to dislodge humans from their vital connection to the land and their community. If a man is defined by something as rudimentary as the color of his skin, then by definition he is little more than a dumb animal or object endowed with no true intrinsic worth. On the contrary, human beings should be defined by place rather than being subject to superficial labels and stereotypes that seek to imprison and limit a person's view of himself or herself, the world, and those around them.

God prepared a place for man and then calls them by the place they are from because it is important to human dignity and purpose.

One of the major issues we see in the so-called "black" communities in the West is that people are no longer defined by a place; there is a diaspora forcibly displaced and oppressed with systemic racism, designed to burden us with the identity-crushing curse of placelessness.

The self-destructive fallout of disconnecting the "black" diaspora in the West from the original places that helped define them as a people and the new places where they are hindered from making meaningful attachments is that the oppressors themselves end up suffering from the same defective sense of identity: they often define themselves by color too.

The other fallout is that those affected on both sides of the displacement issues of the diaspora (oppressor and oppressed) have to deal with the social effects. Men and women created for place, in the image of God, wander the dry land like disembodied spirits, seeking some host to control, manipulate, and ultimately destroy.

As Christians, we need to recover biblical language when talking about people groups, endowing all men and women with the dignity, value, and respect due them as people created to be God's representatives in this place called Earth.

## Placement and displacement in the plans of God: Genesis 11:9

*Therefore its name was called Babel, because there the LORD confused the language of all the earth. And from there the LORD dispersed them over the face of all the earth.*

*—Genesis 11:9*

Babel is one of the most important displacement events in not only Bible history but human history too.

This displacement is not only seen as divine judgment but as a vehicle for God's original purpose of humankind filling the empty spaces of the earth by making places to the ends of the earth.

The people in their rebellion corrupted the sense of place by putting all their emphasis on the place alone and not on the One who provided the place.

Places should not become monuments or idols, as at Babel; be sure that the Lord will disperse the cancerous gathering.

A place can easily be desecrated when it is honored above God and his commands; we see this throughout the world today in both dead forms of so-called Christianity and the monuments of false religions, philosophies, or man-centered achievements.

John 4 liberates place from the locale of the temple in Jerusalem without devaluing the sacredness of the place, instead opening the door to make other places sacred by the worship of God's people.

The exclusivity of the temple as the sacred place of worship has shifted, expanded, or been liberated with a return to the tabernacle model through believers, the church, and its mission.

We will look at the implications of John 4 in the section on God's Body, Believers.

## Displaced by God's call: Genesis 13:14–17

*The LORD said to Abram, after Lot had separated from him, "Lift up your eyes and look from the place where you are, northward and southward and eastward and westward, for all the land that you see I will give to you and to your offspring forever. I will make your offspring as the dust of the earth, so that if one can count the dust of the earth, your offspring also can be counted. Arise, walk through the length and the breadth of the land, for I will give it to you."*
*—Genesis 13:14–17*

This is a different type of displacement, which was not a judgment from God or at the hand of evil men. This displacement was part of a call to faith and, in fact, was a call to better or truer placement by faith in God and the promise of God's Word.

In God's call to Abraham, he was calling him from one place to another. A better way to say it is that God was calling Abraham to a better place, a place that by God's own decree was endowed with far greater promises and significance.

So faith and place are interlinked. We see this today; in the light of the first advent or coming of Christ, we now have a gospel that, at its core, promises a displaced humanity a renewed sense of place and ultimately promises a far greater place as its reward. Jesus has gone to prepare that place, which by faith we look forward to inhabiting.

# Natural displacement: Genesis 12:10

*Now there was a famine in the land. So Abram went down to Egypt to sojourn there, for the famine was severe in the land.*

*—Genesis 12:10*

Some displacement comes about through natural disasters, which God remains in sovereign, providential, and even judicial control over.

Consider the displacement still wrought in the world today through famines, hurricanes, tsunamis, and earthquakes. I think back to 2005 when tsunamis displaced an entire people group; the pictures broadcast by news networks was harrowing and heart-wrenching. I remember rows of dead bodies, killed not by the direct agency of any human but by the groan of the land, a place that continues to reel in the wake of the fall of humankind.

We are reminded in Scripture that the place, the very land and creation itself, groans and longs to be restored. See Romans 8:22–23.

# The promise of a place: Genesis 13:14–17

*The LORD said to Abram, after Lot had separated from him, "Lift up your eyes and look from the place where you are, northward and southward and eastward and westward, for all the land that you see I will give to you and to your offspring forever. I will make your offspring as the dust of the earth, so that if one can count the dust of the earth, your offspring also can be counted. Arise, walk through the length and the breadth of the land, for I will give it to you."*

*—Genesis 13:14–17*

Place is central to the people of Israel. Without God calling Abraham out of a place, into a new place, and further to his call to lift up his eyes from that new place and survey the wider place around him, there would be no land of Israel. As a result, there would be no people of Israel because, without a clearly defined locality or place, humans are not a clear, well-defined people or people group.

There are rich lessons and serious contemporary implications in this passage:

1.  To embrace God's promise of place, we often need to let go of places that people so desperately fight for and that in our own senses would seem best. Abraham let Lot choose what seemed to be the best place according to him, only to receive a far greater place for himself and his offspring.

2. The author makes a point of letting us know that it was not until after Lot and Abraham had separated that God called Abraham to lift up his eyes and receive by faith all the land he could survey. This is true for us too; our "close relative" causing strife and discomfort in our walk of faith is our flesh, and it is in our separation from its ways that our eyes are free to look up and receive by faith God's promise of place for ourselves both spiritually in Christ and physically in this life.

3. There is a prophetic and spiritual element to place too. God tells Abraham to travel through the place that he has promised him as though to occupy and receive it by faith. Hence the rationale for prayer walking.

4. The physical world and actual places really do matter, or God would not have called Abraham to a special place, to look at a particular place and physically walk up and down in that place.

5. The land of Israel, the place God has assigned to Israel, is an everlasting physical gift to the physical decedents of Abraham; this is not allegorical or mystical, it is rooted in the firm ground of reality, which itself is rooted in the firm ground of place.

## Called from one place to another: Genesis 15:7

*And he said to him, "I am the LORD who brought you out from Ur of the Chaldeans to give you this land to possess."*

*—Genesis 15:7*

Called from one land/place to be given another land/place. As much as this narrative of calling, promises, and faith is core to redemptive history, place is at the center of that core.

## Displacement prophesied: Genesis 15:13–14

*Then the LORD said to Abram, "Know for certain that your offspring will be sojourners in a land that is not theirs and will be servants there, and they will be afflicted for four hundred years. But I will bring judgment on the nation that they serve, and afterward they shall come out with great possessions.*

*—Genesis 15:13–14*

God prophesies concerning the coming displacement for the people of Israel.

However, this displacement acted like an incubator to give them a solid base as a people and as a backdrop against which their own sense of place and identity would be more distinctly formed.

We should also consider the unilateral nature of this particular covenant, which at its core has everything to do with place. God declares that he will bring judgment on the place and bring them out of the place himself.

*T*he very first altar we read about in the Bible is the one Noah erects after the flood to make a sacrifice to the Lord in Genesis 8:20.

The word altar in Hebrew is *mizbēaḥ* and appears 403 times. As Vines states, "This word signifies a raised place where a sacrifice was made."[14]

The altar had its own sense of sanctity alongside the house or tent of God (Lev. 21:23; Num. 4:26; 18:3, 5).[15]

Sinai signaled a shift in the way God's people would interact with him as recorded in Exodus 20:22–26. Now altars would be restricted in the way they could be built. What is interesting is that the places where they could be built were not limited; in fact, the implication is that the building of the altar in line with the specifications would cause God's name to dwell in the place, thus making it sacred.

## The Lord will provide: Genesis 22:14

*So Abraham called the name of that place, "The LORD will provide"; as it is said to this day, "On the mount of the LORD it shall be provided."*

*—Genesis 22:14*

---

[14] W. E. Vine, Merrill F. Unger, and William White Jr., *Vine's Complete Expository Dictionary of Old and New Testament Words* (Nashville, TN: T. Nelson, 1996), 3.

[15] Adapted from, Willem VanGemeren, ed., *New International Dictionary of Old Testament Theology & Exegesis* (Grand Rapids, MI: Zondervan Publishing House, 1997), 889.

Abraham was called to build an altar and sacrifice his promised son, Isaac, in faith, believing that God would raise him from the dead in order to fulfill his promise. Abraham showed remarkable faith.

The very building of an altar and making an offering or sacrifice will endow a place with a sense of meaning. Beyond that, it literally will make the place sacred because of what has been built there, to whom it has been dedicated (God), and what has been done there. This, of course, can all work in reverse—if built and dedicated to a false deity, for example.

Abraham does not name the altar but the place. This place is central to the biblical narrative, as the Lord Himself will be provided in this very place as the Lamb of God.

This is re-placement in a sense because Isaac was replaced temporarily by a ram but ultimately by Jesus in the same sacred place.

## Bethel: Genesis 28:13, 16–19

*And behold, the LORD stood above it and said, "I am the LORD, the God of Abraham your father and the God of Isaac. The land on which you lie I will give to you and to your offspring …*

*Then Jacob awoke from his sleep and said, "Surely the LORD is in this place, and I did not know it." And he was afraid and said, "How awesome is this place! This is none other than the house of God, and this is the gate of heaven." So early in the morning Jacob took the stone that he had put under his head and set it up for a pillar and poured oil on the top of it. He called the name of that place Bethel, but the name of the city was Luz at the first.*

*—Genesis 28:13, 16–19*

We have seen altars before, but this one is particularly special. Let's consider the passage.

Jacob was lying on the land itself, actually connected with the place that was promised.

After God announces who he is, he then addresses the place and the connected promise.

This account helps us to have a much better understanding of place, and in particular sacred places because Jacob declares the place to be awesome because of the Lord's presence. This is where we get the definition we stated in an earlier chapter: that a mere space becomes a place and, furthermore, a sacred place when it is endowed with greater value and significance by God's presence and even by God's decree concerning it.

This was not the only time Jacob or other men of God built altars in special places unto the Lord, thus setting the place aside as sacred.

One of the practical purposes of this book is to help us to see the significance of building altars in our own lives again. It is beneficial that we have a special place and time to commune with the Lord; this serves as a type of altar. If yours has broken down, take time to rebuild it by sorting out your daily schedule.

# GOD'S MOUNTAIN: HOREB

rom this point forward in the biblical narrative, the sacred places take on a far more personal nature for God as his own mountain, tent, city, house, incarnation, body, and presence.

Sacred places now come into sharp focus with a mountain that God calls by his own name. We first read about this place in the second book of Moses, Exodus.

## Horeb: Exodus 3:1

> *Now Moses was keeping the flock of his father-in-law, Jethro, the priest of Midian, and he led his flock to the west side of the wilderness and came to Horeb, the mountain of God.*
>
> *—Exodus 3:1*

This is a place like no other. It is called the mountain of God, a title not given to any other place (except maybe the mountain in Eden, referenced in Ezekiel 28:12–19).

This points to the reality that all places do not hold the same intrinsic value.

It is interesting that the place called God's Mountain is named Horeb. The root of this word in Hebrew is *Hrb*, which is a word meaning "dry, desolate, and scorched by heat."

I think God took the worst of spaces, which on its own was dead, dry, and desolate, and endowed this space with the importance and significance of a sacred place by claiming it as his own mountain.

This points to a lesson we see throughout Scripture where God takes the simple things of his creation and by his presence and decree makes them so much more.

Examples of this include the dust of the earth, which he took and breathed into to create man; the simple men he chose to be his apostles and prophets; and even those he chooses to use who are considered disqualified and unworthy by others.

The greatest example of the Lord endowing the dry and desolate with worth is in the Christian life. We are not good in ourselves; we are earthen vessels containing the treasure of God's presence.

God using the dry and desolate makes sense; this way, his glory is clearly defined and cannot be confused with the vessel, platform, or channel he uses.

One example is that of an artist. In order to produce a clearly defined masterpiece, an artist will need a clean, simple canvas. If the canvas was already a masterpiece, then how could the artist's work be clearly defined and recognized?

Again, we can see the biblical theology of place is connected to the higher, central biblical theme of God's glory.

Paul picks this up in 2 Corinthians 4:7, where he states, "But we have this treasure in jars of clay, to show that the surpassing power belongs to God and not to us."

Another interesting point about God's mountain is that it speaks of God's dwelling place as being high and lofty, yet with a sense of humble majesty—in the bush that burns with his glory but is not consumed, in the midst of the dry and desolate space that is Horeb.

In Hebrew, the word *shamayim* that is often translated as "heaven" in its simplest terms means heights or high place.[16]

Note that in the same way that heaven will eventually come down to earth in the New Jerusalem, so there is a picture of heaven coming to earth in the sacred place of

---

[16] Cairns, Alan. *Dictionary of Theological Terms* (Belfast; Greenville, SC: Ambassador Emerald International, 2002).

the mountain of God, Horeb, where the bush burns but is not consumed and God himself calls the place holy ground.

## Holy ground: Exodus 3:4–6

*When the LORD saw that he turned aside to see, God called to him out of the bush, "Moses, Moses!" And he said, "Here I am." Then he said, "Do not come near; take your sandals off your feet, for the place on which you are standing is holy ground." And he said, "I am the God of your father, the God of Abraham, the God of Isaac, and the God of Jacob." And Moses hid his face, for he was afraid to look at God.*

*—Exodus 3:4–6*

God himself declares this dry and desolate Horeb, graced by his presence and appearing as sacred or holy ground. This is one of the first places in Scripture that the Lord distinguishes as holy, set apart, especially sacred as opposed to a mere space or normal place.

The implication is clear. The land was not intrinsically holy because its very name pointed to the unremarkable nature of the space. It is the manifestation of God's presence in the bush that makes the place holy.

In Hebrew, the term holy ground is *qōdeš* (a transliteration of the Hebrew word for apartness, holiness or sacredness[17]) and *ădāmâ* (a transliteration of the Hebrew word for ground or land).

This place was holy in the sense that it was sacred, set apart from the common space, and undefiled. Again I need to emphasize that the land itself had nothing in it to make it holy, as the New Age movement might teach, but it was made holy by God's presence and decree. This is where the title of this book, *Sacred Places*, takes its name from.

The children of Israel return to this sacred place later in the book of Exodus to receive the law and the new covenant with God, commonly referred to as the Mosaic (Moses) Covenant. This covenant is not just given in any old place but specifically in a place of God's choosing.

---

[17] Thomas E. Mccomiskey, "1990 קדשׁ," in *Theological Wordbook of the Old Testament*, ed. R. Laird Harris, Gleason L. Archer Jr., and Bruce K. Waltke (Chicago: Moody Press, 1999), 786.

# A place of agreement: Exodus 19:2–6

*They set out from Rephidim and came into the wilderness of Sinai, and they encamped in the wilderness. There Israel encamped before the mountain, while Moses went up to God. The LORD called to him out of the mountain, saying, "Thus you shall say to the house of Jacob, and tell the people of Israel: 'You yourselves have seen what I did to the Egyptians, and how I bore you on eagles' wings and brought you to myself. Now therefore, if you will indeed obey my voice and keep my covenant, you shall be my treasured possession among all peoples, for all the earth is mine; and you shall be to me a kingdom of priests and a holy nation.' These are the words that you shall speak to the people of Israel."*

*—Exodus 19:2–6*

Horeb is the place where God entered into a covenant with his people Israel, known as the Covenant of the Law.

The mountain the people set up camp by and that Moses ascended to hear from God is the same place where Moses saw the burning bush, Horeb or Sinai.

In this mountain, the whole drama of the contract, covenant, or agreement between God and Israel was initiated by God and submitted to by the people later in the book (Exodus 24:7–8).

*T*he next milestone we will look at in terms of the theology of place in the Bible is God's tent, the tabernacle.

This is the center ground of the theology of place.

## A place for God to dwell: Exodus 25:8–9

*And let them make me a **sanctuary**, that I may **dwell** in their midst. Exactly as I show you concerning the pattern of the **tabernacle**, and of all its furniture, so you shall make it.*

*—Exodus 25:8–9, (emphasis added)*

Let's begin by looking at some of the keywords in this passage. The keywords are all in bold:

1. Sanctuary
2. Dwell
3. Tabernacle

## Sanctuary

The first word is *sanctuary*. The Hebrew transliteration is *miqdāš*, meaning holy place, sanctuary or shrine.[18] The word is actually pronounced "mig-dash" according to Dr. Randall Buth.[19] We will come back to this actual word in a moment; for now, we want to spend a little time looking at the root of this word in Hebrew.

In Hebrew, the word translated as sanctuary (*miqdāš*) has its roots in a word that is simply translated as holy, this word (holy) in Hebrew is *qādaš*, pronounced "qo-des" according to Dr. Buth.[20]

Understanding the roots of the word we are studying (sanctuary) will help us think clearly about the meaning of the word, its significance, and the implications of its use by God and his people.

The Hebrew word *qādaš* is defined as "to be holy, to be hallowed or to be sanctified. It signifies being set apart and separate, either intrinsically (in the case of God) or secondarily (through rituals or contact with what is already holy)".[21]

The earliest root word in this range is *qdš*,[22] which simply means "holy" and is the root word for anything in the sphere of the sacred realm from God himself to the things he endows with holiness by his decree or presence, like places or through the rituals he passes down to his people to consecrate or make a place, thing, or person holy.

Very quickly we are starting to see the implications of this word. There is one who is intrinsically holy—God, namely the God of the Bible, Yahweh. The Bible tells us that this is one of the core attributes that makes Yahweh God. This pure and original form of holiness belongs to God alone.

Sources like the *Concise Oxford English Dictionary*, *Merriam-Webster's Collegiate Dictionary*, and *Merriam-Webster's Collegiate Thesaurus* help bring further definition and clarity to the word *holy* for English speakers.

The word *holy* (including holier and holiest) is an adjective. An adjective is an attribute added to or related to a noun to describe or modify it. A noun is simply the name of

---

[18] William D. Mounce, *Mounce's Complete Expository Dictionary of Old & New Testament Words* (Grand Rapids, MI: Zondervan, 2006), 982.
[19] Hebrew Audio Pronunciations by Buth, Randall, Faithlife 2014–2015
[20] Ibid.
[21] "Holiness," ed. Douglas Mangum et al., *Lexham Theological Wordbook*, Lexham Bible Reference Series (Bellingham, WA: Lexham Press, 2014).
[22] See Thomas E. Mccomiskey in *Theological Wordbook of the Old Testament* for more detail.

a thing, place, idea, or person(s). So we might say that a thing, person, idea, or place is holy, holier, holiest or has the attribute of holiness.

Holy is described as a thing (including persons and places) being dedicated to God or some religious purpose. It also describes a thing as possessing moral and spiritual excellence.

The English word finds its roots in German and is related to the adjective "whole".[23] It is a Middle English word derived from the Old English word *halig*, which is akin to *hal*, meaning whole.[24]

Holy can be used in a number of contexts, including:

1. A thing exalted or worthy of complete devotion because the thing is perfect in goodness and righteousness. This can only properly be attributed to God.

2. A divine thing, again only properly/ultimately attributed to God, but this can be applied to created deities like the faithful created elohim (sometimes called angels) in the unseen heavenly realm.

3. A thing devoted entirely to God or the work of God, like the sanctuary we are studying.

4. An attribute attached to God's own divine qualities like his holy love as opposed to love aside from holiness.

5. A thing venerated as or as if sacred like the Bible as God's Word.

Synonyms are words with nearly or exactly the same meaning as another word in the same language. Synonyms can be useful to help us understand this adjective in various applications and contexts. Synonyms for *holy* include:

- *Blessed* (blessed place)
- *Consecrated* (consecrated place)
- *Hallowed* (hallowed ground)
- *Sacred* (sacred place or space)
- *Sanctified* (sanctified place)
- *Unprofane* (a place that is no longer profane)

---

[23] Catherine Soanes and Angus Stevenson, eds., *Concise Oxford English Dictionary* (Oxford: Oxford University Press, 2004).

[24] Frederick C. Mish, "Preface," *Merriam-Webster's Collegiate Dictionary* (Springfield, MA: Merriam-Webster, Inc., 2003).

Some related words that are not strictly synonyms include *adored, glorified, revered, reverenced, venerated, worshiped, divine,* and *spiritual.*[25]

Among the synonyms for holy, a word of particular interest for us is *sacred.*

Related words for the adjective *sacred* include *sacramental, angelic, godly, saintly,* and *cherished.* The contrasted words are *lay, secular, temporal, earthly,* and *unhallowed,* while the adjective *profane* is a direct opposite (otherwise known as an antonym).

The word *sacred* can carry the meaning of something sanctified, dedicated to, or hallowed by association with God. This, of course, includes physical places.

A less well-known meaning for sacred is *protected* either in the context of laws, customs, or respect for a fellow human against abuse. The synonyms in this sense are *inviolable, inviolate,* and *sacrosanct.* Related words for *sacred* in the protected sense are *defended, guarded, shielded, immune,* and *untouchable.*[26]

In summary, the sanctuary is a holy, sacred, and protected place.

God is holy; the Bible calls him the Holy One and the Holy One of Israel. He is the only Being with this unique title and intrinsic attribute. Here are forty-one verses in which the Hebrew Bible calls God by this name:

- 2 Kings 19:22
- Job 6:10
- Psalm 71:22; 78:41; 89:18
- Proverbs 9:10; 30:3
- Isaiah 1:4; 5:19, 24; 10:17, 20; 12:6; 17:7; 29:19, 23; 30:11–12, 15; 31:1; 37:23; 40:25; 41:14, 16, 20; 43:3, 14–15; 45:11; 47:4; 48:17; 49:7; 54:5; 55:5; 60:9, 14
- Jeremiah 50:29; 51:5
- Ezekiel 39:7
- Hosea 11:9, 12
- Habakkuk 1:12; 3:3

As a sample from this list, Proverbs 9:10 says, "The fear of the LORD is the beginning of wisdom, and the knowledge of the Holy One is insight."

---

[25] Inc Merriam-Webster, *Merriam-Webster's Collegiate Thesaurus* (Springfield, MA: Merriam-Webster, 1996).
[26] Ibid.

The actual Hebrew does not use the term "one" for God; it literally reads as "The Holy" (although English translators are right to add the word one to retain the context that God is the one authentic, unique, original holy one, in a league all by himself, possessing eternal, complete, and total holiness). This is the case with all forty-one references.

God himself is the essence of the attribute of holiness; he is its source and so is utterly possessed with his own holiness and imparts his holiness to his creatures, making them holy too.

The supernatural beings that we sometimes generalize under the word *angels* are also called holy ones. The Bible calls God's people to be saints, which also means holy ones.

It is also worth noting that holiness is not some abstract attribute that can be called upon aside from the person of God. It is a unique part of God's very nature, which, at its source, he alone has the power to truly impart and make available to his creatures as subjects on whom his holiness acts.

Also consider God's creatures as both sentient/thinking, animated creatures (like humans and animals) and the non-thinking, inanimate creations (like rocks, land, and water) and not only in the physical realm but in the supernatural realm too.

So God calls his creation, both natural and supernatural, to live with him, set apart from sin in holiness.

The word translated as "sanctuary" is defined as a construction, which is consecrated and so recognized as a sacred place.[27]

The English word *sanctuary* is taken from the Latin word *sanctuarium* and is used for places dedicated especially for the worship of God or a false god. [28]

A review of the translated word, root word, and its implications point to the fact that the sacred place called the sanctuary was made so by God, the one who is holy, declaring that the space should be made holy for him; calling it a sanctuary confirms that it is, in fact, holy. This will be confirmed later by God's manifest presence filling the sacred place.

---

[27] James Swanson, *Dictionary of Biblical Languages with Semantic Domains: Hebrew (Old Testament)* (Oak Harbor: Logos Research Systems, Inc., 1997).
[28] Willem VanGemeren, ed., *New International Dictionary of Old Testament Theology & Exegesis* (Grand Rapids, MI: Zondervan Publishing House, 1997), 1079.

The startling realization is that the place is related to the Holy One and derives its sacredness from the Sacred One, "the Holy." In fact, by definition it could not be endowed with genuine sanctity in any other way because only the one who is holy can make other things, including places and people, holy by imparting his own holiness by decree (including that protracted through ceremonial rituals) and presence.

Our understanding of sanctuary underlines and give context to the other two words we are interested in in this passage, namely *dwell* and *tabernacle.*

## Dwell

Dwell simply means to live, to stay, or to take up residence, and in light of the sanctified place, the Lord would do this. This is a major movement in the narrative, showing us God's desire to be close to his people, to live with them in a sacred place.

## Tabernacle

Tabernacle is translated from the Hebrew word *miškān* and simply means a dwelling place, place of abode, or tent. The root word is *skn*, which carries the meaning to settle, reside, or to be enthroned.

In the Scriptures, the tabernacle is referred to in various ways, including the Tent of Meeting and the Tent of Testimony. It would contain three sections, the outer court, the Holy Place and the Holy of Holies.

In the outer court, we find a large bronze basin and a large bronze altar. These were used for ritual cleansing and sacrifice.

In the Holy Place, the priest would minister using a table of shewbread, a golden lampstand, and golden incense altar.

In the most Holy Place or Holy of Holies, the ark of the covenant would be housed, and it was from this place above the mercy seat that God would commune with his people through the high priest.

Nothing is spoken about in the Pentateuch (the five books of Moses) more than the tabernacle and the activity surrounding it.

In summary, we can conclude that central to the narrative concerning God, his people, the covenant, the law, and their living together in fellowship and harmony is place, a very special place called the tabernacle, a holy tent enabling God to dwell with his people.

Eugene Carpenter makes a very valid point in the *Evangelical Exegetical Commentary*, where he reminds us that this is the first time God has tented or abided with his people since the sanctuary of Eden."[29] This is true; now we start to see the thread running through Scripture of God setting the stage to draw humans closer to him by making himself accessible.

It is the presence of God that sets the children of Israel aside as God's own people and the tabernacle as God's sacred place of meeting with his people. However, God's presence is not just there for this reason; there is an important practical reason too, which we see throughout redemptive history and that is the purpose of the king, in his kingdom, ruling over his people.

God himself tells Moses in Exodus 29:45–46:

> *I will dwell among the people of Israel and will be their God. And they shall know that I am the LORD their God, who brought them out of the land of Egypt that I might dwell among them. I am the LORD their God.*

There is so much more that can be said about the structure of the tabernacle, its furnishings, and religious activities expressed in sacrifices, feasts and Sabbaths. However, I am going to conclude our study here, as we have established the core purpose of the tabernacle and revealed it to be vitally connected to the theology of place.

A good note to end on is the account of God blessing the newly built tabernacle with his manifest presence. I had this event in mind when formulating the thesis of the theology of place regarding the presence of God endowing a space with a sense of place and sacredness.

> *Then the cloud covered the tent of meeting, and the glory of the LORD filled the tabernacle. And Moses was not able to enter the tent of meeting because the cloud settled on it, and the glory of the LORD filled the tabernacle. (Exodus 40:34–35)*

---

[29] Eugene Carpenter, *Exodus*, ed. H. Wayne House and William D. Barrick, Evangelical Exegetical Commentary (Bellingham, WA: Lexham Press, 2012), Ex. 25:8.

# GOD'S CITY: JERUSALEM

*W*e read about Jerusalem, which was at first called Salem in Genesis 14:18. Later it become a central part of the biblical narrative as King David takes the city and makes it the capital of the kingdom in 2 Samuel 5:6–9.

It would come to be known as Zion, the City of David, and the city of God. We will take a brief look at the significance of the city, a place that God chose to dwell in through the Psalter (the book of Psalms), which takes us beyond the mere history of the city, recorded in the Bible and other literature, revealing to us the spiritual significance of this place, the most hotly contested and loved place on Earth.

## The city of God: Psalm 46:4

*There is a river whose streams make glad the city of God, the holy habitation of the Most High.*

*—Psalm 46:4*

This passage is quite clear, it states that there is a place called "the city of God." This is not referring to a spiritual place but a physical place, and all the evidence suggests this is the city of Jerusalem, the capital of the ancient kingdom.

As a city, it holds a unique place in history and theology because no other city is given this title of ownership by God himself.

The verse goes on to say that this is a holy habitation of the Most High, so God is not just associated with or owns the city but lives in it and by his presence makes it holy.

This flies in the face of the way we think today, where one place is no different from another. However, the fact remains no other place on earth was ever called God's holy habitation.

We have already studied the tabernacle, and it seems from the language in this psalm that God's purpose in the tabernacle, of dwelling among his people, is extended to the entire city of Jerusalem.

## The joy of all the earth: Psalm 48:1–3

*Great is the LORD and greatly to be praised in the city of our God! His holy mountain, beautiful in elevation, is the joy of all the earth, Mount Zion, in the far north, the city of the great King. Within her citadels God has made himself known as a fortress.*

*—Psalm 48:1–3*

Mount Zion, which is a substitute name for Jerusalem, is called the joy of all the earth in this passage. This is not said of any other city, which again sets the very place apart from all others.

The reason for this is expressed clearly in the passage; it is because within this city God has revealed himself. God choosing to reveal himself in one place as opposed to another points to the importance of place in God's redemptive plans.

This revelation also points to intimate relationship between God and the inhabitants of his city. This points to the wider theme of our biblical theology, which highlights God's desire to dwell with his people, in the same place.

This city of the great King is the City of David and will one day be the City of David's greatest son, the Messiah Jesus Christ. The city continues to hold significance for God's kingdom on the earth and his redemptive plans for his elect people in Christ.

A final observation from this passage is that the inhabitants of the city are called to praise God greatly. This is particularly true of the special place Jerusalem but also unlocks a subtle pattern we will see throughout the Bible.

This pattern is that God seeks to be praised in every place on the earth, by all peoples, and with this time of global praise will also come an age when the knowledge of the Lord will fill the earth. This is where God is taking history, to the glory of his name and the joy of all peoples. He will rule as King over all the earth with a global, glorious kingdom.

We read about this age in a number of places in the Bible. Here are just four examples:

**Habakkuk 2:14:** *"For the Earth will be filled with the knowledge of the glory of the* LORD *as the waters cover the sea."*

**Numbers 14:21:** *"But truly, as I live, and as all the earth shall be filled with the glory of the* LORD *..."*

**Psalm 22:27:** *"All the ends of the earth shall remember and turn to the* LORD*, and all the families of the nations shall worship before you."*

**Isaiah 11:9:** *"They shall not hurt or destroy in all my holy mountain; for the earth shall be full of the knowledge of the* LORD *as the waters cover the sea."*

Knowledge about God's glory and intimate, experiential relationship with the Lord will fill the earth. It will be found in every nation, tribe, and tongue. We have begun to see glimmers of this with the spread of God's kingdom through the church, but the actual age of the universal knowledge of the Lord and the full rule of his kingdom is still to come.

## Zion, God's dwelling place: Psalm 76:2

*His abode has been established in Salem, his dwelling place in Zion.*
*—Psalm 76:2*

Salem and Zion are the same place, Jerusalem. Salem is the original name of the city, meaning peace. The name Zion has become synonymous with the heavenly Jerusalem and even heaven itself.

The verse declares that the place God dwells, his abode, is Jerusalem.

This would be a good point to study a possible objection to the whole notion of place, found in the gospel of John, when Jesus engages with the Samaritan woman at the well in Syacar.

# The liberation of places to worship: John 4:20–24

*"Our fathers worshiped on this mountain, but you say that in Jerusalem is the place where people ought to worship."*

*Jesus said to her, "Woman, believe me, the hour is coming when neither on this mountain nor in Jerusalem will you worship the Father. You worship what you do not know; we worship what we know, for salvation is from the Jews. But the hour is coming, and is now here, when the true worshipers will worship the Father in spirit and truth, for the Father is seeking such people to worship him. God is spirit, and those who worship him must worship in spirit and truth."*

*—John 4:20–24*

We pick up the account where the conversation turns to places of worship, and observe the authoritative and prophetic declaration of Jesus in response to the woman's sectarian view on places of worship, which she is actually using as a diversionary device to take attention away from herself.

Jesus begins by announcing that an age is coming that will see worship liberated from any one specific location, whether that was a legitimate sacred place like Jerusalem or a traditional one like Mount Gerizim.

Jesus, however, goes on to correct the woman's faulty view of true worship by pointing out that her people do not even know what or whom they are worshiping. He does not sit on the fence and say, well, both sides are wrong, or partly right, he comes down very clearly on the side of the Jews and their Scriptures, identifying himself as a Jew in both body and belief.

He affirms that worship should not be held in Mount Gerizim as the Samaritans with their truncated Bible (just the law of Moses, with no other parts of the OT) taught, but that the Jews were, in fact, correct concerning the proper way of salvation and worship of the true God, Yahweh.

The second part of Jesus's answer can be interpreted as doing away with places entirely, requiring only a genuine and authentic heartfelt worship informed by the Word (as opposed to that not informed by the Word as seen in the Samaritans). However, I believe that will be taking the statement too far.

John 4 liberates place from the locale of the temple in Jerusalem without devaluing the sacredness of that place; instead it opens the door to make other places sacred by the heartfelt worship of God's people across the earth.

[78]

Rather than being a stumbling block to the theology of place, this passage is a necessary balance and corrective to the concept of place today. Place has evolved along with other things like the altars and sacrifices found in the narrative of redemptive history.

Also even if we did away with the importance of place based on this passage, it would only be in regard to places where worship should be done; the underlying concept of places and sacred places remains as a constant of our existence and God's redemptive purposes.

The exclusivity of the temple as the sacred place for worship has shifted, expanded, or even been liberated with a return to the tabernacle model through believers, the church, and its mission in the earth, which we will pick up in more details in our chapter on being place makers.

In conclusion, the city of Jerusalem remains a unique and special place to and for God, and itself will be replaced with a new city in the new heaven and earth bearing its name, thus upholding its status as a special city above all other cities, a place set aside from others by God's decree and presence.

This reality shines some light on the history of wars over the Holy City and the current conflicts and tension in the region, which all ultimately center on the land of Israel and its historical capital as an exalted land and city, for a chosen people, through God's own purposes by election of the Jewish people and the later election of the church from every nation, tribe, and tongue.

We have a more detailed treatment of the last point in our historical case study chapter on Israel.

# GOD'S HOUSE: THE TEMPLE

*T*he structure built as the permanent replacement to the tabernacle, as God's abiding place among his people and as the center of religious life for the believing community, is commonly called the temple or, more specifically, Solomon's temple.

However, the terminology used in Scripture is closer to house than temple, which makes sense, as it is a place for God to abide or live among his people rather than a cultic temple graced with his presence on the odd occasion.

God desires to live among his people, not just to be worshiped but to actually walk in fellowship and the joy of covenant relationship each day.

## The house is built: 2 Chronicles 3:1

> *Then Solomon began to build the house of the LORD in Jerusalem on Mount Moriah, where the LORD had appeared to David his father, at the place that David had appointed, on the threshing floor of Ornan the Jebusite.*
>
> *—2 Chronicles 3:1*

This is the first temple built for God in the OT. A special place had been prepared for it by David the great king and psalmist of Israel. The place, including its surrounding area, is not new to the unfolding biblical narrative; we have seen it before and will see it again. This was the traditional region in which Abraham bound Isaac to be offered as a sacrifice (Gen. 22:2) and the eventual location of the sacrifice provided in place of Isaac through the offering of Jesus on the cross (Matt. 27:33, Mark 15:22; Luke 23:33; John 19:17). This site is indeed a special place unlike any other.

God had previously appeared to David on this specific site after he built an altar there in repentance (2 Sam. 24:18–25; 1 Chr. 21:18–30). These passages provide solid evidence that the Lord had established the space on the threshing floor as sacred by virtue of his presence, as evidenced in his appearance to David and by the altar built to honor and appease him there.

While there are questions regarding the historical evidence[30] that this is the exact same site as Abraham's offering of Isaac, it is fair to say that the region was the same. The readers of the chronicle at the time understood this implication because they already had the Abrahamic account from Genesis. Therefore, the temple being built here added to the sanctity of the structure, as it reached back in redemptive history to the Lord's promise of sacrificial provision for his people, which is what the house of the Lord existed to provide, through the sacrificial system of the Levites.

As Christians, we attach special significance to the site because it is in the same area that Jesus died on the cross, called Golgotha.

Modern-day Judaism and Islam also attach very special significance to the site.

Jewish tradition teaches that the cornerstone of the temple was the rock Abraham used to attempt the sacrifice of Isaac, and that this historical event acts as the archetype or foundation to all temple sacrifices.[31]

This rock became known as the foundation stone. According to legend, it was the place of creation, the very foundation on which the world was built, and Abraham would later attempt to offer Isaac on the same rock. It is the foundation of the temple and even a rock that blocks up waters of the abyss, keeping demonic forces sealed below.[32]

---

[30] See James R. Davila, *The Anchor Yale Bible Dictionary*, 1992 and Jeremiah K. Garrett, *The Lexham Bible Dictionary*, 2012, 2013, 2014, 2015.

In contrast to Davila, see Avraham Negev, *The Archaeological Encyclopedia of the Holy Land*, 1990 and T. C. Mitchell, *New Bible Dictionary*, 1996.

[31] Jeremiah K. Garrett, "Mount Moriah," ed. John D. Barry et al., *The Lexham Bible Dictionary* (Bellingham, WA: Lexham Press, 2012, 2013, 2014, 2015).

[32] Edward P. Sri, *Mystery of the Kingdom: On the Gospel of Matthew* (Steubenville, OH: Emmaus Road Publishing, 1999), 97.

I have been to Jerusalem a number of times, and these traditions are still believed today, according to an official epitaph to the foundation stone in the precinct of the Western Wall.

Muslim tradition agrees with much of the Jewish tradition regarding the foundation stone but goes further to say that it was the site from which Mohammed ascended to heaven. This is why the structure they built over the supposed foundation stone is called the Dome of the Rock, the rock being this foundation stone. This site, and its associated Al-Aqsa Mosque, is one of the oldest and third-most revered site in Islam, built on the temple mount itself in 692 AD.[33]

All this talk about foundation stones and rocks is significant; these are mostly legends with no historical support, yet Jesus knew that men would put their faith in the place itself rather than in him. Thus, he challenged the traditional belief and import given to this supposed foundation stone by declaring himself to be the true foundation stone.

Jesus said of himself that he was the cornerstone and that the truth that he is the Christ was the foundation upon which he would build the church, and the gates of hell would not be able to prevail against them. This may be a reference to the belief that the foundation stone plugged up the forces of hell.

Jesus also taught that truly believing his teaching and living it out would be the equivalent to a man who built his house on a rock and so was able to withstand the storms of life.

As we mentioned before, when looking at John 4, the exclusivity of the temple as the place of worship has been surpassed as well as the significance of the foundation stone because Jesus is the foundation stone for the true houses of God, manifested in the earth corporately and individually through those who put their trust in the Rock.

Much of our earlier study about the sanctity of the tabernacle applies to the temple. I do not want to go into a large amount of detail about the temple; however, it suffices to say that, like the tabernacle, it points to the significance of places and sacred places, in particular, in redemptive history and ultimately points forward to Christ.

---

[33] For more detail, see *Encyclopedia Britannica Noet Edition*, 2015 or F. L. Cross and Elizabeth A. Livingstone, eds., *The Oxford Dictionary of the Christian Church*, 2005.

In conclusion, as we saw with the tabernacle, the Lord endorses the building of the House by filling it with his presence, which, by virtue of himself, sanctifies the place as holy.

This whole section has seen the placement of God's house through its building and consecration in God's city, Jerusalem. Now we will go on to briefly review displacement and re-placement in regard to the temple.

## The house is destroyed

The first great displacement for both the City of Jerusalem and the house of God in particular came in the form of God's ordained judgment through the Babylonian ruler Nebuchadnezzar in approximately 587 BC as recorded in 2 Kings 25:8–21 and 2 Chronicles 36:18–19, which reads:

> And all the vessels of the house of God, great and small, and the treasures of the house of the LORD, and the treasures of the king and of his princes, all these he brought to Babylon. And they burned the house of God and broke down the wall of Jerusalem and burned all its palaces with fire and destroyed all its precious vessels.

See additional references here: 2 Kings 25:8–21; 2 Chronicles 36:18–21; 1 Chronicles 6:15; 9:1; Ezra 5:12, 14; 6:5; Jeremiah 1:3; 39:8–10; 52:12–27, 29; Daniel 5:2.

Much of the work of the major prophets leads up to this judgment, while most of the smaller prophets are in context to the aftermath of the destruction and the desire to rebuild the sacred place in the Holy City.

A new concept for the Jews living in captivity in Babylon was how they as a believing community could practice their faith faithfully while living in exile and without the central holy place of the temple.

This is where we first see the introduction of synagogues and the liberation or extension of holy places from a single locale as was the case with the temple, this paved the way for modern-day Judaism and, by extension, Christianity.

The second displacement in this regard came in 70 AD as prophesied by Jesus, who laments over the coming destruction in Matthew 23:37–38 and Luke 13:34–35, which reads:

*O Jerusalem, Jerusalem, the city that kills the prophets and stones those who are sent to it! How often would I have gathered your children together as a hen gathers her brood under her wings, and you were not willing! Behold, your house is forsaken. And I tell you, you will not see me until you say, "Blessed is he who comes in the name of the Lord!"*

Later in the same Gospel, Jesus appears to prophecy about the actual destruction of Jerusalem and the temple, see Luke 19:43–44.

*For the days will come upon you, when your enemies will set up a barricade around you and surround you and hem you in on every side and tear you down to the ground, you and your children within you. And they will not leave one stone upon another in you, because you did not know the time of your visitation.*

In fact, Jesus makes reference to the destruction of the Temple multiple times in the gospel records, including Matthew 24:2, 26:61, Mark 13:2, Luke 21:6, and John 2:19.[34]

Jesus's prophesy came to pass in 70 AD under Titus of Rome, who fulfilled the abomination of desolation by desecrating the holy place of the temple and going on to utterly destroy the structure.

## The house is rebuilt

In between the two great displacement events, with regard to God's house, was the re-placement of the house.

The rebuilding is recorded in Ezra. Here is a passage about the beginning of the restoration in Ezra 3:11–13:

*And they sang responsively, praising and giving thanks to the LORD, "For he is good, for his steadfast love endures forever toward Israel." And all the people shouted with a great shout when they praised the LORD, because the foundation of the house of the LORD was laid. But many of the priests and Levites and heads of fathers' houses, old men who had seen the first house, wept with a loud voice when they saw the foundation of this house being laid, though many shouted aloud for joy, so that the people could not distinguish the sound of the*

---

[34] Read more about this in R. A. Guelich, "Destruction of Jerusalem," eds. Joel B. Green and Scot McKnight, *Dictionary of Jesus and the Gospels* (Downers Grove, IL: InterVarsity Press, 1992), 175.

*joyful shout from the sound of the people's weeping, for the people shouted with
a great shout, and the sound was heard far away.*

This temple was less ornate but no less sacred. This serves as a useful corrective to
many church traditions that have a warped view of place, which the Puritans rightly
reacted against. The place is not made sacred by decorations and ornate furnishing;
rather, the place is made sacred by the decree and presence of God.

We read later that the building work was successful in Ezra 6:14:

> *And the elders of the Jews built and prospered through the prophesying of
> Haggai the prophet and Zechariah the son of Iddo. They finished their
> building by decree of the God of Israel and by decree of Cyrus and Darius and
> Artaxerxes king of Persia;*

Notice the passage declares that the rebuilding was according to God's sovereign
decree as the ultimate King over his people but also under the decree of the world
leaders at the time and the spiritual leaders of the faith community in Israel.

As we mentioned in our opening thesis, it is the decree of God that makes a place
sacred. However, this is not without the obedience, faith, and activity of God's
people. In this sense, God's people are the place makers as his representatives or
image bearers. We will spend more time talking about this in the place makers
chapter.

# GOD INCARNATE: JESUS

*N*ow we turn to the New Testament, where God comes closer than ever through the incarnation of his Son, Jesus the Christ. Jesus tabernacled,[35] as it were, in the body prepared for him and tabernacled with his people for the time of his incarnation on the earth both before and after his resurrection.

## Immanuel, God with us: Matthew 1:21–23

*"She will bear a son, and you shall call his name Jesus, for he will save his people from their sins." All this took place to fulfill what the Lord had spoken by the prophet: "Behold, the virgin shall conceive and bear a son, and they shall call his name Immanuel" (which means, God with us).*

*—Matthew 1:21–23*

In this account, one of God's ministering spirits named Gabriel spoke to Joseph in a dream concerning the God-Man, Jesus, who would be born through the virgin Mary. To be sure, we mean virgin in the sense that she had never had sexual intercourse, not just in the sense that she was a young woman.

We hear that his name will be Jesus because of the redemptive mission he has come to accomplish for God's elect people. Matthew, the apostle and author of this gospel, who himself was an eyewitness to the life, ministry, death, bodily resurrection, and

---

[35] Or lived in a holy tent, if the body can be considered as a place in which the spirit dwells.

ascension of Jesus, adds an editorial note to the gospel record by quoting the Hebrew Bible and declaring unequivocally that Jesus is the fulfillment of this prophecy found in Isaiah 7:14.

The name Immanuel is also interpreted to ensure there is no confusion. It means that God is with us, and indeed he was—in a way that mankind had never known before. God came closer and more clearly than any other time in redemptive history, he became incarnate, born into Adam's fallen race to save them.

The name and function of Immanuel points to the big Bible theme of God with his people, in the same place.

God had been moving toward this more perfect expression of Immanuel through the other tabernacles of redemptive history, including the mountain, the tabernacle, and the temple or house, but they all pointed to the Son of God, Jesus the Christ.

But how was this thing that Sinai, the tabernacle, and the temple had pointed to going to be possible? How could God be with men? There was only one answer: God would have to become incarnate in time and space through birth. This is explained further in the next two verses.

## The Word made flesh: John 1:1, 14

*In the beginning was the Word, and the Word was with God, and the Word was God ...*

*And the Word became flesh and dwelt among us, and we have seen his glory, glory as of the only Son from the Father, full of grace and truth.*
*—John 1:1, 14*

The explicit implications of these verses are clear: the Word is God and yet district from the Father because the Word is God and is with God. The second verse tells us that this Word became flesh.

This shows that Jesus did not merely have a human origin but was eternal with God and yet is God himself and that this eternal Word became a man. The previous verse explains how this was achieved.

He did not just appear in human form, as he would have done in an OT appearance known as a theophany. This was different; God actually became a fully fledged 100 percent man while remaining in essence 100 percent God. This is where we get the unique term for Jesus, the God-Man.

## The humble God: Philippians 2:5–11

*Have this mind among yourselves, which is yours in Christ Jesus, who, though he was in the form of God, did not count equality with God a thing to be grasped, but emptied himself, by taking the form of a servant, being born in the likeness of men. And being found in human form, he humbled himself by becoming obedient to the point of death, even death on a cross. Therefore God has highly exalted him and bestowed on him the name that is above every name, so that at the name of Jesus every knee should bow, in heaven and on earth and under the earth, and every tongue confess that Jesus Christ is Lord, to the glory of God the Father.*

*—Philippians 2:5–11*

This verse shows us the heart of God our Father and Jesus, who emptied himself so he could be born in the likeness of men to save us. All humanity is called to bow in reverence to Jesus as King and confess that he is the Sovereign Lord of all creation.

In a sense, Jesus was displaced from his glory with the Father in heaven (John 17:5, 24) so that he could be placed in the body or tent prepared for him (Hebrews 10:5) so that humankind's relationship could be re-placed before God, in the right standing or righteousness that God's holy love desires and demands.

Jesus is the greatest of all place makers, in fact he said he would go and prepare a place for us so that we could be together in the same place forever in heaven.

## The place of the skull: John 19:16–19

*So he delivered him over to them to be crucified. So they took Jesus, and he went out, bearing his own cross, to the place called The Place of a Skull, which in Aramaic is called Golgotha. There they crucified him, and with him two others, one on either side, and Jesus between them. Pilate also wrote an inscription and put it on the cross. It read, "Jesus of Nazareth, the King of the Jews."*

*—John 19:16–19*

The cross was ground zero for God's attack on the kingdom of darkness, the center ground of the drama of redemption, the pinnacle of human achievement in Jesus the man and divine action in Jesus the God. It was the scene of the sacrifice of the God-Man, for God's holy love, to redeem the fallen race of men and establish the kingdom of God on earth. There is nothing more important than the cross in the Christian mind, faith, and practice.

One of the first deeply theological books I ever read was the late John Stott's *The Cross of Christ*. In it he lays out the centrality of the cross for our faith in historical, practical, and theological terms. He goes on to explore the significance of this great work of Christ in providing a penal substitutionary atonement for all those who would put their faith and trust in him.

All the gospel writers agree that the crucifixion did not just happen in some undesignated place but was in a very specific, almost appointed place called Golgotha or the Skull or the place of the skull. See Matthew 27:33, 39; Mark 15:21–22; Luke 23:33; and even Hebrews 13:12–13.

It seems that with the imagery of death, this was the most cursed of places and yet this is where the Son of God died. And that is the scandalous beauty of God's work of redemption and the gospel message we have been entrusted with.

It is this place where sin did most abound, on this dark place, on the cursed earth that Jesus poured out his blood, like a simultaneous high priest and sacrificial lamb, for the sins of the human race. His connection to our sin was through the place he had come to inhabit with us, the cursed earth.

Years before, the same earth was cursed as a result of man's treason in the sanctuary of Eden and later opened its mouth to receive the innocent blood of Abel; now this same cursed earth received the blood of the Son of God. The curse set in motion by the rebellion of the first Adam was reversed by the obedience of the eschatological (last) Adam.

Place underpins much of the scene at the cross. Jesus wears a crown of thorns, the thorns that came and thrived as part of the curse the sin of man had inflicted on his domain by breaking allegiance with God his King.

These thorns were long and sharp. They pierced deeply into the head of the redeemer, and his blood—the innocent blood that makes atonement for sin because life is in

[89]

the blood—touched the thorns, the symbol of sin's curse and death; then the curse is broken.

Take a moment and sing praise to the Lamb of God who takes away the sin of the world, the seed of the woman, the seed of Abraham, the great Lion of the Tribe of Judah, the greatest son of David, Daniel's Son of Man, the Messiah, the King, the Christ of Peter's confession, the Alpha and Omega, the one who is worthy, the God of our salvation, our victorious savior, the Servant-King, Jesus.

## The place shakes: Matthew 27:50–51

*And Jesus cried out again with a loud voice and yielded up his spirit. And behold, the curtain of the temple was torn in two, from top to bottom. And the earth shook, and the rocks were split.*

*—Matthew 27:50–51*

Jesus's death shakes the earth, the cursed place, as the chains of sin were broken and the effects of the curse were put in reverse. In a spiritual way, manifest in the physical sense, the earth mourns the death of the Son of God.

Matthew's intention as an author is clear: as a witness to the events, he is conveying to us that they are directly linked, that the death of the Son of God had an effect on the place in multiple ways. There was an earthquake, the ground was split, and the veil in the temple was torn.

The splitting of rocks may seem insignificant, but it is not. Firstly, it tells us that this was no small shaking; and, secondly, it points to a deep spiritual reality. The dearth of Christ caused great shockwaves in the spiritual and physical realms. The splitting of the rocks was symbolic of the breaking of the "curse of place" and placelessness imposed by God as a judgment in Eden, in a symbolic way pointing forward to the ultimate end of Jesus's work.

The split rock also echoes the event that would happen in three days' time, when we would see the full reversal of death, the death that judicially entered the world as a penal judgment and consequence for the high treason of man and woman. At the resurrection, we would again see the movement of the place with rocks rolled and the ground shaken.

The holy place is forever changed; the torn curtain, possibly as a result of the earthquake, holds particular significance for us as students of God's Word, but also for the Jews at the time. These lessons could have included the following:

1. The end of God's dwelling in the Holy of Holies.
2. The end of the sacrificial system.
3. The sorrow of the Father for his Son, like a father tearing his garments.
4. Judgment on the corrupt leaders at the time.
5. Pointing to the prophesied destruction of the temple.

Throughout church history, many possible interpretations have been put forward. The list above is one I've devised myself, but there are more. A full overview has been made by Daniel M. Grutner in *Themelios: Volume 29*; it makes for interesting reading if you have the time.

One interesting interpretation I picked up when reading this was the tearing of the veil opening the new and living way for humanity to approach God through the blood of Jesus. This points to the spiritual realities of the veil and the work of Christ on the cross as mentioned in Hebrews 6:19, 9:3, and 10:20.

Grutner mentions in his conclusion the parallel between the veil in heaven—which conceals God's abode—and the veil to the most Holy of Holies—which was God's abode on earth, like a heaven on earth. He goes on to say that this then could point to the rending of the heavens or the opening of heaven's doors, signifying the start of the last days, which Jesus inaugurated. He notes the following Scriptures regarding the opening of access to heaven: Revelation 3:7–8; 4:1; 11:19; 15:5; 19:11.[36]

I think this is a great insight to the deeper and symbolic meaning of this event, which is recorded in all the gospels. This interpretation lends weight to our assertion regarding the central theme of God dwelling with his people in the same place.

## The garden of resurrection: John 19:41–42

*Now in the place where he was crucified there was a garden, and in the garden a new tomb in which no one had yet been laid. So because of the Jewish day of Preparation, since the tomb was close at hand, they laid Jesus there.*

*—John 19:41–42*

---

[36] Daniel M. Grutner, "The Rending of the Veil Matt. 27:51a: A Look Back and a Way Forward," *Themelios: Volume 29, No. 3, Summer 2004*, 2004, 14.

We began the story in the garden of Eden, the original sanctuary of Yahweh with man but also the scene of the greatest crime in the history of humanity, the tragic fall of Adam's royal line and the subsequent judgment.

Here we are in another garden, but now comes the twist in the narrative, the turning point; the tide turns, the kingdom of darkness is on the back foot, and the kingdom of light is gaining ground and pressing forward. The King is alive.

This is it. This is the good news. This is what we run from place to place proclaiming: that the King has come and has been victorious in his battle with sin, death, and the devil.

Jesus literally conquered death, and he did this by reversing the effects of the fall, in a full and eternal bodily resurrection. The fact it was a "bodily" resurrection should dispel any subtle Gnostic and Dualistic views that have diluted our taste for God's glory and sacredness in the physical world.

Jesus not only rose bodily, he rose in glory, in a body transfigured and transformed by the glory of God touching his flesh, the dust of the earth.

The fact that Jesus rose in a garden was no accident. God, the ultimate and original storyteller, is weaving a tale of redemption and a beautiful narrative of salvation for the same race of men he had placed in the garden. God now invites all men and women to come to another garden, the resurrection garden, and see that the Son is risen, the battle is won, and now we can walk in fellowship and worship with God again in the cool of the day.

Consider resurrection for a moment. Why bother? Why not just exist in the spiritual, nonphysical world? Why is that not the end? Why resurrection?

Because God's creation is good, the physical world was his idea, the body was his idea, the housing of spirit beings was his idea, the human race was his idea, and he has not changed his mind. Place is central, crucial, and foundational to the very purpose of God in creation and redemption. Jesus rose and came back to the earth, living here again for over a month, although in an elevated state. He will return here in the end, and one day the city of God will be here. Resurrection is God's way because place matters.

## A place prepared: John 14:2–3

*In my Father's house are many rooms. If it were not so, would I have told you that I go to prepare a place for you? And if I go and prepare a place for you, I will come again and will take you to myself, that where I am you may be also.*

*—John 14:2–3*

This verse is one of the strongest in favor of the theology of place as an overarching theme in the Bible and as a large part of the ultimate end of the Bible's narrative, of God's purposes in election, his story of redemption, motivated by his own holy love.

I am so excited about the place Jesus has prepared for us. He has offered his shed blood in heaven's tabernacle for all his elect sheep that he has redeemed by his blood. We have so much to look forward to.

In a later chapter about heaven, we will spend some time looking at the intersection of earth and heaven in the New Jerusalem (Rev. 3:12; 21:2) and consider our prepared place in this new city of God, which the saints of old looked forward to (Heb. 11:10) rather than varied faulty concepts of heaven being beyond and removed from God's good and soon to be purified and perfected creation (see 2 Peter 3:7–12).

*N*ow is the time to bring this home (pun indented). As believers, we exist as God's body, his image bearers and representatives on the Earth. In a sense, we are God's government in his creation, his council on the earth.

God now Tabernacles in us through God the Holy Spirit, the third person of the Trinity.

## Filled with God: John 14:15–17, 25–26

> *"If you love me, you will keep my commandments. And I will ask the Father, and he will give you another Helper, to be with you forever, even the Spirit of truth, whom the world cannot receive, because it neither sees him nor knows him. You know him, for he dwells with you and will be in you ..."*

> *"These things I have spoken to you while I am still with you. But the Helper, the Holy Spirit, whom the Father will send in my name, he will teach you all things and bring to your remembrance all that I have said to you."*
> —*John 14:15–17, 25–26*

This passage follows on from the last reference we looked at from John's gospel, where Jesus said he was going to prepare a place for us. The setting is the Last Supper held at Passover, and Jesus is preparing, comforting, and charging his disciples for his imminent arrest, suffering, death, resurrection, and ascension.

This is an amazing development in God's story of redemption. First we were blown away by the reality that God came and lived in a tent of flesh with us as an actual man, Jesus the Christ, Immanuel, God with us. Now God goes even further by committing himself in this new covenant to live inside each believer and to be in the midst of the new believing community of Jesus's disciples.

Think about that for a minute. God himself now lives in believers. The believer is like the house of God in Jerusalem, where God lives in holiness and exerts his power and authority over that place. An even better analogy is that we are like the sanctuary of the tabernacle, holding the presence of God and a place in which God dwells like the house of God, only this house is on the move.

This passage is where we first hear about the promised Holy Spirit, but it is certainly not everything the Bible has to say on the phenomenon of being filled with God the Holy Spirit. Additional references from both testaments include but are not limited to:

Exodus 31:3; 35:31

Deuteronomy 34:9

Joel 2:28–29

Luke 1:15, 41, 67; 4:1; 10:21; 24:49

John 1:33; 3:34; 7:39

Acts 1:4–5, 8; 2: 2–4, 16–18, 33; 4:8, 31; 6:3–5; 7:55; 8:15–17; 9:17; 10:38, 44–47; 11:15–17, 24; 13:9, 52; 15:8; 19:6

Romans 7:6; 8:4–6; 15:13

Galatians 3:2–5; 5:16, 22–23, 25

1 Corinthians 12:13

2 Corinthians 3:17; 5:1; 6:6

Ephesians 5:18–20

If you have taken time to read the passages above, you will see that the Holy Spirit serves many functions in our lives, he is the ultimate author of the Scriptures, the one who brings us from death to life, our guide, teacher, the one who helps us, our intercessor, the one who convicts of sin, the one who empowers us and produces fruit in us.

The Holy Spirit living inside Christians is one of the great pinnacles of redemptive history; he is the down payment on our eternal inheritance, the seal of our redemption.

Our earlier study on the word *sacred* of course applies to God the Spirit because he is the "Holy" Spirit, and the places in which he dwells are made holy by virtue of his presence. It is the Holy Spirit who we have seen throughout redemptive history from the moment he hovered over the face of the placeless waters at creation to the work of regeneration he accomplishes in believers causing them to be born again.

It is God the Holy Spirit who sanctifies and makes holy, he is the great place maker by his very presence, carrying out the Father's decrees and making effectual the Son's work.

As believers, we should honor the God inside us as holy by living holy lives in union with Christ. Some teach that the Holy Spirit is not God while others teach that the Son, Jesus the Christ, is not God, still other confuse the persons of the one God. To be clear, we will take a moment to look at our biblical and historic beliefs concerning the Tri-Unity of God.

## The Trinity

The Christian teaching on God is distinguished from all other religions, systems of belief, or cults in its understanding of the three in oneness or tri-unity, specifically the eternal coexistence of the Father, Son, and Spirit, who remain equal in all the attributes that make God who God is.

See Appendix A for a list of God's attributes compiled for a six-week apologetics course I wrote for Worldwide Mission Fellowship in November 2015.

And the catholic (Universally accepted) faith is this: That we worship one God in Trinity, and Trinity in Unity; Neither confounding the persons nor dividing the substance. For there is one person of the Father, another of the Son, and another of the Holy Spirit.[37]

This quote is from one of the ancient creeds of the faith, written some time before 428 AD, commonly called the Athanasian Creed. Although not written by Athanasius, it

---

[37] *Taken from the* Athanasian Creed, Source, *Historic Creeds and Confessions.* (1997). (electronic ed.). Oak Harbor: Lexham Press.

deals with the doctrine of the Trinity, which he was famous for defending centuries before.

It makes clear the central tenet of the doctrine of the Trinity, which is that God is one in essence with three distinct persons, and that one person should not be confused with another, yet all three are the one God, not three gods.

The New Bible Dictionary summarizes this point well by affirming that, as Christians, our beliefs regarding the Trinity have three basic tenets:

1. there is one God;
2. the Father, the Son, and the Spirit are each fully God;
3. each is a distinct person.[38]

This brief detour has been taken to remind us that the permanent indwelling of the Spirit of God in the believer is an absolutely mind-blowing reality; we are talking about God, not just a spirit, power, or philosophical notion. God lives inside the believer, as Paul reminds us in a later section.

## Together in one place Acts 2:1–4

> *When the day of Pentecost arrived, they were all together in one place. And suddenly there came from heaven a sound like a mighty rushing wind, and it filled the entire house where they were sitting. And divided tongues as of fire appeared to them and rested on each one of them. And they were all filled with the Holy Spirit and began to speak in other tongues as the Spirit gave them utterance.*
>
> —*Acts 2:1–4*

This event, the full coming of the Holy Spirit to live in and among believers, was the birth of the church. It is significant that these first Jewish believers all had to be in one place. Think about it: the Spirit transcends time and space because he created them, so why would the foundational members of the church, both men and women have to be in one place in agreement or one accord, as the KJV puts it? Could it be again the place has a significant part to play in the story?

The place was a house, not a synagogue or the temple or some other special venue, it was a normal place. This alone holds a huge amount of significance; it seems now that

---

[38] M. Turner and G. McFarlane, "Trinity," in *New Bible Dictionary*, ed. D. R. W. Wood, I. H. Marshall, A. R. Millard, J. I. Packer, and D. J. Wiseman, 3rd ed. (Downers Grove, IL: InterVarsity Press, 1996), 1209.

God's people can gather anywhere, and he would then sanctify that space by coming by God the Spirit and filling the place or rather by filling the people in the place.

The story of the place makers has begun! But it was all started and is sustained by the ultimate place maker, the one who hovers over the placeless creation brooding, being, in holiness and love—the God who created every space and place and time itself.

Contrast this story of God the Spirit entering a place with the time he entered the temple or the sanctuary. In those stories, there was much ceremonial holiness and rituals, and when he came it was to be in the place, not the people.

Also in the accounts of God coming as the Spirit to dwell in a place, there would be warnings and accounts of death to those who infringed on his holiness. There was an unapproachableness to his glory and presence that was unlike anything any human had ever seen.

Now something has changed, the Spirit came, but the climate and conditions are different; Jesus has changed something. Could it be true? Could it be as he had always said from the first word of his ministry, that the kingdom had come and things had changed? Had the way to God been opened up, had the ordinances, rituals, types, and shadows been done away with? Would God and humankind dwell together so freely?

Everything that Jesus said about the kingdom of God; the effect of his birth, life, death, resurrection, ascension, enthronement at the right hand of his Father; and the coming of God again—but this time not the Son, but God the Spirit—had all been true. The Spirit of God entering this normal place was evidence of this, and the effect on this scared little band of believers was proof to the world that the Spirit had come.

Another consideration in regard to place and the room is that places can be used by God and his people for sanctification and to find agreement and unity.

This event as well as the resurrection and appearances of Christ gave precedents to the church to infuse their lives with a theology of place by meeting together on the Lord's day in honor of his resurrection and the coming of God the Holy Spirit at the birth of the church.

One final consideration is that this was a place of empowerment, a place where the disciples were empowered by the Spirit of God for the mission God had given them to do. The staggering reality is that they would not have to visit this place to be charged up or pay homage but became the carriers of God in the earth themselves, as vessels of the Spirit to accomplish his will in the earth.

One more thing: note the church was born in Jerusalem, God's city, not in any other city, and it was from here that it spread to every other place.

The rest of the book of Acts details the adventure of the Spirit of God though the apostles as they set about fulfilling the Great Commission by proclaiming the gospel of the kingdom all over the world, making places for God to dwell via his people and rule via the Spirit.

A good way to end this section is to reflect on the prophetic words of Jesus concerning the purpose of the event that shows the centrality of place for the church and its mission in Acts 1:8:

> But you will receive power when the Holy Spirit has come upon you, and you will be my witnesses in Jerusalem and in all Judea and Samaria, and to the end of the earth.

## Bodies as temples: 1 Corinthians 6:19–20

> Or do you not know that your body is a temple of the Holy Spirit within you, whom you have from God? You are not your own, for you were bought with a price. So glorify God in your body.
>
> —1 Corinthians 6:19–20

The Bible teaches that the body is a temple or house, which means something lives inside the body; more than one thing can even live in one body. I know that all sounds a bit mystical and farfetched, but it is what the Bible actually teaches as you can read for yourself in the verse above. Also just pause for a minute and think about our own existence, talk to yourself now in your mind, pause and assess your feelings and thoughts now, and you will quickly realize you are more than just a body.

Still not convinced? Okay, look at this. Jesus spoke of his own body as a temple in John 2:19–21:

> Jesus answered them, "Destroy this temple, and in three days I will raise it up." The Jews then said, "It has taken forty-six years to build this temple, and will you raise it up in three days?" But he was speaking about the temple of his body.

Jesus's teaching on the spiritual realm precludes or makes the assumption that his hearers understand that spirits live inside bodies. In Luke 11:24–26, Jesus teaches us:

> *"When the unclean spirit has gone out of a person, it passes through waterless places seeking rest, and finding none it says, 'I will return to my house from which I came.' And when it comes, it finds the house swept and put in order. Then it goes and brings seven other spirits more evil than itself, and they enter and dwell there. And the last state of that person is worse than the first."*

The point made is clear. There is also an interesting sidenote here in regard to the theology of place. The evil spirits go to waterless or dry and desolate places. They are placeless beings that have been disembodied as judgment and need a place to dwell in. The places they dwell in are people, the actual material bodies of men and women.

James agrees with the teaching and basic presupposition of both Jesus and Paul when he uses the following example in his teaching on the necessity of genuine, active faith in James 2:26: "For as the body apart from the spirit is dead, so also faith apart from works is dead."

While we are talking about the subject of spirits and bodies, let's look at one more example, which shines a light on the nature of the unseen realm, the centrality and importance of place—even for the spirits God has created, which each have their place in a material house, in other words a body.

Jude verse 6 states:

> *And the angels who did not stay within their own position of authority, but left their proper dwelling, he has kept in eternal chains under gloomy darkness until the judgment of the great day—*

At first glance, it just looks like these angels (created spirit beings) left their own homes or land in some sort of rebellion, going beyond their allocated authority and so have been judged. However, there is more to the text than this. All commentators agree that the angels (the actual word translated as angel in Hebrew is almost always *elohim*, simply meaning a created divine or spiritual being as opposed to the eternal (not created) divine being [Elohim] who is Yahweh) spoken about here are the same ones found in Genesis 6:1–4 where we read (emphasis added):

> *When man began to multiply on the face of the land and daughters were born to them, the sons of God saw that the daughters of man were attractive. And*

[100]

*they took as their wives any they chose. Then the Lord said, "My Spirit shall not abide in man forever, for he is flesh: his days shall be 120 years." **The Nephilim** were on the earth in those days, and also afterward, when the sons of God came in to the daughters of man and they bore children to them. These were the mighty men who were of old, the men of renown.*

Traditional Jewish and Christian commentators agree that these sons of God (created Elohim, often translated as angels) took on a physical form and had actual sex with actual women, which produced actual giants known as Nephilim.

With this in mind, consider the passage in Jude again; it is not only saying they left their allotted place like a building or land but left their own heavenly bodies and took on bodies in this realm and then went far beyond their allotted authority as God's creations. They overstepped the mark and committed a grievous sin by transgressing the physical realm from their spiritual realm and joining sexually with human women to produce hybrid offspring that should never have existed.[39]

Remember spiritual beings need a place to live in and cannot just dwell in any place they choose but in the place or body that God has assigned either by grace (in creation and life) or in judgment (in damnation and death).

Back to our main passage: as believers, we are called to live holy lives because the One living inside us, the One who has made our body his place of dwelling is Holy. He is literally holy in his essence; at his core, he is the source of all holiness and sanctifies as holy that which he graces with his presence.

We are sanctified, made holy, as God's houses on the earth and in light of the God who lives in us with his holy nature, which itself has sanctified our nature. We must live out that miracle, act out that holy life, allowing the Spirit of God, the great place maker to express his holy love through us, so that we as carriers of God, the greatest treasure, can carry him and his presence across the earth to every dry and desolate place. Filling the earth with his presence.

So the call is simple, we need to make the conscious choice to honor the holy God residing in our bodies, the place he has chosen to live in the earth instead of a single building (note buildings are often made from the materials of the earth, reflecting the human body made from the same material).

---

[39] See Herbert W. Bateman IV, *Jude: Evangelical Exegetical Commentary* for a more detailed discussion of the connection between Jude 6 and Genesis 6.

The practical application is that we turn away in mind and action from sin. The biblical word for this is repentance, which is inextricably linked to genuine saving faith. For example, we cannot in good conscience choose to live in a known sin like fornication in its many forms. This is the example Paul uses too because sexual sin has a direct effect on the body unlike many other sins.

## Conformed to his image: Romans 8:28–30

> *And we know that for those who love God all things work together for good,*
> *for those who are called according to his purpose. For those whom he foreknew*
> *he also predestined to be conformed to the image of his Son, in order that he*
> *might be the firstborn among many brothers. And those whom he predestined*
> *he also called, and those whom he called he also justified, and those whom he*
> *justified he also glorified.*
>
> *—Romans 8:28–30*

The first part of this passage is popular, and for good reason—it reminds us that God is sovereign and is working all things out according to his purposes for those who are called and reciprocate that call by loving the Lord.

However, the passage should be read in full to get the richer context, the following two verses encourage us further regarding God's love for us, not just our love for him, and is designed to strengthen our hope and resolve in God's election of us as his chosen people.

Mapping this passage out can be useful, so here it is in eight points, first as a summary and then expanded and explained.

I've done this almost in note format, to help you think about each of the key words in context and to give you some insight into the way you too can break a passage down into its component parts to see the message of the whole by stating that which may seem obvious. This is one of my own Bible study methods that believers have used for centuries in various ways:

### Summary

1. God *predestined* those he *foreknew.*
2. The *predestination* is to be *conformed.*
3. The *conformation* is to the *image* of *Jesus.*
4. Jesus as the *image* has *primary place* in *God's house.*

5. The *predestined* have been *called* by *God*.
6. The *called* have been *justified* by God.
7. The *justified* will be *glorified* by God.
8. God is *sovereign* to bring this *all* to pass for the *called*.

## Expanded and explained

1. "For those whom he foreknew he also predestined"

   God *predestined* (prepared and designed a destiny for)

   those he *foreknew* (not in the sense of knowledge because God knows everything, but in the sense of intimacy, relationship, and life. Like when the Bible says Adam knew his wife, it means they consummated their covenant relationship in the most intimate way possible).

2. "to be conformed"

   The *predestination* (that which was planned by God)

   is to be *conformed* (to be changed, comply with a standard and become like someone in nature).

3. "to the image of his Son,"

   The *conformation* (the thing changed to)

   is to the *image* (likeness, reflection, or representation)

   of *Jesus* (The Son of God, the God-man who lived a perfect and righteous life in submission to his Father in his incarnation).

4. "in order that he might be the firstborn among many brothers."

   Jesus as the *image* (the standard and example to look to and model or be conformed to)

   has *primary place* (firstborn does not mean he is a created being but that he is the preeminent Son in God's family of elect spirits and humans. He is above them in essence because he is God and proved it categorically in his incarnation and current status as the God-Man, the only one who could legally [in accordance with the requirements of God's holy love] redeem the fallen race of men and the creation subject to men. Only the Lamb

[103]

was worthy to open the seals in the book of Revelation. Jesus is the Lamb of God.)

in *God's house* (God's image bearers in heaven and on the earth, the divine councils of the Most High God, created and conformed to his image as his representatives. God's government. God's elected officials).

5. "And those whom he predestined he also called"

The *predestined* (those for whom God made a plan that will come to pass because he has decreed it as the sovereign King)

have been *called* (summoned by God's decreed will, which cannot be resisted unlike his commanded will, which can)

by *God* (Yahweh, the God of the Bible, the one eternal God, the triune God of the Bible who is one unique essence with three distinct persons, in this context it is the person of the Father in the Godhead that has summoned us).

6. "those whom he called he also justified,"

The *called* (those summoned by God's decreed will as sovereign King over his creatures)

have been *justified* (made just as if we never sinned, by the finished work of Christ on the cross, which satisfies the requirements of God's holiness and God's love or, in short, which satisfies God's holy love. This is a present state.)

by God (same as the by God above).

7. "and those whom he justified he also glorified."

The *justified* (those made just before God by the finished, complete, and eternal work of Christ on the cross, who have had the righteous, perfect life of Christ imputed or given to them in exchange for their own imperfect and sinful life)

will be *glorified* (this is a future state that points forward to the end of the predestined plan that God has for those he has called. The elect will receive glorified bodies in the resurrection and live in the glory of God's presence in the new heavens and earth, ruling with him from the capital city, the New Jerusalem, heaven on earth)

by God (same as the by God above).

8. "And we know that for those who love God all things work together for good, for those who are called according to his purpose."

God is *sovereign* (this cycles us back to the start of the passage to explain the opening statement in context. God is sovereign in that it is his purpose that will come to pass)

to brings this *all* (the trials and victories in the life of the believer who was foreknown to God in intimacy and holy, electing love before the world began)

to pass for the *called* (are those who respond to the call and show evidence of that response in their full and free love for God. These are the ones known intimately to God [foreknown], whose lives and end were planned ahead of time [predestined], who have been transformed [conformed] to the likeness [image] of the Son [Jesus], and who God has made just [justified] and will one day ennoble, exalt, promote, and honor [glorify]).

The part of this passage that concerns us most is being conformed or transformed to and by the image of Jesus.

God created us to be his image bearers, that is to be his representatives, ruling on his behalf on the earth as we read in Genesis 1:26–27:

> Then God said, "Let us make man in our image, after our likeness. And let them have dominion over the fish of the sea and over the birds of the heavens and over the livestock and over all the earth and over every creeping thing that creeps on the Earth." So God created man in his own image, in the image of God he created him; male and female he created them.

However, in the fall, the image of God we were to represent or reflect in the world as his council or government in the earth was distorted as we became self-centered by representing ourselves, like a mirror turned in on a mirror seeing only ever decreasing images of what humans should be, or worse, we reflect the fallen ones, the evil spirit beings who rebelled against God their creator.

[105]

In the 2015 course "Hold and Advance," which I wrote and delivered for Worldwide Mission Fellowship, I mentioned one of the fundamental realities for us as humankind, which is that we are built to relate, built to have relationship and live in community, and this extends beyond the physical realm to the unseen, spiritual, or supernatural realm, where man will by nature and necessity be aligned in allegiance to one deity or another. Either we are aligned to the spirit beings/elohim that God created who have rebelled against him and were never created to be worshiped, or we align ourselves in allegiance, faithfulness, and relationship as in a covenantal marriage with Yahweh, the one and only eternal, triune God, who created all things both seen and unseen, the only one truly deserving the allegiance of the creatures he has made in all realms.

In Christ, our allegiance and relationship with God is reconciled, and we begin to reflect God as God always intended, as his image bearers in the earth. We are the ones who proclaim the gospel of the kingdom, the word and decrees of God in this earth; we are his hands and feet. As we take up our place of authority in the earth, God is reflected, and his presence by proxy, in us, is able to make the desolate sacred, turning empty spaces into places, sacred/holy places where his glory is on display and his name is glorified.

Jesus was the perfect image of God to us, as mentioned in 2 Corinthians 4:4 and Colossians 1:15, so we now reflect him—the original and greatest place maker—to the world around us as referenced in Ephesians 4:24 and Colossians 3:10.

# GOD'S PRESENCE AND
# GLORY: HEAVEN

*W*e come to the end of the Bibles narrative, the glory of God's presence, a place called heaven.

In many ways it is our understanding of heaven that has been infected by Dualistic and Gnostic misrepresentation the most. As we are about to see, heaven is a very tangible place and will actually be on the earth itself in the end as the ultimate sacred place.

It is important to mention the current culture's preoccupation with heaven tourism in the proliferation of books and accounts of those who have apparently visited this divine realm, with conflicting and unbiblical accounts. We, however, will be looking at the biblical view of heaven, which of course is the only valid one, despite the apparent experience of the modern heaven tourists.

The basic definition of heaven is the dwelling place of God, where his throne room is, in the unseen realm. It is a created place like every other place because only God has Aeism or true eternality in that he was never created, had no beginning, and has always been. Hence his name "I AM."

A small but important point is that we say God has "always been" not "always been there," as that gives the impression that "there" has always been too, making it equally eternal with God whether "there" is heaven or some other place. Again the point is, God is the only one that has no beginning, every other animate or inanimate thing has a beginning, even if after that initial beginning the creature lasts forever like a spirit being (angel) or the spirit of a human being or God's created dwelling place, heaven.

## The prepared place: Revelation 21:1–3

*Then I saw a new heaven and a new earth, for the first heaven and the first earth had passed away, and the sea was no more. And I saw the holy city, new Jerusalem, coming down out of Heaven from God, prepared as a bride adorned for her husband. And I heard a loud voice from the throne saying, "Behold, the dwelling place of God is with man. He will dwell with them, and they will be his people, and God himself will be with them as their God.*

*—Revelation 21:1–3*

This is the final vision of the Bible, the end of the story, and yet this is not the heaven we read about in nomenclature. Rather than being a spiritual place in the clouds without form or physical presence, it is a very tangible, material place. A great city … on Earth.

Unlike the Gnostics taught, the physical or material world is not evil; this is an insulting lie from the enemy to fly in the face of the Creator. Think about it for just a minute, who made the physical world? Not just this earth, but the entire physical realm, the whole universe? It was God, his own original idea. He made it all and said it was good (not perfect, but good).

If material was inherently evil, then how can we explain the initial creation or the incarnation of God the Son as a man who though incarnated in flesh remained without sin? This makes the simple point that the physical world is good and God-breathed.

In the hands of God, the physical creation can be made new and restored to his original purpose. Aside from God, the original place maker, the creation is disconnected from the source of all life and in a perpetual sate of death and decay.

This passage tells us that the New Jerusalem comes down from heaven itself as a bride prepared for her husband. This is the place that Jesus went to prepare for his people.

Cities are of God. We can fall into the error of thinking only the open spaces and rural areas are what God intended on the earth, but God did not intend his six-day creation to be the end of creative work in the cosmos. As God's image bearers, we are supposed to create, build, and be creative like him, working for him and as unto him to perfect the creation.

When God created the earth, he said it was good, not perfect. If it were perfect, he would have said so; he made the earth to be filled and to be dominated by his own royal family through the decedents of his son, Adam.

When God created the earth, the Bible tells us he finished the work he had intended to do. However, the psalms tell us what the end of this task was. It was not an end in itself; it was preparation for man's flourishing and enjoyment, to God's happiness and glory. See Psalm 8:6–8 and 115:16.

When Genesis 1:1 tells us that God created the heaven and the earth; it does not only mean that he made the earth out of noting, it also carries the meaning of him preparing the earth for the habitation of humans.

All creation was made before man was made, so in a real sense, the creation was prepared for humankind. The word *prepared* is an adjective essentially meaning to make something ready. The synonyms for prepared include: made ready, set up, equipped, organized, arranged, primed, geared up, made, formulated, planned, and put in order

In Exodus 23:20 we hear God tell Moses that an angel would go before them to the land he had prepared for them to occupy. Jesus picks this theme of a prepared place when he declares he will go and prepare a place for us in John 14:2–3. The shadow from Exodus and the prophetic promise of Jesus from John see their fulfillment and realization in the heavenly city prepared for the earth, particularly for God's elect people.

A place has been prepared which we in faith can look forward to.

The New Jerusalem in a way redeems God's creation as good because it serves as a bridge between heaven and earth, just like an embassy is as much a part of its home country as the country itself, so the New Jerusalem serves as an embassy for heaven, bringing heaven to earth in a very real, material, tangible, and spiritual way.

As inhabitants of the New Jerusalem, we are both citizens of heaven and earth, serving as God's image bearers, his ambassadors to the rest of creation.

We end this subject by reminding ourselves of the sacred words of Scripture in Hebrews 11:16, which states:

*But as it is, they desire a better country, that is, a heavenly one. Therefore God is not ashamed to be called their God, for he has prepared for them a city.*

## The joy of his presence: Matthew 25:21

*His master said to him, "Well done, good and faithful servant. You have been faithful over a little; I will set you over much. Enter into the joy of your master."*
*—Matthew 25:21*

Although this is only a parable, it does provide us with some insight regarding the coming judgment as well as the joy, rewards, and responsibility connected to our prepared place in heaven.

The place God has prepared for us will bring us great joy, and it is the same thing that brings him joy as well as being in his presence. We are permitted access to this place by his grace for our joy, but also as a reward for fruitful faithfulness.

This place of joy and the coming responsibilities of the world to come should motivate us to live lives worthy of the one who has called us.

We are encouraged to look to our King again, who has gone before us and endured hardship and suffering in this life with his eyes fixed on the joy set before him, in the presence of his Father and his people in Hebrews 12:1–2:

*Therefore, since we are surrounded by so great a cloud of witnesses, let us also lay aside every weight, and sin which clings so closely, and let us run with endurance the race that is set before us, looking to Jesus, the founder and perfecter of our faith, who for the joy that was set before him endured the cross, despising the shame, and is seated at the right hand of the throne of God.*

John Piper calls the promises of God's Word the promise of "future grace." In particular, this applies to the place of joy and reward called heaven for those who overcome. The grace that has been promised to us should have a sanctifying effect on our thoughts, words, and actions. As John puts it, "the promises of future grace are the keys to Christ-like Christian living."[40]

I don't want to misrepresent Piper's book because it is not just about the future grace promise of heaven, but of the grace to overcome in the real trials that we face each

---

[40] John Piper, *Future Grace* (Sisters, OR: Multnomah Publishers, 1995), 13.

day no matter how small or big. However, the principle most assuredly applies to the grace of a place in heaven, in the very presence of God.

The Apostle John also teaches that the promise of God's grace to us in not only the immediate but the ultimate future—in our resurrection, glorification, and placement in the joy of his presence—will have a purifying effect on our lives as he encourages us in 1 John 3:2–3.

> Beloved, we are God's children now, and what we will be has not yet appeared; but we know that when he appears we shall be like him, because we shall see him as he is. And everyone who thus hopes in him purifies himself as he is pure.

So live in holiness before God with the joyful hope and assurance of your prepared place in both heaven and the Heavenly city—the embassy of heaven on the new earth, the New Jerusalem—which Jesus has prepared for you by God's grace and as a reward for fruitful obedience.

God's grace in the past, present, and future as well as God living in you as his house, by his Spirit, will aid you in your walk of holiness and purity. Providing you both the strength and the mercy you need as a pilgrim in this world, to make it to the place he predestined for you in glory.

## The other place: 2 Thessalonians 1:5–10

> This is evidence of the righteous judgment of God, that you may be considered worthy of the kingdom of God, for which you are also suffering—since indeed God considers it just to repay with affliction those who afflict you, and to grant relief to you who are afflicted as well as to us, when the Lord Jesus is revealed from heaven with his mighty angels in flaming fire, inflicting vengeance on those who do not know God and on those who do not obey the gospel of our Lord Jesus. They will suffer the punishment of eternal destruction, away from the presence of the Lord and from the glory of his might, when he comes on that day to be glorified in his saints, and to be marveled at among all who have believed, because our testimony to you was believed.
>
> —2 Thessalonians 1:5–10

There is a place of ultimate displacement that has also been prepared. It in a sense is the opposite of heaven, mainly because it is away from the manifest presence of God, in particular it is away from the joy of his presence. This place is called by a number of names, including hades, hell, eternal fire, the lake of fire, and the second death.

This is a place you really want to avoid. Thankfully, God has made a way of escape through and in order to satisfy his own holy love. God has made a way of escape through the gospel of the King and his kingdom, which has triumphed over darkness as the emancipator and leader of a new humanity, created anew in him. All debts owed for sin have been paid, and the penalty of death and separation from God served by the penal, substitutionary sacrifice of the King himself, Jesus the Christ.

This is the ultimate displacement because in the mind of the triune God, the proper place for all creation is in his presence, partaking in the joy and glory of the Trinity. As our passage makes clear, hell is judgment first because it is away from his presence.

"Eternal destruction, away from the presence of the Lord and from the glory of his might," as we read in the Scripture, reminds us that the judgment of hell is everlasting and final. There is no opportunity to escape once the threshold of death has been passed unless that threshold is transgressed by a temporary miracle of God in a person's bodily resurrection, which is highly unlikely.

The Bible teaches us that this place was not made for human residency but for the fallen elohim of God's house, the spirit beings who rebelled, namely the devil and his angels. As Matthew 25:41 says, "Then he will say to those on his left, 'Depart from me, you cursed, into the eternal fire prepared for the devil and his angels.'"

However, one of the realities of our existence is that we align ourselves either to the true God or a false one, false in the sense that no created being is on par with God or should be worshiped. These beings are actually real; they really are created divine beings, or elohim, that have rebelled against God and seek to deceive mankind and destroy man's relationship with the Trinity.

The following is a summary I wrote about the nature of sin for the Hold and Advance apologetics courses © 2015 Worldwide Mission Fellowship:

1. **Origin?** Sin originates in *created beings* (men and spirits)
2. **Nature?** It is deeply connected to relationship, *allegiance*, and rebellion in context to God or other gods (elohim)
3. **Consequence?** *Relational issues* at all levels (with God, spirits, people, and self); *punishment/judgment*
4. **Remedy?** Salvation through Jesus is the *ONLY* remedy

The wages of sin is death, not in a temporal sense only, as in the cessation of life in this house or body. There are eternal effects of death as a judgment for sin on the true self, known as the soul or spirit of man.

However, the second point I made about the nature of sin is really important for us to understand. Sin, at its core, has to do with our relationship to the spiritual realm and, in particular, our allegiance to God or demons. This is why sinners end up in the place prepared for the devil and his angles, because they are spiritually aligned with them in a rebellious relationship against Yahweh; it is this vital connection that sees man in the presence of his chosen deity for all eternity.

The question every human being must ask is: Where will I place my allegiance? That which man is essentially attached to, which draws and anchors him to one place or another, either to heaven and the presence of the God to whom we have sworn our allegiance, or to hell and the demons (false gods) we have been deceived into casting our lot in with, to our own destruction.

Choose eternal placed-ness in God through Christ and turn away from eternal displacement, away from the presence of the Lord, in the presence of damned spirits who are at war with God and his creation, hell-bent on your destruction and displacement from the presence of God.

For the glory of God and your joy, I appeal to you by his mercy, grace, and Spirit that you turn from the deceiving spirits leading you astray to destruction and choose the place called heaven and its King, God.

# SECTION 4

---

# NARRATIVE

# GOD WITH HIS PEOPLE

ave you read a good book or seen a good movie recently? When I think about the books or films I have enjoyed in the past, the crucial element was narrative—a good story over and above special effects and clever wordplay.

John Bunyan, C. S. Lewis, and J. R. R. Tolkien all understood the importance of narrative in their respective masterpieces, which are all allegorical tales pointing to deep and biblical truths.

Non-Christian authors and producers are aware of this principle too. Take Ed Catmull, the co-founder of Pixar Animation Studio, who retells the story of its founding in his book *Creativity, Inc.* He makes the point that the success behind *Toy Story*, and everything else produced by Pixar, was not the advances in 3D animation but a good story. Narrative was the main thing, the most important element in each production. This is the same for other masters of screen and stagecraft like William Shakespeare, Steven Spielberg, and George Lucas.

We all love good stories. Our preferences may lead us to various formats, like books or films. We also differ in the genres we enjoy, like comedies or dramas. A consistent theme is that the stories we enjoy most or find most compelling, are the ones with good narrative, which includes good character development, plot lines, and themes, not to mention the necessity of a clear, convincing, and relatable beginning, middle, and end.

This attraction to stories is a result of the reality in which we find ourselves, as a result of God's direct creation. We are narrative creatures, driven by stories, worldviews, and big plot lines or metanarratives. These frameworks help us understand and interpret, well, everything.

An example narrative in which people find themselves is the one presented by naturalism. This asserts that there is no God, no supernatural, no purpose or design. This is the underlying framework for the theory of evolution and its related philosophies.

The biblical worldview or narrative consists of three major building blocks—a beginning, middle, and end, as it were—these are Creation, Fall, and Redemption.

Zechariah 14 is a chapter about the coming day or age of the Lord. There is a lot to learn from the passage, especially with regard to place because God's city, Jerusalem, is central to the prophesied events of that day.

One of the central declarations is found in verse 9, "And the Lord will be king over all the earth. On that day the Lord will be one and his name one."

The Lord our God is King, and one day he will rule over the entire earth in a very physical and immediate sense, not just in the spiritual sense that he is King and rules now.

This passage, along with many others, paints a picture of where human history is heading and shows us the ultimate aim and end of the Bible's great narrative.

We see God with his people in various ways throughout history coming ever closer to the goal of creation, which is that God might dwell in the same place as his creation, in holiness and love, reigning as their King in his kingdom.

Here is a map of the events of history with regard to God living in the same place as his people:

1. **4142 BC,**[41] **The Garden:** At creation, God and man walked together in the garden of Eden in close fellowship before this was ruined by man's rebellion. The garden was the first sanctuary or sacred place meant for the communion and fellowship of God with man.

   **Scripture reference:** Genesis 2:7–8, 3:8

2. **1444 BC,**[42] **The Tent:** God ordered and designed the building of the tabernacle so he could be with his people as a holy God and make them a holy people so they might dwell together.

   **Scripture reference:** Exodus 25:8, 40:38

3. **1400 BC,**[43] **The Land:** God prepared a land that he determined to dwell in with his chosen people, Israel. He led Joshua in the conquest of this Promised Land.

   **Scripture reference:** Joshua 1:11, 24:16–18; Ezekiel 36:28

4. **1004 BC,**[44] **The City:** God declared Jerusalem to be his city and the place where he dwells. David the greatest of all Israel's kings conquered the city and made it the capital of God's land and nation, Israel.

   **Scripture reference:** Psalm 46:4, 48:1–3, 76:2

5. **966 BC,**[45] **The House:** King Solomon was commissioned by his father, David, to build a house for God that would serve as a sanctuary so that God could dwell among his own people.

   **Scripture reference:** 2 Chronicles 3:1; 1 Kings 8:27–30

6. **5 BC,**[46] **The Son:** God came as Jesus the Christ, Son of the Living God, Immanuel—meaning God with us. The Word, who was with God and was

---

[41] J. B. Payne, *The International Standard Bible Encyclopedia, Revised,* 1979–1988.

[42] Sharon Rusten with E. Michael, *The Complete Book of When & Where in the Bible and throughout History* (Wheaton, IL: Tyndale House Publishers, Inc., 2005).

[43] Walter A. Elwell and Barry J. Beitzel, *Baker Encyclopedia of the Bible* (Baker Book House, 1988).

[44] Israel P. Loken, *The Lexham Bible Dictionary,* 2012, 2013, 2014, 2015.

[45] Sharon Rusten with E. Michael, *The Complete Book of When & Where in the Bible and throughout History* (Wheaton, IL: Tyndale House Publishers, Inc., 2005).

[46] France, R. T. "Jesus Christ, Life and Teaching Of." Edited by D. R. W. Wood, I. H. Marshall, A. R. Millard, J. I. Packer, and D. J. Wiseman. *New Bible Dictionary* (Leicester, England; Downers Grove, IL: InterVarsity Press, 1996).

God, became flesh and dwelled with us in the same place as us, and even in our place, to save us and reconcile us to God. To the end that we might be together with God in the same sacred place forever.

**Scripture reference:** Matthew 1:21–23; John 1:1, 14; Philippians 2:5–11

7.   **33 AD,**[47] **The Spirit:** God is here now, in the midst of his people collectively as the church, the called out and collected, through God the Holy Spirit. God came at Pentecost and now tabernacles with believers, living in the body of each believer. God is with us.

**Scripture reference:** John 14:15–17, 25–26; 1 Corinthians 6:19–20

8.   **???? AD, The Kingdom:** This timeline will culminate at the consummation of all things when the kingdom proclaimed in the gospel and prophesied in the Scriptures comes in fullness, with God reigning on the earth as King over a global kingdom from the New Jerusalem in the midst of the people he has so lovingly redeemed.

**Scripture reference:** Revelation 21:1–8

A possible summary statement might read something like this:

God dwelling happily with his people in holiness and love (holy love) as their victorious King, in a kingdom reflecting himself, to the joy and satisfaction of his children and the glory and fame of his name.

—C. J. Scott, 2016

---

[47] J. D. G. Dunn, "Spirit, Holy." *New Bible Dictionary*. (Leicester, England; Downers Grove, IL: InterVarsity Press, 1996).

We must be balanced and led by the text when looking at the Scriptures, so this section serves to show the theology of place and, in particular, the biblical theology of "God with his people" in the wider context of other biblical themes and to ensure that we do not swap neglecting the point for overemphasizing it.

I mention this being *a* rather than *the* major biblical theme because it is one among other major biblical themes that are very important for us when we read the Bible as a single narrative. I have listed the major biblical themes here. This is not an exhaustive list, but twelve important ones are as follows:

1. Jesus the Christ
2. The gospel or salvation
3. The story of redemption or redemptive history
4. Israel and God's people
5. The covenants of God
6. The love of God
7. The sovereignty of God
8. God as King and the kingdom of God
9. Relationship with God
10. Faith in God and his Word/promises
11. The holiness of God or God as Judge
12. The glory of God

I will take some time to talk about each of these briefly. Entire works have been written on each of these, which does them far more justice than can be done in this small section of a relatively small book.

## Jesus the Christ

Everything in the OT points forward to Jesus, while everything in the NT points backward to Jesus. Jesus is therefore at the center of all Scripture. Jesus is also the ultimate interpretative key for all Scripture being the center and end of everything.

On the road to Emmaus, Jesus taught his disciple that all the Scriptures were pointing forward to him in Luke 24:27 and later in verse 44:

> And beginning with Moses and all the Prophets, he interpreted to them in all the Scriptures the things concerning himself ...

> Then he said to them, "These are my words that I spoke to you while I was still with you, that everything written about me in the Law of Moses and the Prophets and the Psalms must be fulfilled."

Also in Matthew 5:17

> "Do not think that I have come to abolish the Law or the Prophets; I have not come to abolish them but to fulfill them."

The Apostle Paul also picks this up in the following summary statement taken from his second letter to the believers at Corinth (2 Corinthians 1:20):

> For all the promises of God find their Yes in him. That is why it is through him that we utter our Amen to God for his glory.

Other considerations are that he is the one who starts the story in creation and ends it in the consummation of all things. As the Scriptures say, he is the Alpha and Omega.

I find that this is one of the strongest central themes in all of Scripture. When I'm not sure about a passage in terms of relevance and application, I put Jesus in the middle of it or use him as a lens to see it through, and it always helps.

## The gospel or salvation

One of the most important messages in Scripture is the gospel or good news about salvation through Jesus.

The work of Jesus Christ, in his incarnation, life, death, resurrection, and ascension brings salvation to God's people.

In some ways, this is the practical center of the Scriptures and even human history.

There are many aspects to the central theme of the gospel, including prophesies leading up to it, the event in history when salvation was won, the working out of that salvation in the life of the believer, the spread of the gospel throughout the earth and over the ages, and the ultimate end of the gospel in the redemption of the body at the final resurrection.

The gospel is a great key for interpreting, applying, and understanding the Scripture, much like the person of Jesus the Christ.

Along with this gospel-centered approach are the important ways and doctrines of salvation, which are among the most important teachings of Scripture.

There are important distinctions here like reformed soteriology (the study of salvation), otherwise known as Calvinism versus more modern ideas like Arminianism. I come down clearly on the biblically balanced Calvinist side of this debate in the vein of teachers like Charles Spurgeon, John Piper, John MacArthur, D. A. Carson, R. C. Sproul, Francis Chan, Wayne Grudem, Ray Comfort, etc.

## The story of redemption or redemptive history

The biblical narrative or story is an important concept that has gained traction in recent years.

It is a method that seeks to trace the worldview, narrative, and macro—or overall storyline—of the Bible and thus discover its ultimate theme and message.

This is often known as redemptive history or the story of redemption. It explores the way that God has progressively revealed himself and made redemption possible, culminating in Jesus the Christ.

The ultimate theme of the Scripture in this case is redemption of a people and even creation to God.

I have employed the narrative approach in my attempt at biblical theology in regard to place and see redemptive history as a vital part of the thread tying all Scripture together.

# Israel

The physical and later the spiritual Israel or the people of God is seen as one of the continuing and central themes of Scripture for many.

There is often controversy in the way this central theme is applied where some say that the church has wholesale replaced the nation of Israel; this is known as replacement theology, which we will address in a latter chapter as a faulty understanding.

I agree that Israel is both physical and spiritual centrally important to understanding the Scriptures, and I believe the theology of place plays a major role in this regard.

I will argue in a later chapter for balance with this theme so that the reality of God's people as the spiritual Israel is not maligned or discounted in an overreaction to replacement theology and anti-Semitism and at the same time there is a place in our biblical theology for Israel and its land.

## The covenants of God

The covenants or agreements God makes with humans over time are a central part of the Bible's story and are key to understanding the Scriptures in context.

The division of the covenants is a controversial area. Many, myself included, believe in covenantal theology, which affirms that there are essentially two covenants—the old and the new—and that all other covenants are subordinate and in context to either one or both of these covenants.

The two main covenants are the OT through the law of Moses and the NT through the grace of Jesus Christ as John puts it in John 1:17, "For the law was given through Moses; grace and truth came through Jesus Christ."

The other biblical position is that of dispensationalism, which sees various dispensations of salvation by various methods culminating in the dispensation of grace, which we are in now. There is a lot of good to be found in the dispensational method too. I think we can learn from both covenant and dispensational approaches to understanding covenant.

I do not hold to a classical position on either of these views. My view is a hybrid of both, which sees the ages in terms of the covenants without discounting the continuation and future real life fulfillment of covenant promises to Israel (not the church as Israel).

"A" MAJOR BIBLICAL THEME

Some of the most important covenants in the Bible are as follows:

- The Noetic Covenant (the one God made with Noah)
- The Abrahamic Covenant (the one God made with Abraham)
- The Mosaic or Law Covenant (the one God made via Moses)
- The New Covenant (the one Jesus made)

## The love of God

A popular and important theme in the Bible is the love of God, seen in all the previous themes mentioned.

This theme has been abused and skewed by so-called liberal theologians who have a weak concept of the love of God, which discounts all God's other attributes, and in so doing, have formed a false god of love who endorses everything, judges nothing, and accepts everyone to heaven regardless of anything.

As I have mentioned in other places in this book, the love of God is a holy love.

The true love of God is certainly a central theme in the message and story of the Bible.

## The sovereignty of God

God's sovereignty speaks to his ultimate rule and control over all. It is the glue that holds the coherent story of redemption together. God's sovereign rule is that which brings history to its ultimate end and sees his plans come to pass. I definitely see this theme played out and running through the Scriptures as a constant.

## God as King and the kingdom of God

This is related to the last point in major ways. God as King is central to the role he plays in the Bible's narrative.

In relation to the kingdom, this is the part the creation and God's people play in relation to him as King.

## Relationship with God

We have been designed for relationship, and even God is centered around the inner trinitarian relationship between Father, Son, and Spirit.

[125]

This is again a constant and ultimate theme.

## Faith in God and his Word/Promises

Related to the gospel and covenant themes but with a focus on faith versus unbelief.

## The holiness of God or God as Judge

A clear theme in the Scriptures from Genesis through to Revelation, it is central to the theology of place too.

This theme has fallen on hard times, but it is as crucial to the Bible's narrative as the love of God is.

## The glory of God

All these themes culminate in the glory of God; all things exist ultimately as a result of and to the honor of his glory.

I see these as the central themes of the Bible without discounting the importance of other themes like worship, justice, repentance, prayer, grace, mercy, and any number of important subjects, which are all subordinate to and included in the central themes above.

## The synthesis: The King's narrative

The concept of God as King with his people in one place incorporates all the central themes of Scripture. Consider the following statement, highlighting each of the twelve central themes:

God's purpose in creation is for the sake of his own *glory (12)* and pleasure as *King (8)*, through the expression of his *holy love (6)*, that love experienced in his holy unity as the one eternal Trinity. God seeks to dwell in holiness with the creatures he has made a *covenant (5)* with in love through the incarnation, life, death, resurrection, ascension, and return of *Christ (1)* as King, to reign over those elect people, *saved (2)* by the King's *sovereign (7)* mercy and grace, through *faith in the King's Word and promises (10)* found in the *good news (2)* about his *kingdom (8)*. The King exacts perfect, holy *judgment (11)* on all rebels in his realm as King over all that is in the seen and unseen worlds of humans and angels. *Redemptive history* will end with the King living together in perfect *relationship (9)*, in a *sacred place* with a *sacred people (4)*, while the rebels will live in eternal displacement away from the presence of the King.

—C. J. Scott, 2016

It is within this grand story, this metanarrative, that the deepest questions of the human experience are answered as outlined in the Total Truth course © Worldwide Mission Fellowship 2016. They are as follows:

*Who are we?* Creatures, human beings, distinctly male or female. Created in the image of God, endowed by God with qualities like worth, dignity, and reason. Created as persons with the capacity for choice, relationship, allegiance, and belief.

*Where and when do we live?* The good creation made by God, designed to be inhabited and explored. We live after the fall; the universe is broken. We also live after the cross, so we can be redeemed, but before the new heaven and earth, when redemption will be full.

*What's wrong with the world?* The sin of Adam and Eve has placed mankind and all creation into a fallen state of rebellion against God. Sin brings death to all it touches. Creation is under the holy anger and judgment of God. Sin is a root cause of evil, pain, and suffering in the world.

*How can the world be fixed?* Through the liberating truth of God, expressed most clearly through the Bible and in particular through the gospel or good news of Jesus the King, his victory, and his kingdom.

*What is life/reality all about?* God has a purpose in creation, to express his love so that he may be glorified and that humans might love God, being satisfied, happy, and flourishing in fellowship together with God in his good creation.

# THE GOSPEL: THE KING, HIS TRIUMPH AND KINGDOM

*T*his central theme of Scripture is also the essential story of the good news or the gospel.

The gospel is defined as the Christian message, which is the announcement of "good news" proclaimed by Jesus regarding the arrival of God's kingdom, with reference to his mission and identity as the King or Messiah.

The English term *gospel* is from Old English *gōd*, which means "good," and *spell*, which means "tale, talk," so you could say the good story, this is translated from the Greek word *euangelion* from *eu*, which means "well," and *angellō*, which means "to announce."[48]

This word *euangelion*, in the ancient world, was often used in the context of a king's victory or triumph and the proclamation of that victory and new rulership by his heralds, who would go before him to let the inhabitants of the land know that the old ruler or enemy had been defeated and the new king's rulership had begun.

In the NT, the gospel is often used in this context too, it is an announcement—a good announcement that is proclaimed everywhere, openly, publicly, boldly, and clearly by the ambassadors of the king, seen first in his apostles and soon in all believers.

---

[48] Sources include K. Schenck, *Dictionary of Jesus and the Gospels, Second Edition*, 2013, and Moisés Silva and Merrill Chapin Tenney, *The Zondervan Encyclopedia of the Bible, D-G*, 2009, 2.

Let's look at a few Scriptures to see how Jesus being King, and by extension his kingdom, are an essential core to the gospel itself.

## Jesus opens his ministry as King: Mark 1:14–15

*Now after John was arrested, Jesus came into Galilee, proclaiming the gospel of God, and saying, "The time is fulfilled, and the kingdom of God is at hand; repent and believe in the gospel."*

—*Mark 1:14–15*

These are the first recorded utterances we have of Jesus in public ministry. He begins by announcing or proclaiming the *gospel of God*. This news, this story, is God's, the God of the Scriptures who had revealed himself throughout the narrative of redemptive history as the God who draws near to redeem and dwell with his people.

He is the God who had inspired the prophets to declare, though through a veil, that one day, fuller, more perfect, and permanent redemption would come; true salvation was on its way, and God himself would come closer than ever before. This is the good news that Jesus so boldly and truly proclaimed to God's people, Israel.

Jesus is quoted as saying *the time is fulfilled*, he does not say it shall be or is about to be but that it is fulfilled and this is because he has come, the God-man, the promised King and Messiah who would overthrow the reign of the usurping evil prince, Satan, with his kingdom and instead begin the eternal establishment of God's kingdom in the earth, which had been prophesied by God himself in the garden in Genesis 3:15 and continues to be built upon as the biblical story unfolds by God's prophets.

This is it, the sovereign, decisive act of God in redemptive history, at this particular time, in this particular place, comes God incarnate. Once again, God has entered human history, invading the enemy territory, but this time it is not just an attack, it's an occupation. This is the great battle that all the other attacks on the enemy's kingdom had been leading up to; now comes the Son, the King. He mounts the attack himself; the time to defeat the enemy is here.

God has come as King and, by extension, his kingdom has come; the enemy's kingdom is now in its final days. This is why the arrival of Jesus in redemptive history signals the start of the final or last days—the enemy's days are now numbered. His strongholds are about to be besieged by the Lamb of God, and the effects of the fall that gave him the right to the tyrannical rule of men is about to be reversed. Jesus will demonstrate this reversal of the suffering and death of the serpent's kingdom in the healings and miracles he will perform as evidence that God's kingdom is on its way to overthrow the dragon king once and for all.

The *kingdom is at hand,* according to Jesus. This is where we get the theological position of the now-and-not-yet nature of the kingdom of God. It is here in a very real way, and yet not here in the fullness that it will be at the end of the age.

In one sense, the enemy has been severely wounded, and his time is now limited. At the same time, there is a gradual progression of the kingdom being advanced to reach every place and people on the earth through the spread of God's story, the gospel, and God will act again in the final decisive act, the final victory over the enemy once and for all when the kingdoms of this world become the kingdom of our King forever (Revelation 11:15).

The final part of Jesus's statement connects the proclamation of God's story, the announcement of the long-awaited news that his kingdom has come and will come in fullness, to the response this news demands—repentance and belief in those who hear.

Core to the gospel is the call to action, the requirement on those hearing to respond in one way or another. Do we celebrate with the King and the coming of his kingdom by denouncing our allegiance to the serpent's kingdom, do we turn our back on the domain of the dragon and instead turn to the true King, to live in his kingdom? Or do we stand against the advancing army of God's kingdom and suffer the consequence of defeat without surrender, leading to punishments for our treason toward the true King and suffer the same judgment as the usurper, the devil? The choice really is yours.

Jesus announces the imminent and present kingdom of God in the voice of both a promise fulfilled and something to rejoice in but also with a warning. This later, cautionary stance reminds us of the serious implications the coming of God's kingdom will have on those who are living under the wrath of the King for their rebellion. Jesus makes an appeal, in light of the coming kingdom—which is God's, and so is holy—warning men to repent, switch their allegiance, or suffer the consequences.

You may disagree with the ultimate rule of God as King, but that changes nothing; God is God, his kingdom will reign forever, and those opposed to his kingdom will be conquered by it in either repentance or judgment. Will your relationship to the kingdom of God be as a grateful citizen, the beneficiary of the King's magnanimous grace, or that of a rebel, faithful to the usurper's kingdom, tied to the fate of the evil one?

# Kingdom authority driving the commission: Matthew 28:18–20

*And Jesus came and said to them, "All authority in heaven and on earth has been given to me. Go therefore and make disciples of all nations, baptizing them in the name of the Father and of the Son and of the Holy Spirit, teaching them to observe all that I have commanded you. And behold, I am with you always, to the end of the age."*

*—Matthew 28:18–20*

This is an earth-shattering text. Look at what Jesus actually says here. He has won authority in heaven and earth as the God-man, the new leader of the new humanity. Jesus has just declared that his rule as King has begun. The enemy has been defeated in his death but most importantly in his resurrection.

The resurrection of Jesus vindicates and validates his claim to be the promised King, the Son of Man who would rule over all.

The commission Jesus gives to us is in light of the authority he has been given. It is in the spirit of that authority and because of this new rule that we go and proclaim this new rule and new ruler, Jesus Christ the King, and his kingdom.

This is why we spread throughout the earth. In every place, we proclaim the good news of God's victory and the actual coming of his kingdom to overthrow the enemy's kingdom in that place and for that people. The coming of God's stronghold in place of the enemy's stronghold and of the true ruler, the servant King, who through his own sacrifice and resurrection has established the kingdom and opened the door for people of every nation, tribe, and tongue.

Jesus's declaration of authority shows the extent of his rule is beyond the earth and beyond the physical realm. It extends to the entire cosmos and the spiritual realm of spirit beings as well as the temporal realm of men. Coupled with this is a call to universal, global mission. The whole creation needs to hear this, needs to know about the new kingdom and its King, to know the work he has done and the message he teaches, the story he tells, and the news he brings about God and his kingdom.

This all echoes the prophecy in Daniel 7:13–14, which tells us the Son of Man, whom Jesus referred to as himself and proved himself to be, would one day rule over all people in the earth. The Son of Man would be King over a global kingdom, this is the authority that Jesus has been given and will be consummated at the end of the age.

The commission is to make disciples, those faithful in their allegiance to the King, those who will themselves become ambassadors of the King and his kingdom and not just citizens of the kingdom living on the benefits of the kingdom but not following in the steps of the King, who himself lived as a servant to all.

We are called to make disciples—not converts or even believers—but disciples, those committed to growth and fruitfulness in their own lives in the King's house while living lives concerned not only with their own well-being in the safety of the kingdom but willing to join the army on the front lines, expanding the kingdom across the earth.

This also echoes the theology of place in the gospel message because we are sent to all the earth, to all peoples in every place, carrying the message of the King, and the Spirit of the King, bringing the very presence of the kingdom as we stand and bear witness to the King's rule. We stand as a proxy for him, as official ambassadors. As we spread spatially and ideologically throughout the earth, so does the kingdom of God as we make mere places into sacred places filled with those who have sworn allegiance to the King.

It is significant that Jesus does not spread the kingdom himself; he inaugurates it and commissions his followers, the subjects of his kingly rule to expand his kingdom in the realm in which they have been called to be his image bearers, his representatives, government, or ambassadors. We as human beings that have been redeemed to carry the presence of God throughout the earth making sacred that which was once profane.

Just like God's ways with prayer, he desires that we act on behalf of the world he created for us. We have work to do in the kingdom of God; we have advancements to make and ground to hold. We have been called to hold and advance the kingdom of God to the glory of God for the joy of all peoples.

Teaching the truth of the kingdom of God as Jesus taught it is the gospel, it is not about a single event with a single decision; the teaching we are called to perform in the great commission is the ongoing teaching that builds disciples and, thus, builds the kingdom numerically and in the comprehension of its members and their obedience to the requirements of God's narrative, the gospel.

The kingdom is not a place of anarchy; it is a place ruled by God, and his dictates must be obeyed. The gospel call has at its core the imperative of belief and repentance. Will we believe the claims of God's story? Will we adhere to the call of his narrative? Or will we buy the lie of the serpent king, who has been wounded and restricted, who is now in the spasms of death as the kingdom of God spreads like an antidote attacking the virus of sin, death, and decay, reversing the effects of the fall and, as Jesus said, making all things new?

An essential part of the great commission, which empowers us to perform it and is a part of the message itself, is that God is with us. Jesus said he would be with us till the end of the age. This is the whole point of the kingdom of God; it is a place where God seeks to dwell with his people, and it is because he dwells with us now that we can be effective in advancing the kingdom.

Jesus himself taught us in the parable of the marriage supper that it is God's desire to dwell with man, that this is at the heart of the kingdom, and that the opposite of this was the displacement of one from that kingdom, whether Satan (Luke 10:18) or man (Matthew 22:1–14).

## The King's love, the heart of the gospel: John 3:16–17

*"For God so loved the world, that he gave his only Son, that whoever believes in him should not perish but have eternal life. For God did not send his Son into the world to condemn the world, but in order that the world might be saved through him."*

*—John 3:16–17*

When I speak about God as King, I mean the one essence of God—therefore, all three persons. The Father is King, the Son is King, and the Spirit is King because God is King, and they are all one God.

We should be truly grateful that our God is a loving King; he does not seek to exploit, manipulate, or abuse his people. His love for humankind motivated him to give his Son, and so in the trinitarian sense, God gave himself and paid the ultimate price for us.

God's love for humans is made clear in this passage; the extent of his love is seen in that which he gave—the greatest thing he could ever give, himself.

The reach of both the kingdom and its associated message mean that there is no restriction to those who can believe and so not perish but have eternal life. Any person can hear the King's message and respond by switching allegiance to him and thus becoming a part of his kingdom and so escape the fate of those who stand against him.

At the center of all God's redemptive activity throughout history is his holy love.

[133]

## Jesus is Lord, so Jesus is King: Romans 10:9–17

*Because, if you confess with your mouth that Jesus is Lord and believe in your heart that God raised him from the dead, you will be saved. For with the heart one believes and is justified, and with the mouth one confesses and is saved. For the Scripture says, "Everyone who believes in him will not be put to shame." For there is no distinction between Jew and Greek; for the same Lord is Lord of all, bestowing his riches on all who call on him. For "everyone who calls on the name of the Lord will be saved." How then will they call on him in whom they have not believed? And how are they to believe in him of whom they have never heard? And how are they to hear without someone preaching? And how are they to preach unless they are sent? As it is written, "How beautiful are the feet of those who preach the good news!" But they have not all obeyed the gospel. For Isaiah says, "Lord, who has believed what he has heard from us?" So faith comes from hearing, and hearing through the word of Christ.*

*—Romans 10:9–17*

That was a long passage to quote but a really important one. This passage is from Paul's letter to the Romans. It lays out in practical terms the way salvation works from a human perspective as a responsible, moral being.

This is so important because the Bible is full of teaching regarding the election of God's people and God's decisive action in saving every one of his elect. This passage shows us the other side of the choice versus election coin. It assures us that in full compatibility with God's elective love, humans have a response to make to the encroaching kingdom, the undeniable personality that is the King, Jesus, and must engage mentally and volitionally with the content and claims of the gospel message.

In line with this practical call for a response is the equally practical call to go and tell people, to expand the kingdom by proclaiming God's story in all the earth as commanded at the great commission.

## Praise to the King: 1 Timothy 1:17

*To the King of the ages, immortal, invisible, the only God, be honor and glory forever and ever. Amen.*

*—1 Timothy 1:17*

John Pipers says, "Missions is not the ultimate goal of the church. Worship is. Missions exists because worship doesn't. Worship is ultimate, not missions, because God is ultimate, not man."[49]

This is so true; we were created to worship God in holy love, and God is at the center of everything; he, not man, is uppermost in his own affections, and he himself is the greatest treasure there is. He is the worthiest, and his glory is the highest good and goal there is. Indeed, we are saved to worship the Father in spirit and in truth.

Jesus, our great Savior King, is worthy of our praise, worship, adoration, and allegiance. We should live in light of his grace and for his glory, for the rise of his fame in the earth and the spread of his kingdom to the very ends of the cosmos. Our hearts' desire should be in line with the prophecies of the book—that the whole earth might be filled with the knowledge of the glory of the Lord, like the waters cover the sea.

We should not hamper our faith and expectations by putting too much confidence in or focus on our model of the timing and sequence, of events in the last days. Our goal should remain the royal charge, the holy aspiration, the glorious call of the kingdom: to see the earth filled with worship toward God through Jesus Christ.

To see the spaces and places of the earth become sacred places through the worship of God's people to their immortal King should be our sacred ambition.

There is a song called "Saviour King" by Marty Sampson from Hillsong, which beautifully captures the nature of Jesus as our Lord and King but also our Saviour and Shepherd who laid down his life for the sheep.

Take a moment to praise our King today. This is the essence of the call in the gospel message: we believe God's Word, repent, and turn toward God in worship as prescribed in his word and in line with the cry of our regenerated hearts.

Other songs from our rich Christian history, which celebrate God, and especially Jesus as King, include:[50]

- "All Creatures of Our God and King"
- "All for Jesus"
- "Angels We Have Heard on High"
- "At Calvary"

---

[49] John Piper, *Let the Nations Be Glad! The Supremacy of God in Missions* (Grand Rapids, MI: Baker, 2010).
[50] *Logos Hymnal*, 1st edition. (Oak Harbor, WA: Logos Research Systems, Inc., 1995).

- "Christ the Lord Is Risen Today"
- "Come, Thou Almighty King"
- "Come, Thou Long-Expected Jesus"
- "Crown Him with Many Crowns"
- "Hallelujah Chorus"
- "Hallelujah, What a Savior!"
- "Hark! the Herald Angels Sing"
- "It Came upon the Midnight Clear"
- "Joy to the World!"
- "Lead on, O King Eternal"
- "My Country, 'Tis of Thee"
- "O Come, All Ye Faithful"
- "O for a Thousand Tongues"
- "O Little Town of Bethlehem"
- "O Worship the King"
- "Onward, Christian Soldiers"
- "Praise Him! Praise Him!"
- "Praise to the Lord, the Almighty"
- "Silent Night, Holy Night"
- "Since I Have Been Redeemed" (the first song I could find with the term "Savior King" written by Edwin O. Excell)
- "Stand Up, Stand Up for Jesus"
- "Standing on the Promises"
- "Take My Life and Let It Be"
- "The First Noel"
- "There Is Power in the Blood"
- "We Three Kings"
- "What Child Is This?"

Many of these hymns are in the public domain and can be found in most hymnbooks or online for free, one of the songs from this collection was "Lead on, O King Eternal" by Ernest W. Shurtleff:

> Lead on, O King eternal,
> The day of march has come;
> Henceforth in fields of conquest
> Thy tents shall be our home:
> Thro' days of preparation
> Thy grace has made us strong,

[136]

*And now, O King eternal,*
*We lift our battle song.*

*Lead on, O King eternal,*
*Till sin's fierce war shall cease,*
*And holiness shall whisper*
*The sweet amen of peace;*
*For not with swords' loud clashing,*
*Or roll of stirring drums;*
*With deeds of love and mercy*
*The heav'nly kingdom comes.*

*Lead on, O King eternal,*
*We follow not with fears;*
*For gladness breaks like morning*
*Where'er Thy face appears;*
*Thy cross is lifted o'er us;*
*We journey in its light:*
*The crown awaits the conquest;*
*Lead on, O God of might.*[51]

## Biblical thinking about salvation

The following is adapted from the 2015 Apologetics course "Hold and Advance" I wrote for Worldwide Mission Fellowship. It reminds us about some of our core beliefs regarding a biblical understanding of salvation.

We begin with the five solas (*sola* is Latin for alone) or the five exclusive claims for the biblical understanding of the necessary components that lead to saving faith. These are that salvation and the life of the believer is:

1. Sola Scriptura (from "*Scripture* alone")
2. Solus Christus (in "*Christ* alone")
3. Sola gratia (by "*grace* alone")
4. Sola fide (through "*faith* alone")
5. Soli Deo gloria (to "the *glory of God* alone")

---

[51] *Ibid.*

Another important element for the way we think of salvation as a God-centered act would be to consider the biblical and historical five points of the doctrines of grace, sometimes called the five points of Calvinism. These are:

1. Total Depravity—Man is *dead* in sin
2. Unconditional Election—God's *sovereign* choice, special love
3. Limited Atonement—Accomplished and *applied* to the elect
4. Irresistible Grace—Saved by God's *decisive* grace
5. Perseverance of the Saints—Security, *endurance*, holiness

In summary, the following will help us continue to think of the salvation that the King provides:

1. *5 Alones (Sola's)*—Scripture alone, Christ alone, grace alone, faith alone, and to the glory of God alone.
2. *5 Points*—Total depravity, unconditional election, limited atonement, irresistible grace and perseverance of the saints.
3. *Extremes*—Legalism seeks salvation through morals. Antinomianism (anti-law) seeks to abuse the grace of God.
4. *Security*—Our salvation is eternal and sure.
5. *The Evangel*—The gospel of the victory and reign of the King.

Salvation comes from God by his grace, for his elect through faith, according to the Bible, to God's own glory and is sure and eternal.

It is the free call of the gospel message but is not an excuse to sin (antinomianism/anti-law) nor needs additional human works (legalism/religion).

# SECTION 5

---

# HISTORY

# HISTORICAL CASE STUDIES

We all have a history. Some of us are well acquainted with ours, while many are ignorant of theirs. Are you aware of your own history—the histories of your family, town, country, and faith?

If we do not know where we are coming from, it is hard to know where we are going or to learn the lessons offered by the past. It can be hard to fully comprehend our present condition without knowledge of the past events that gave rise to our current state.

In my own case, I live in the United Kingdom, but my parents are from another island, Jamaica. That gives me a basic understanding of my family line: we are part of the African Diaspora in Europe. I am the descendant of "black" slaves from Africa who survived the transatlantic slave trade. My ancestors were slaves in the island of Jamaica. This is the case for me, my family, and many friends. This history and the subsequent years of personal, institutional, and even legislated racism have contributed to a sense of placelessness and general disenfranchised state in the "Black" Diaspora.

With this knowledge, we can use the liberating truth of the gospel as a remedy to the scars left by sin and are reminded that our history is rooted in the deeper history of the entire human race, going right back to God's creation of Adam, his subsequent fall, and God's mission to redeem the fallen race of men.

Place is not just a subject of philosophy or theology, but as we stated in the opening chapter, it is very much a part of our everyday lives and plays an important role in world history.

We are going to take some time now to look at two very important and connected areas of world history, which both play a central part in "place" and in whom "place" has played a big part.

Our subjects of study are the nation of Israel and the entity called the church. By no means are these the only historical phenomena worthy of study in regard to place, but from our biblical presupposition they are the most important.

# ISRAEL

*A*s a people group, none have been molded and given their sense of identity by the land or place associated with them and the God of that place like the Jewish people.

There are other people groups who have survived from ancient times, like the Egyptians and Ethiopians of northern Africa, but the story of the Jewish people is so interwoven with their land that, apart from their land as a backdrop, they lose some of their distinction and definition among the nations of the world.

The other distinguishing factor is their monotheistic religion, worshiping the one true God and not an idol or physical thing but in accordance with their sacred text now canonized in the OT.

Even secular Jews take their sense of identity as a people from their ancient roots in a promise regarding a land by a God recorded in the pages of their sacred text.

To help orient ourselves regarding the historical realities of Israel as a people, nation, and land, we turn to that most trustworthy text of ANE antiquity, the Bible.

## A place of promise: Genesis 15:7

*And he said to him, "I am the LORD who brought you out from Ur of the Chaldeans to give you this land to possess."*

*—Genesis 15:7*

*W*e covered this verse back in our chapter regarding biblical theology. We mention it again here because this is not some legend or cleverly devised fable (2 Peter 1:16–21[52]), this is an event in human history. This actually happened, possibly in around 2082 BC.

Other biblical authors quote this event as history, not legend or a theological abstract. Here are just three authors who refer to the historical event and its theological implications:

Nehemiah in Nehemiah 9:8:

> *You found his heart faithful before you, and made with him the covenant to give to his offspring the land of the Canaanite, the Hittite, the Amorite, the Perizzite, the Jebusite, and the Girgashite. And you have kept your promise, for you are righteous.*

Luke in Acts 7:6–7:

> *And God spoke to this effect—that his offspring would be sojourners in a land belonging to others, who would enslave them and afflict them four hundred years. "But I will judge the nation that they serve," said God, "and after that they shall come out and worship me in this place."*

Paul in Romans 4:18:

---

[52] This reference is a major proof text for our presupposition regarding Scripture as God's inspired Word; in part it reads: "For we did not follow cleverly devised myths when we made known to you the power and coming of our Lord Jesus Christ, but we were eyewitnesses of his majesty ... no prophecy of Scripture comes from someone's own interpretation. For no prophecy was ever produced by the will of man, but men spoke from God as they were carried along by the Holy Spirit."

*In hope he believed against hope, that he should become the father of many*
*nations, as he had been told, "So shall your offspring be."*

The most important person to mention Abraham as a real historical figure and so
confirm the reality of the events of his life, including God's promise of a place to
dwell, was Jesus, who said in John 8:58:

*Jesus said to them, "Truly, truly, I say to you, before Abraham was, I am."*

Jesus also mentions Abraham as a real person in Matthew 8:11, 22:32; Mark 12:26;
Luke 13:16, 28, 16:23-30, 19:9, 20:37; and the passage we took the previous verse
from in John 8:33–56.

The fact is, theological truth cannot be founded on legends because this would mean
that the ideals of our theology are built on lies, fear, and falsehood. Our faith, by
necessity, is rooted in the ground of reality, history, the real world, right there and
then, related to right here and now.

This is the ground we give up when we submit to Dualistic and Gnostic tendencies,
which separate historical facts and theological truth when they are inextricably
linked.

Our God is the God of the spirit, truth, history, facts, science, knowledge, and
wisdom all at the same time. Our divisions are foolish and immature knee-jerk
reactions to past or potential overindulgence or emphasis on any number of the
multifaceted parts of reality, juxtaposing one against another to make adjustments
resulting in a lopsided and distorted view of reality.

Our God is the God of the real world in which exists ultimate truth, rooted in the
ground of that real world, created and sustained by him. So, no, this was not made up
or embellished by postexilic scribes. This is a history recorded with consideration to
the theological implications of the clear, honest worldview of the author and original
readers regarding the nature of reality, including the supernatural realm.

## Origin of the name Israel: Genesis 32:28

*Then he said, "Your name shall no longer be called Jacob, but Israel, for you*
*have striven with God and with men, and have prevailed."*

*—Genesis 32:28*

The origin of the name of the people and land of Israel lies in the story of Jacob's wrestling with this spirit being, who was likely an angel from Yahweh who spoke on behalf of God as a representative from God's heavenly council/government and renamed the man Jacob to Israel in approximately 1908 BC.

Hosea also mentions this event as historical in Hosea 12:4:

> He strove with the angel and prevailed; he wept and sought his favor. He met
> God at Bethel, and there God spoke with us—

As a direct descendent of Abraham, the land and name became synonymous as did the descendants of Jacob, now named Israel, although often still referred to as Jacob.

The name's meaning comes from the event of Jacob's wrestling and the wider context of his walk of faith with God up to that point of his life. It literally means, "he (who) struggles with God."[53]

This same name was applied to the seventy people who enter Egypt in 1876 BC;[54] it is applied to the decedents of these people and the land they would come to own.

## The best place on Earth: Ezekiel 20:6

> On that day I swore to them that I would bring them out of the land of Egypt
> into a land that I had searched out for them, a land flowing with milk and
> honey, the most glorious of all lands.
>
> —Ezekiel 20:6

Every place on Earth is not automatically endowed with the same importance or value as every other place; by the very definition of place as we understand it in this book, that would be illogical.

Against the skewed egalitarian thought forms of our culture, God in his usual sovereign (all free, all powerful ruler, owner, and King), elective (the one who freely chooses, electing according to his own holy love and purposes for his glory) and salvific stance (with salvation in mind, again to the glory and fame of his name) declares (from his place as eternal, omniscient, wise, creator King) the value of this land, this particular place above all others.

---

[53] Warren Baker and Eugene E. Carpenter, *The Complete Word Study Dictionary: Old Testament* (Chattanooga, TN: AMG Publishers, 2003), 486.
[54] Sharon Rusten with E. Michael, *The Complete Book of When & Where in the Bible and throughout History* (Wheaton, IL: Tyndale House Publishers, Inc., 2005).

I know; it doesn't sit well with our fallen nature and its warped sense of what is right and wrong and what is true, fair, and expected. As crushing as it is to human pride and thought, God is sovereign, and by his decree the elect are elected, this does not apply only to creatures but places, which as we state in our thesis, are made places and furthermore sacred places by his decree and presence.

The space God graces with his presence or blesses with his words can never be the same; as King, he is the one who does not change. It is he who is holy and so affects all that he comes into contact with in presence and by his words, which themselves are endowed with power, because of the one who speaks. This applies to God alone.

So Israel is the best land in the earth, and God chose this as the best, not the biggest or most famous, but the best for his chosen people. It is a chosen land for a chosen people. The choice was not made by humans, but by God in the very real history of creation and redemption.

## An appointed place: 2 Samuel 7:10

*And I will appoint a place for my people Israel and will plant them, so that they may dwell in their own place and be disturbed no more. And violent men shall afflict them no more, as formerly,*

—*2 Samuel 7:10*

Places are appointed by God; I know based on the text, I'm simply stating the obvious, but it is the obvious that we so often miss.

This verse is referring specifically to a social, ethnic group—the Jews—defined by their ancestry, language, land, and faith.

God has a twofold action here with regard to place and the people of Israel:

1. He will make the decision to prepare, select, and appoint a place for his people.
2. He will take the decisive act to plant his people in that place.

God also has a threefold purpose here with regard to place and the people of Israel:

1. That they would dwell and thrive in the appointed place
2. That they would be safe in the appointed place
3. That they might find rest in the appointed place

Paul picks up this general point regarding God appointing places too in Acts 17:26:

*And he made from one man every nation of mankind to live on all the face of the earth, having determined allotted periods and the boundaries of their dwelling place,*

I don't want to short change you on the last verse and its wider passage, but this will be picked up in a later part of the book in the application section.

## A land to dwell in: Ezekiel 28:25

*"Thus says the Lord GOD: When I gather the house of Israel from the peoples among whom they are scattered, and manifest my holiness in them in the sight of the nations, then they shall dwell in their own land that I gave to my servant Jacob.*

—*Ezekiel 28:25*

Not Uganda or any other place but the historically, linguistically, and geographically specific place called by the name of its people, Israel. My particular juxtaposition with Uganda will make sense later.

The land was not given as a temporary stage for the story of redemption to be played out on. Instead it served a very practical and wider theological purpose; it was a place for the Jews to dwell.

Somewhere to dwell, as we mention in our section on philosophy, is a core aspect of human existence and one of the underlying principles of reality itself. Not to mention a theological constant reaching back from the mind of God in creation to the glory of God in the consummation. All things are underpinned by the destiny of creatures in proximity to God with regard to place, across the realms of creation.

The scattered or displaced Israel was regathered or re-placed in the past in regard to their exile to Babylon and their return to the land of Israel some years later.

This principle of regathering is a pattern with regard to God's people Israel. After almost a two-thousand-year hiatus, we have seen this, in a sense, played out before our own eyes, in the modern world with the reestablishment of Israel as a nation state in 1948.

*B*efore we go any further in our study, we need to appeal for historical honesty. The rules applied to the critical study of historical records regarding many ancient lands and people enjoy a certain liberality that is not afforded to the study of the ancient land of Israel and its people.

In a related sense, the veracity of the historical documents contained in the Bible are treated with hubris and mistrust; they are not given the same credibility afforded to other historical documents from the same or later periods.

So my appeal is to those who are involved in critical analysis and interpretation of historical data to treat both Israel and the Bible with the historicity they deserve alongside other works and artifacts of antiquity.

This inherent distrust of Israel and the Bible, propagated by a deceptive secular humanist elite, does not only abuse us in academics but reaches more popularly and harmfully into our media reporting and therefore into nomenclature in an increasingly aggressive secular culture, driven by the presuppositions of modernity and postmodernity.

## Canaan

The land has had a change of name a few times in history; it was first called Canaan, named after the Canaanite people who first occupied the land in the post-flood world, according to the table of the earliest post-flood people groups, often referred to as the table of nations in Genesis 10:15–19.

## Israel

At the time of Joshua and Judges, the land become known by the people who had come to possess the land, and so it was called Israel. This is clearly evidenced from the biblical text in the book of Joshua and throughout the OT.

It is also attested to in an ancient artifact from Egypt called the The Merneptah Stele, also known as the "Israel Stele" dated to approximately 1230 BC. Part of this poem regarding Merneptah's (the son of Rameses II) victory over Libya reads as follows:

*Plundered is the Canaan with every evil; Carried off is Ashkelon; seized upon is Gezer; Yanoam is made as that which does not exist; Israel is laid waste, his seed is not;[55]*

The monument records the victory in poetic, songlike form, so it is not a valid historical record of that event itself (poems and songs exaggerate, etc.), but it is a reliable source in regard to the lands and peoples of the Ancient Near East in the 1200s BC.

## Palestine or Judea?

The name Palestine is not used once in the Greek NT. At the time of Jesus and the writing of the New Testament, the land was known as Judea, named after its historical people group or nation, the Jews.

The land historically known as Canaan, Israel, or Judea was changed in name to Palestine by the Romans in 135 AD in honor of the ancient enemies of Israel, the Philistines, who lived in the southern coastal region called Philistia. This area included famous Philistine cities like Gath (the place Goliath came from).

So let's be clear: the Romans took the general name of the coastal areas and expanded its scope by applying it to the entire region as a punishment for the second Jewish revolt or uprising. However, succeeding empires had various names for the area.

As these empires have risen and fallen, the term has fluctuated in importance and use. For example, under the Ottoman Turks it was not used to refer to the entire region.

Looking back to antiquity, some claim that Herodotus in his *Histories* (440 BC) was the first to use Palestine as a name for a region. Louis Feldman points out that the Greek historian Herodotus speaks inaccurately here because he was only familiar with the southern coastal area, which was actually called Philistia or Palestine.

Throughout the duration of the Greek Empire, and for a large part of the Roman, the area was called Judea. This was the official name for the area, according to the historians of the time, like Josephus. The historians, leaders, and officials would always distinguish between the two (Judea versus Palestine) as distinct areas.

---

[55] James Bennett Pritchard, ed., *The Ancient Near Eastern Texts Relating to the Old Testament,* 3rd ed. with Supplement (Princeton: Princeton University Press, 1969), 378.

It is not until after the second Jewish revolt against Rome, known as the Bar Kochba revolt, named after Simon bar Kosiba, who was said to be a false messiah of sorts. He was also accused of persecuting Jewish followers of Jesus and was instrumental in the uprising.

The name, in light of this revolt, was officially changed from the province of Judea to the province of Syria Palestina as a punishment to the people by the notably brutal General Hadrian.

Artifacts from the time, like coins and military documents, make a firm case for 135 AD as the date that the name was changed. Many authors after the change continue to refer to the area as Judea.

In the Byzantine period, the term became the accepted name of the area. It was revived in the Enlightenment and passed on to modern times, taking us up to the British Mandate, which ended in 1948 with the reestablishment of Israel as a nation and a return to the ancient name of a large part of the land.[56]

It is noteworthy that as a noun denoting a people group, the term Palestinian does not occur even once in the ancient world. Not once. Not even after the change to the name of the province by Rome in 135 AD.

The current concept of a Palestinian people group seems to be a modern invention in light of the formation of the present state of Israel and the ideological and racist resistance to this, motivated by traditional interpretations of Islam in the surrounding nations like Egypt, Syria, Iran, and Saudi Arabia.

Before the re-formation of Israel in 1948, the land had become placeless, with no people or hope. Mark Twain, the famous American author from the 1800s, is quoted as saying the following concerning the land after visiting it during his travels:

> *Palestine sits in sackcloth and ashes, desolate and unlovely. It is a hopeless, dreary, heartbroken land.*

Dr. Theodor Herzl, a prominent Zionist who lived at the same time as Mark Twain, said of Palestine:

---

[56] Frederick J. Murphy, "Palestine and Israel, Terminology For," ed. Katharine Doob Sakenfeld, *The New Interpreter's Dictionary of the Bible* (Nashville, TN: Abingdon Press, 2006–2009), 358.

> *There is a land without a people. There is a people without a land. Give the land without a people to the people without a land.*[57]

So here we have two well-known, credible witnesses from the 1800s, before the terrible events of the First and Second World Wars, who comment on the land as being desolate and without people. It is noteworthy that neither were resisted in their times for these assertions because they were true, and there was no thought of this place, held as sacred by so many, ever becoming a political entity again.

The hope of the Zionists seemed unattainable and even undesirable; that is, until world events took such a horrific turn that the Zionist vision of a place for the Jewish people in their historical homeland now seemed like a necessary reality.

---

[57] J. Vernon McGee, *Thru the Bible Commentary*, electronic ed., vol. 3 (Nashville: Thomas Nelson, 1997), 514.

# THE DISPLACEMENT OF THE
# SHOAH (HOLOCAUST)

*T*he attempted annihilation of all nine million Jews in Europe by Hitler and his Anti-Semitic Nazi party from 1933 until their defeat in 1945 is known in Hebrew as the Shoah or in English as the Holocaust. It stands as a testament to the depravity of man.

Hitler understood the importance of place, as does Satan. The spirit that empowered his diabolical thinking and actions, which at their root involved the wholesale displacement of the Jewish people in Europe.

The forced displacement began with boycotts, riots, and abuse fueled by centuries of so-called Christian anti-Semitism derived from errant teaching like extreme replacement theology, which affirms that God is finished with National Israel as a people, and the place. This is inconsistent with the Bible and its revelation of a God who keeps his promises and covenants.

I want to make the point here that true Christianity, as taught in the Bible, would not promote hating any people group and would never condone racism in any of its forms. Those were and are now nominal so-called Christians and are not actually full-blown disciples of Jesus Christ, who himself was a Jew and is still a Jew today as he sits enthroned beside his Father in heaven as the resurrected Jewish God-man.

There are many sources where you can read more details regarding the Holocaust. In preparing this section of this book, I read the following, which you may find useful too:

- *Encyclopedia Britannica Noet Edition*, 2015.

- Jennifer L. Koosed, *The New Interpreter's Dictionary of the Bible*, 2006–2009, 1–5.

- Jacob Neusner, Alan J. Avery-Peck, and William Scott Green, Eds., *The Encyclopedia of Judaism*, 2000.

- Carl F. H. Henry, *God, Revelation, and Authority*. (Wheaton, IL: Crossway Books, 1999).

- David E. Holwerda, *Jesus and Israel: One Covenant or Two?* (Grand Rapids, MI; Leicester, England: William B. Eerdmans Publishing Company; Apollos, 1995).

- Michael L. Brown, *Answering Jewish Objections to Jesus: General and Historical Objections.* (Grand Rapids, MI: Baker Books, 2000), 1.

*E*retz Yisrael simply means "Land of Israel" the true name of the historical Roman province of Judea, later called Palestine. The history of this place is rich for many people but none more than the most famous and longest-lasting inhabitants, the Jews.

> *Even non-Jews (such as Napoleon, in his manifesto to the Jews of Asia and Africa to re-establish themselves under his auspices in Palestine [1799]; Henry Dunant, the founder of the Red Cross, in his efforts to organize Jewish colonization there; Lord Shaftesbury, Lord Palmerston, and other Englishmen, in their sympathetic support; and Laurence Oliphant in his scheme in Gilead [1890]) realized the hold which the idea of a Jewish State in Palestine had on the Jews.*[58]

The political movement by European Jews to re-establish a sovereign Jewish state in the historical and biblical land of Israel is known as Zionism. The movement began in the 1800s before the World Wars. The term was first used by an Austrian Jewish journalist named Nathan Birnbaum in 1890. Although this was before the term was coined, the idea was well known and gaining a new momentum from thinkers like the German Jew Moses Hess, who said that the Jews in the diaspora would never give up hope of a restored Jewish State.[59]

Later thinkers and activists pick up on this same sentiment, drawing the Jewish people to a place of their own again away from the displacement and cold of the diaspora. One of the most famous was Theodor Herzl, who wrote a book called *The Jewish State*, calling for the establishment of a nation state for the Jewish people as a remedy to the anti-Semitism experienced by the Jewish diaspora in Europe. Herzl led the way in organizing and forming Zionism into the political movement we see today.

The Bible would often refer to Zion, which is literally a hill in Jerusalem, to speak of the entire city of Jerusalem and sometimes the entire land. It is often used in a deeper messianic and spiritual sense in relation to the place. This is one of the reasons

---

[58] Paul Goodman, "ZIONISM," ed. James Hastings, John A. Selbie, and Louis H. Gray, *Encyclopædia of Religion and Ethics* (Edinburgh; New York: T. & T. Clark; Charles Scribner's Sons, 1908–1926), 855.
[59] A. James Rudin, "Zionism," *The Encyclopedia of Christianity* (Grand Rapids, MI; Leiden, Netherlands: Wm. B. Eerdmans; Brill, 2008), 857.

it was chosen by the nationalist thinkers and founders of Zionism as the root word of their movement.

A well-known medieval Jewish poet who lived in Spain between 1085 and 1140 is just one voice from across the centuries that echoes the constant connection the people of Israel have had with the land of Israel, in one of his poems quoted in *The Jewish Encyclopedia* (1901) as follows:

> *Zion, wilt thou not send a greeting to thy captives.*
>
> *Who greet thee as the remnant of thy flocks?*
>
> *From West to East, from North to South, a greeting,*
>
> *From far and near, take thou on all sides.*
>
> *A greeting sends the captive of desire, who sheds his tears*
>
> *Like dew on Hermon; would they might fall on thy hills*[60]

Another poem by the same author is quoted in *The Jewish Encyclopedia*, again displaying the desire among the Jewish people throughout the ages to dwell in their own place or land again:

> *Lo! sun and moon, these minister for aye;*
>
> *The laws of day and night cease nevermore:*
>
> *Given for signs to Jacob's seed that they*
>
> *Shall ever be a nation—till these be o'er.*
>
> *If with His left hand He should thrust away,*
>
> *Lo! with His right hand He shall draw them nigh.*[61]

This was the heart and soul of Jewish life, seen in the works of their artists, the words of their leaders, and the remembrance kept at every Passover, while in their

---

[60] Isidore Singer, ed., *The Jewish Encyclopedia: A Descriptive Record of the History, Religion, Literature, and Customs of the Jewish People from the Earliest Times to the Present Day, 12 Volumes* (New York; London: Funk & Wagnalls, 1901–1906), 666.

[61] Isidore Singer, ed., *The Jewish Encyclopedia: A Descriptive Record of the History, Religion, Literature, and Customs of the Jewish People from the Earliest Times to the Present Day, 12 Volumes* (New York; London: Funk & Wagnalls, 1901–1906), 348.

relatively modern exile or displacement as a people, where they would say "Next year in Jerusalem."

The JPS dictionary confirms this, informing us that the traditional phrase is a common tradition for the Pesach Seder. To end with the declaration, which in Hebrew would sound like "le-shanah ha-ba'ah be-Yerushalayim."[62]

This all points to the fact that the Jewish people had "place" in their hearts; and not just any space, but their own place, God's city, Jerusalem. This shows the heart's desire of the Jewish people is to be in their own land.

The power of place, and this sacred place in particular, has a magnetic pull on its people, that even after thousands of years they still heard the call to come and dwell, to come and be in the land, made a place for them by God's own decree and personal presence.

My point in mentioning art, poems, sayings, hopes, and dreams is that it is not some soft sentimentalism at all, but a firm connection, a cord that ties the people back to their ancient land, through countless cultures and ages, while in a perpetual state of displacement.

No other people had among their number those who would long to go back to Israel, for no other people had been there in any prolonged and meaningful sense other than the Jews.

No other people group has an annual religious feast that includes any statement regarding Jerusalem as a matter of course. Only the Jews. Again, this makes a case for their unique connection, heritage, and right to the place.

However, we do find references to Jerusalem and Israel in some Christian art and thought. When thought of biblically, this is not a look at the place with the mind to displace the original and rightful inhabitants of the land but focuses on the wider, deeper, eschatological and spiritual reality the land and its city point to.

The issue is that the extreme presupposition called "replacement theology" infected pure Christian thought and behavior toward the Jews, especially in those only called Christian in name rather than in faith and practice (the type who would go on to murder people just because of their race or religion).

---

[62] Joyce Eisenberg and Ellen Scolnic, Jewish Publication Society, *The JPS Dictionary of Jewish Words* (Philadelphia, PA: Jewish Publication Society, 2001), 117.

It is worth noting that historically, many Christians have supported the Zionist position regarding a restored Jewish state in their ancient homeland. One example is William Blackstone, who urged four hundred prominent leaders in America to sign a declaration calling for a Jewish state in 1891.

> *Zionism received its most powerful impetus by the recognition on the part of the British Government of the historical connexion of the Jewish people with Palestine and the claim which this gives them to reconstruct Palestine as their national home.*

> *There are in England traditions, dating back to Puritan times, which favour the restoration of the Jews to their ancient country. It was also in England that the first society for the Jewish colonization of Palestine was formed by George Gawler in 1845. George Eliot's Daniel Deronda (1876) was in those days a remarkable revelation of the Jewish nationalist aspirations of a Gentile, while the romanticism of Benjamin Disraeli, with his strong Jewish sympathies, gave a glamour to the idea of the restoration of Israel, with which the English-speaking world is familiar through the Bible.[63]*

---

[63] Paul Goodman, "ZIONISM," ed. James Hastings, John A. Selbie, and Louis H. Gray, *Encyclopædia of Religion and Ethics* (Edinburgh; New York: T. & T. Clark; Charles Scribner's Sons, 1908–1926), 857.

# REPLACEMENT THEOLOGY
# VERSUS RE-PLACEMENT
# THEOLOGY

*M*ichael J. Vlach's articles in the *Conservative Theological Journal* have been a great guide to help us understand the nature and history of replacement theology. I would recommend it to anyone who wants to read more about the subject. Other notable authorities include David H. Stern, Arnold G. Fruchtenbaum, Chuck D. Pierce, Rebecca Wagner Sytsema, and C. E. B. Cranfield.

Voices for a biblical type of replacement theology include Cornelis P. Venema and Michael Horton.

## What is replacement theology?

Replacement theology can be defined from an ecclesiastical perspective (study of the church) as the view that Israel has been permanently replaced by the church. Equally from an eschatological perspective (study of the last things) the belief affirms that Israel no longer figures in God's plans in anyway, they have been cast off and utterly surpassed by the church. I would also say that the system is underpinned by a subtle Dualistic and Gnostic undertone that exalts spiritual realities at the expense of physical ones, seen most clearly in the allegorizing of OT promises.

One of the questions theologians seek to answer is the relationship between Israel and the church: Is the church the continuation of Israel (traditional covenant theology) or an entirely distinct from Israel (classical dispensational theology)? I am of the view that the truth lies somewhere in between the two. They are indeed distinct; at the same time, they are spiritually connected while there are areas of both continuity and discontinuity.

## The roots of replacement theology

There are four factors that contribute to the church's historical and current position on replacement theology, none of these are rooted primarily in the Scriptures but in historical, social, and political events. These include:[64]

1.  *Decreasing Jewish influence in the early church.* The church began with all Jewish leaders and believers; however, as the message successfully spread and the first generation began to die out, the church became Gentile by majority and so organically moved away from its Jewish roots.

2.  *The destructions of Jerusalem in 70 and 135 AD.* This was an earth-shattering event that would have fueled a belief in believers at the time that God did indeed appear to be finished with Israel, with the displacement from the land and the destruction of the temple. It seemed plausible that the church was the new Israel.

3.  *Jewish-Christian hostilities.* There were radical Jews like Simon bar Kosiba, the instigator of the second revolt, who was infamous for persecuting believers in Jesus. It is from this time that anti-Jewish polemics start to appear in Bible commentaries.

4.  *The church's appropriation of the Jewish Scriptures.* This early practice of applying the OT Scriptures to themselves paved the way for the errant view of replacement theology.

## Extreme (unbiblical) replacement theology: Israel is done away with

Extreme replacement theology is a negative and erroneous concept. It essentially asserts that, due to the Jews rejecting Jesus as the promised Messiah/King and his gospel of the kingdom of God (which is not true, all the first Christians were Jews), God judicially and permanently replaced Israel with the predominately Gentile church.

There is another extreme that goes in the other direction, which is called two-covenant theology. This position was recently embraced by the Roman Catholic Church. It states that there are, in fact, two active, parallel major covenants, one for the Jews and another

---

[64] Based on the work of Michael J. Vlach in "Has the Church Replaced Israel in God's Plan? A Historical and Theological Survey of Replacement Theology," *Conservative Theological Journal Volume 4* (2000).

for Christians and that the Jews have their own way of salvation quite removed from Christ. This is not just a theological aberration, disagreement, or mistake, this is rank heresy. Jesus is the only way to salvation for all descendants of Adam.

So on the one hand, extreme replacement theology teaches that God has finished his dealings with Israel as a people, while two-covenant theology makes way too much of his continued dealings with the nation to the exclusion of Christ. [65]

We will find the balance of true newness (some may call replacement) and continuity from the Scriptures, a truth that has been taught and defended well by the authors I mentioned above, if you are interested in doing more research on the topic.

The late Reverend Professor Charles E. B. Cranfield mentions the following in his commentary on Romans 9:1–11:36:

> It is only where the Church persists in refusing to learn this message, where it secretly—perhaps quite unconsciously! —believes that its own existence is based on human achievement, and so fails to understand God's mercy to itself, that it is unable to believe in God's mercy for still unbelieving Israel, and so entertains the ugly and unscriptural notion that God has cast off His people Israel and simply replaced it by the Christian Church. These three chapters emphatically forbid us to speak of the Church as having once and for all taken the place of the Jewish people. [66]

The Bible refutes the extreme case at every turn:

1. The Bible does not teach that Israel is ever permanently rejected; this is evidenced in the teachings of both Jesus and Paul.

2. The title "Israel" is never used of believers in the general sense. At most it is possibly mentioned in a spiritual sense, which does not lead to the conclusion that the actual Israel is done away with.

3. It is a flawed presupposition to say that the church must become the new Israel to have OT Scriptures applied to it. This is possible without that unnecessary jump; for example, believing Gentiles can become sons of Abraham without becoming Jews.

---

[65] See the summary by Cornelis P. Venema, "The Church and Israel: The Issue," *Tabletalk Magazine, October 2012: The Church and Israel* (Sanford, FL: Ligonier Ministries, Inc., 2012), 9.

[66] C. E. B. Cranfield, *A Critical and Exegetical Commentary on the Epistle to the Romans*, International Critical Commentary (London; New York: T&T Clark International, 2004), 448.

4. Jews and Gentiles are equal spiritually both in sin and in Christ. However, this fact does not preclude that God's functional dealings with the Jews as a distinct people has ended.

5. Hebrews 8:8–13 sees the New Covenant spoken of by Jeremiah 31–34 applied to the church, this does not mean that it cannot be applied to Israel too in the last days.[67]

## Normal (biblical) replacement theology: One new man

There is a type of theology often called replacement theology, but it really is not, or if it is then it is the right and biblical type.

The Bible teaches one way of salvation in Christ for both Jew and Gentile and that these two are one new man in Christ. This replaces the old order of things in which someone needed to ceremonially become a Jew through circumcision and keeping of the covenant of the law with its animal sacrifices to be saved.

In Romans 1:16, Paul makes clear that this is the one way of salvation but he simultaneously makes it clear that the distinction between particular people groups still exists by the fact that he mentions them. He also points to the fact that God's redemptive purpose for the Jews is not done away with or superseded but fulfilled in Christ.

Jesus really does replace things like the Passover Lamb and all the sacrifices with the truth that these shadows pointed to, and in so doing he fulfills many promises. However, in many cases, his coming serves as confirmation and makes possible the future fulfillment of Israel's specific promises.[68]

It is entirely biblical to affirm, as the Bible teaches, that Jesus has come and both fulfilled the law and surpassed the old order of sacrifices and priests as taught in Hebrews.

---

[67] Based on a list by Michael J. Vlach, "Has the Church Replaced Israel in God's Plan? A Historical and Theological Survey of Replacement Theology," *Conservative Theological Journal Volume 4* 4, no. 11 (2000): 32.

[68] Cornelis P. Venema, "The Church and Israel: The Issue," *Tabletalk Magazine, October 2012: The Church and Israel* (Sanford, FL: Ligonier Ministries, Inc., 2012), 9.

## What do I mean by re-placement theology?

My play on words is nothing to do with the church as a "nation" replacing Israel as a nation. The church is not a nation; it is far more than that, it is the body of Christ, comprised of a new humanity, superior to the old only by God's mercy and grace, encompassing Jews and Gentiles from every nation, tribe, and tongue.

I'm alluding to God's purposes in taking the displaced and emplacing them again, re-placing them in safe and sacred places for their flourishing and his glory, in accordance with the redemptive history of the Scriptures and God's dealings with humans and in particular with his people, the Jews.

We believe in the God who has re-placed Israel in their ancient land for his glory and their joy, found in the salvation provided by Israel's King, Jesus.

The reason I juxtapose my term *re-placement theology* against the errant teaching of extreme replacement theology is because of the future promises to Israel, which replacement theology does away with by spiritualizing and allegorizing them. It does this by reading them all into the church. This is diametrically opposed to the biblical promise and pattern of physical, literal fulfillment and re-placement, in accordance with God's promises, which the coming and work of Christ should give us more confidence in, believing them rather than explaining them away as spiritual realities only.

There is no room in this book for an exposition of Romans 9–11 regarding the restoration of Israel (the ethnic, social, and political people group) in the real world in the actual place called Israel, but with the added element of faith in Christ and the engrafted Gentiles without discounting the truth regarding the spiritual aspect of Israel as encompassing all God's people, redeemed in Christ.

# THE STATE OF ISRAEL

*T*he land was first occupied by Israel in 1200 BC, that is over three thousand years ago.

Look at this timeline adapted from Arnold Fruchtenbaum's list of historical and archeological periods. I have summarized it to give a high-level picture of who was in the land and when. In my summary, this will consist of twelve overlapping periods, starting and ending with Israel as the controlling force.[69]

1. 1200–587 BC, Israelite (613 years)
2. 587–536 BC, Babylonian (51 years)
3. 536–332 BC, Medo-Persian (204 years)
4. 332–63 BC, Greek or Hellenistic (269 years)
5. 63 BC–324 AD, Roman (387 years)
6. 324 AD–638 AD, Byzantine (314 years)
7. 614–629 AD, Persian (15 years)
8. 638–1517 AD, Muslim (879 years)
9. 1099–1187 AD, Crusaders (88 years)
10. 1517–1917 AD, Turkish or Ottoman (400 years)
11. 1917–1948 AD, British Mandate (31 years)
12. 1948–Present AD, Israelite (68 years)

It is noteworthy that no single people group outside the various Muslim occupations has lived in this place as the controlling state for a longer period than the Jews.

Whether ruling or not, the Jews have lived in the land for three thousand years, whether their numbers were in the millions, thousands, or just a few hundred.

## A place formed by law, not conquest

Desperation in the early 1900s led Herzl, the leader of the Zionist movement, to seriously consider a ludicrous offer from the British government to establish a Jewish state in Uganda… yes you heard me right Uganda. It is at this point that Chaim

---

[69] Arnold Fruchtenbaum, *A Study Guide of Israel: Historical and Geographical* (Tustin, CA: Ariel Ministries, 1994), 8–9.

Weizmann rose to prominence in a new generation of Zionist leaders. He vehemently opposed the Uganda plan and steered the Zionist movement to focus on the ultimate goal of a state in the only place it should be, the land of Palestine, ancient Israel.

Weizmann, who moved to England in 1904, had a major impact on influential Christians like Arthur J. Balfour, who later became the foreign secretary. In 1917 through Weizmann's efforts, the British government of David Lloyd George sent a letter to Lord Walter Rothschild, which later became known as the Balfour Declaration, it reads as follows:

> His Majesty's Government view with favour the establishment in Palestine
> of a national home for the Jewish people, and will use their best endeavours
> to facilitate the achievement of this object, it being clearly understood that
> nothing shall be done which may prejudice the civil and religious rights of
> existing non-Jewish communities in Palestine or the rights and political status
> enjoyed by Jews in any other country.[70]

This later paved the way for the UN General Assembly Resolution 181, which called for Palestine (modern-day Jordan and Israel) to be divided into separate Jewish and Arab states.

History teaches us the inescapable fact that Israel was formed legally, not by war and conquest but with the open and legal processes in place for the formation of an official state and nation in the post-WWII and the post-Holocaust world in 1948.

It can be argued that some of the greatest nations of the world, including America, were not formed in a peaceful and legal sense but by war, exploit, genocide, slavery, and rebellion.

My nation, England, is not off the hook; we are historically guilty of pillaging the world, perpetrating unjust wars of conquest abroad, and exploiting and enslaving peoples just like our transatlantic cousins did.

In fact, look at the formation and unfolding history of every nation and you will see war, upheaval, atrocities, injustice, and exploitation of their own people, others, and the very place itself. With this shared history in mind, it is with great hubris that the world sits in judgment of Israel and derides their wars with hostile aggressors from the surrounding nations.

---

[70] Paul Goodman, "ZIONISM," ed. James Hastings, John A. Selbie, and Louis H. Gray, *Encyclopædia of Religion and Ethics* (Edinburgh; New York: T. & T. Clark; Charles Scribner's Sons, 1908–1926), 858.

The so-called Palestinians were never an official people or state, to be oppressed, occupied, or squeezed out of the land. At best they were nomads and migrants from surrounding regions passing through or living in the land, at worst they are people sent in by the enemies of Israel at its formation to occupy the land and disrupt the peaceful settlement of the legal new nation.

The place, Israel, is at the center of political life for the world, exactly because it is not just any old space; it is a place that God has endowed with worth by his decrees concerning it, the covenants he made regarding it, and his personal manifest presence in it throughout redemptive history. Not to mention the platform on which the Son of Man took center stage of history, theology, and philosophy as the Last Adam, the one and only unique God-man.

Places matter, Israel matters. Until the Church understands that, we will miss an important part of our mission in the earth, not only in regard to Israel but to all peoples in all lands.

## Wars defending place

The wars the modern-day state of Israel has had to go through have been nothing short of a fight for survival. A fight to hold on to the place declared to be theirs by God, man, and law.

On May 14, 1948, the very night that Israel was declared an independent state no longer under the control of the British, the surrounding Arab nations—ideologically racist against Israel—attacked, bombing Tel Aviv and marching their armies into Israel, starting a war, over a place for a people that lasted for more than a year.

In the years that followed, there were more wars over this place, the home for the Jewish people, often driven by a murderous Islamic ideology that has caused Middle Eastern countries to live in oppression (a reality the Western world is only now waking up to with the advent of groups like ISIS). I will not go into great detail in this book; the point is made by the war of independence alone. But to give a full picture, the major wars included:

1. The war of independence, 1948–49.
2. The war in the Sinai, 1956.
3. The six-day war, 1967.
4. The Yom Kippur war, 1973,

5. The Invasion of Lebanon, 1982 [71]

## Place, traded for peace

Despite these wars, aggression, terrorism, and unbalanced treatment by the global community and press, the government of Israel, with a clear understanding of the importance of place (or land) has gone as far as to trade place for peace.

This is a fact of geopolitical history, but it also teaches us a lesson, or should I say asks us the question: Should we trade place for peace?

I think the answer is an emphatic no because the whole concept of place is that of ownership, destiny, safety, and belonging, and when these are traded, the bullies or antagonists will have invaded a place that belongs to you, occupying that place so it is no longer safe etc. under the pretense of peace.

When we consider this in a spiritual sense, our enemy Satan is always looking for a foothold, a place that is ours that we will give him for the peace found in surrendering in our fight against him and his ways. If it is not him, then it is our flesh seeking the peace of its own appeasement and comfort.

This can even be played out in the real world in social and political spheres, just like we have seen in Israel.

The principle remains, do not trade place for peace or anything else; it is simply too important to you as a person, to the collective human experience, and to the plans of God.

## Two states in one place

It is noteworthy that it was the case from 1948, when the region called Palestine was divided into an Arab state known as Trans Jordan or just Jordan and a Jewish state known as Israel, that the "Arabs" got the larger portion; just look at a map.

Talk of further division and reduction of the Jewish state is unfair.

Two states in one place; this is the noble effort of Israel's government and her allies. However, this flies in the face of another place principle, which is that one place should not encroach on another. Each is unique, sovereign, and endowed with

---

[71] Dates sourced from "Arab-Israeli Wars," *Encyclopedia Britannica Noet Edition* (Chicago, IL: Encyclopaedia Britannica, 2015).

its own sense of meaning and worth. When these collide in a forced or contrived manner, the result can only be disruption and conflict.

This applies in a social context too, where we try to force multiculturalism on our people, with the result that the worldview of humanism or the most dominant voice wins out in a new intolerance. This new stance is usually less tolerant than the "old tolerance" or the intolerance, which itself is sometimes hypothetical, which our contrived forcing together was invented to avoid.

The Bible teaches us that it is God who sets boundaries for lands and peoples, for the flourishing of all peoples so they can come together willingly and not have their mixing and working together legislated to such a degree that it is forced.

This is, however, a complex issue because humans are sinful and so without some control or intervention, the strong would oppress and stifle the weak … but this line of discussion takes us down a rabbit hole. Back to the historical context of the people of Israel in the place called the land of Israel.

## True restoration

The true restoration of Israel, the one that goes beyond the secular one we observe now, will be accomplished by the King of Israel, Jesus Christ, at his return; the current restoration is just a foreshadowing of that.

The restoration the Bible speaks of is epic, with global implications, supernatural phenomena, and a central focus on the Son of Man, Jesus Christ.

We long for that day and believe with firm hope and sure faith that it will come to pass because Jesus is the Amen, the tried, tested, and proven guarantee that all God's promises indeed shall come to pass.

A bricks-and-mortar kingdom is coming, which does not negate the fact that a very real spiritual kingdom is here now in multiple ways through Christ, as we will discuss and explain next.

## Now and not yet

Much of the OT is fulfilled in Christ and points to spiritual realities now and not yet realized in the kingdom of God. This is a concept referred to as "now and not yet."

This is an important idea to help us understand the flow of the Bible's narrative. Without it, the situation can seem that promises have either changed or were never fulfilled in Christ.

Many of the now elements of the kingdom are to do with the spiritual coming of the kingdom of God and the salvation provided by Jesus. The not yet aspects are the real-world reflections and consummation of these spiritual realities in the eschaton or last days. These will be with a real world ethnic people of Israel who have accepted the "now" spiritual aspect of the kingdom and its King, their Messiah, Jesus.

# AN APPEAL FOR BALANCE

ornelis Venema mentions that the Israel versus the church debate needs to maintain the Apostle Paul's balance, not separating them nor displacing one with the other.[72]

I completely agree. One of the issues that quite often arises is that of extremes, polemics, and straw man hypothetical arguments. To polarize around one strain of truth from the Scriptures at the expense of others that appear to the human mind to create a paradox is neither healthy nor safe.

The Bible calls us to check, study, and rightly dissect the Word of God with the right spirit and by the light of the Holy Spirit.

My appeal to believers is to be balanced. To accept all that the Bible teaches regarding God's people, an important concept in this book, which I would summarize as follows:

1. The gifts and callings of God are irrevocable, this is mostly because of God's own holy love, an essential element of his character.
2. God does not lie. If God said it, he will bring it to pass.
3. God has not cast off his people Israel in this sense:
    a. From the start of the church, Jews were saved by God's grace before and just like the Gentiles.
    b. Today, Israelites are still saved as messianic believers.
    c. The mode of salvation has changed as Jesus has fulfilled and superseded the temple and sacrifices as taught in Hebrews.
    d. The not yet of the kingdom including the actual rule of Christ as King on David's throne from Jerusalem will still happen in the specific and promised Jewish context.
    e. The promises will be fulfilled by and in context to the incarnation, perfect life, suffering, death, resurrection, ascension, and return of Jesus Christ, the God-man and prophesied seed of Abraham, Israel's Messiah King and the Son of Man.

[72] See the actual statement, Cornelis P. Venema, "The Church and Israel: The Issue," *Tabletalk Magazine*, *October 2012: The Church and Israel* (Sanford, FL: Ligonier Ministries, Inc., 2012), 9.

f. There has always been a distinction between believing/obedient Israel and unbelieving/disobedient Israel. The former are and always have been part of the olive tree; the later are naturally part of the tree but cut off for unbelief.

4. The spiritual realities that are now a certainty in light of Christ's first advent do not take away from the above but add to its fullness and richness. The new spiritual realities include:

a. The universal body of Christ is grafted into God's People Israel and, so, are God's people.

b. Jewish and Gentile believers constitute the kingdom of God on earth.

c. Believers become a part of the commonwealth of Israel.

d. Spiritual aspects and reflections of the promises are available for all believers in Jesus whether Jew or Greek.

e. Believers do become true inward Jews (they are never said to become outward Jews; this would defy logic and science).

5. Believers are united as one new man without the distinction between national Israel with its related purposes in God's plans and the church with God's destiny for it, becoming confounded, replaced, or superseded by each other.

6. We should note that the ultimate destiny of all believers is to dwell in the same place as God forever.

7. The physical world is not inherently evil; it was created good by a good Creator, who will see his purposes played out in the physical realm, with a physical Israel when he fulfills his actual prophesies in light of and through Christ.

In conclusion it is so crucial that the church regains a biblical understanding of the now and not yet nature of the kingdom and the purposes of God in the physical world as being of great and eternal importance not instead of but aligned to the spiritual realities that underpin and are affected by the physical realm.

We need to drop our tendency and trajectory from Gnostic ideas toward a warped Dualistic view of reality and the Christian faith, to one that his rooted in the here and now, looking forward to the not yet but near. A real faith, for real people in a real place called Earth.

God came close for a reason, well for many reasons, but at least one of them was to remind us that the created realm was good and that the physical world holds worth to its creator. So much so that the high price of redemption was paid in "the flesh" through the broken physical body of Jesus to save God's people here, now, and in eternity.

A return to this fundamental way of thinking, this balanced and biblical view, is the only way forward as we seek to think biblically about God, his people, places, and of course salvation, which leads me on to the next point.

## Real love

In recent years, I have been very concerned that overreaction to the extreme views of replacement theology and anti-Semitism harbored in the church has led to a dangerous precedent of reaching out to, embracing, encouraging, and "loving" the Jews aside from the gospel.

This is not really loving the Jews; it is impotent and has little lasting impact. The fact remains that to truly love the Jews is to preach the gospel of the kingdom, which is ultimately the only path to life, joy, and peace for all mankind in every place.

Show the love of Christ to Jewish people today by pointing them to their King, the Messiah, Jesus.

You may need to take the time to explain to them that expressions of hate toward the Jews by those who claim to be Christians is not consistent with Christian belief, and those who practice hate like this show themselves to be not Christian at all but abusers of the name of Christ.

Another good thing to point out is the Jewish roots of the faith, Scripture, and even current practice and belief, especially the fact that the early church comprised of Jews who believed that Jesus was the promised King, the Son of Man, the Messiah.

# THE CHURCH

My first memory of church was attending a church called Christ Church on Brixton Road; it was an Anglican Church of England establishment. The building was old and ornate. The priest was friendly, but the service itself was quite boring, this is of course clouded by the perception of my mind as a child and the fact that I was not a believer at the time, being no more than seven years old.

While in primary school I also attended St. Johns, this was in Brixton on Vassal Road. This was a classic looking church with a large steeple and belfry. This was also a C of E Church but was larger and more prestigious than Christ Church. It felt cold and dry.

When on summer holidays, I had my first experience of a different type of church. My maternal grandfather was a bishop and grandmother a pastor of a predominantly black congregation in West Ham. They rented the space of a Baptist Church. Their services were more lively and a lot longer.

When I turned eleven and started secondary school (this is what you might call high school). A family friend came to our home and shared the gospel with us. As a family we started attending a very small, eccentric little church in Vauxhall where they would pray for a couple of hours before the service began. For me, my brothers, and sister, this was simply unbearable.

One of the older sisters in that church introduced us to a church in West Norwood, Worldwide Mission Fellowship. I remember the first time I arrived at the church. We were early for the evening service, so we caught the choir—then called Youth Aflame, now called Sincere Praise—practicing a few songs; I was blown away. Lots of people came and gave me a really warm greeting. The service was great. That was it; I had found my home.

I attended the next week's morning and evening services and began attending the Sunday school. This church with its vibrant worship, fervent prayer, warm fellowship, and challenging expository preaching has been my church home ever since.

The church is a unique phenomenon in the world. Consider her beginning—born into persecution and oppression, and yet the church thrived and became the greatest force for change and good in the earth, as those entrusted with the gospel of God's kingdom and the King, Jesus.

What makes the church an important historical case study is that we would be served well to learn the lesson of our past, to see how an understanding of place and our position in the physical world has shaped the thoughts, behavior, mission, and overall witness of the church.

I should begin by making clear that I'm not talking about any one institution, movement, or denomination, and certainly not the Roman Catholic Institution. I am talking about the true church, across all denominations, cultures, times, and—yes—places.

Jesus said of the church in Matthew 16:18–19:

> And I tell you, you are Peter, and on this rock I will build my church, and the gates of hell shall not prevail against it. I will give you the keys of the kingdom of heaven, and whatever you bind on Earth shall be bound in heaven, and whatever you loose on earth shall be loosed in heaven.

## A strong place in the Spirit

A place built by Jesus in the spirit by the Spirit.

This is not a contradiction to one of the premises of the book regarding the importance of place because that truth translates to the spiritual, mental, emotional, and physical realms.

Consider the language used by Jesus, who himself was a builder working with stone and timber. Jesus in another place calls himself the rock, the chief cornerstone, and teaches that those who apply his teaching are like those who built their house on the rock. Peter goes on to call us stones in a house.

All this building imagery is important; it highlights some important points for us, including:

1. Jesus's theology was aware of the centrality of place. He affirms and comforts his followers that he has built them like a building and no storm of hell could prevail against them. He assures his people that they will endure.

2. Christ is central to his own theology and ours because it is the confession of Peter that Jesus is the Christ the Son of the Living God that we are built on, the firm foundation of our confession of Christ. We are not founded on any efforts or institutions of men. Peter, Israel, or any organization is not our foundation. Faith in the person of Jesus, the revelation of the Father, and the Word of God—this is our foundation.

3. The devil seeks to displace humnity and, in particular, believers.

4. God is the one who wants us to be an emplaced people in the Spirit, in the fellowship of the church. With that sense of purpose fueling our mission and helping form our identity.

5. The parallel importance of the physical and spiritual world.

6. Jesus is, among many other things, a place maker, as the one who builds, sustains, and preserves the church.

7. The settled and secure place of the church in the spirit is the precursor to the authority of the church as ambassadors of God's presence and place (heaven) in the earth.

## What is a biblical church?

We should consider the following when thinking about a biblical church, just because something's called church or Christian does not mean it is. The following basic list is taken from the apologetic course I created in 2015 for Worldwide Mission Fellowship called Hold and Advance:

1. **Ecclesia**—An elect, called out, gathered people in Christ. The church, God's elect and "called out" people.
2. **Catholic**—The universal, true church, which spans across time, place, and culture. Not to be confused with "Roman Catholic."
3. **Not legalistic (legalism)**—Salvation through keeping moral laws, the heresy that we are saved by works.
4. **Not without law (antinomianism)**—Anti-law, the heresy that sin no longer matters in Christ.
5. **Grace**—God's unearned or deserved special, particular, personal love. Getting what we do not deserve.
6. **Faith**—Trust in God and His Word, especially the word of the gospel message.
7. **Biblical**—Founded on the apostles, with elders who both pastor and teach. Jesus is the cornerstone of our life and practice, according to his Word, which is the bedrock.
8. **Body**—Diverse gifts and peoples unified by one Spirit and Truth.
9. **Purpose**—Evangelize, teach, build, represent, worship and glorify God.
10. **Sacraments**—Baptism and communion as signs and seals.
11. **Growth**—True believers will develop and grow spiritually.
12. **Fellowship**—Family, instruction, service, encouragement.
13. **Affections**—Joyful service, heartfelt emotions for God.
14. **Results**—Bearing spiritual fruit in various ways, including the salvation of others.

The church built by Jesus is universal, transcending time and place, unified around the truth, founded on Jesus the Christ, the Son of the Living God himself.

We are called to be and make disciples ("only believe" thinking is wrong).

We are God's people on the earth, his witnesses and representatives.

## Ambassadors of the place maker

Now we turn to the history of the church in the earth. From the birth of the church it has been growing. This growth was prophesied by Jesus and is indicative of the symbolic or spiritual arrival of God's kingdom on earth through his people, which itself points forward to the literal kingdom that will be on earth, and just like the Christian mission began in Jerusalem, the actual coming kingdom will be headquartered in Jerusalem too.

This growth was empowered by God himself as the Holy Spirit but actively accomplished by believers—citizens of God's kingdom. Heralds of the King proclaim the news of the King's kingdom, his person, glorious victory over the enemy's kingdom, the life now available through his accomplishments, the call on all creatures in all realms to bow to him as King and receive his royal pardon for rebellion, treason, and allegiance with the enemy and the coming fullness of the kingdom when the King returns.

It is the ambassadors of the King and his kingdom from Paul some two thousand years ago to the church planters like the founders of my own church, Dennis and Anita Greenidge, that are advancing God's kingdom.

God the original place maker of heaven and earth, then as redeemer through Jesus, makes a place in the real world for believers. This is in the presence of God, which will be here on the earth in the end and spiritually a place is made called the church or body of Christ. This body manifests itself in actual gatherings, often in buildings of all shapes and descriptions. It is this God that the church over the ages has imaged, reflected, and represented when we went out as heralds of the kingdom, ambassadors of the place maker.

## An urban movement

Christianity has historically proven itself to be an urban movement, nearly always starting in the city. First in Jerusalem and moving to other cities in the area.

In God's strategy to spread the news of the kingdom, this makes sense. Cities are densely populated places, unlike the wide-open spaces of the wilderness or countryside, so it's the perfect place for the holy town criers to go and announce the good news: the King and his kingdom have come, are here, and will come in fullness soon.

The reformers continued this pattern of working where the people are, in the place in which they live. Owen Chadwick in his book about the early reformation notes the following three elements of the reformed mission to and from cities in Europe:

1. the city council would become the controller of church affairs;

2. transform worship to be understandable and accessible by the people;

3. take "misused" trust funds and use them for social care.[73]

## Place and "Christian" terrorists, crusaders

It is important that we are honest with the record of history. There are many dark moments in what is commonly understood to be Christian history. The reality is that Christian by definition is not one who can harbor hate or commit acts of genocide.

However, nominal Christians who take on the name Christian based on the country they are from or the "religion" passed down to them from their forefathers have no living relationship with the Lord and so would be capable of anything.

The crusades commissioned by the Roman Catholic Church and the acts of the crusaders themselves were one of these dark moments in the history of the so-called church.

The very purpose for the crusades points to the importance of place in the human psyche and in the religious mind. It shows us that apart from Christ, the importance and centrality of place can drive men into gross wickedness to both man and land.

The Crusades began as a mission by any means necessary to capture Israel and Jerusalem for the Pope. The sacred nature and rich scriptural history of the so-called Holy Land made it the prize of corrupted ruling powers of the Roman church. They were not content with relics and artifacts; it was the very place, the land itself they wanted to claim for themselves. One of the reasons is that the possession of the land would add legitimacy to their faith's claims as being rooted in the firm ground of world history, played out in and around the place called Israel, later known as the province of Judah, most recently called the province of Palestine.

The Byzantine powers had fallen in the east to the Seljuk from Turkey. In 1095 the Byzantine emperor appealed to the Pope and western powers to help him get the holy land back from the Muslim Turks. Pope Urban, a very eloquent speaker, gave a sermon in France, where he called for holy war. The response from the crowd of clergy, soldiers, farmers, and men from every walk of life was a resounding, "God wills it."

---

[73] See the following for the full list, Owen Chadwick, *The Early Reformation on the Continent*, ed. Henry Chadwick and Owen Chadwick, *Oxford History of the Christian Church* (Oxford; New York: Oxford University Press, 2001), 95.

These men became the first crusaders and marched on Jerusalem successfully in 1099 AD. Much like the jihadi terrorists of our day, they believed their war was the will and work of God and that it earned them special pardon before God.

In this campaign and the years that followed, the crusaders were guilty of persecuting the Jews and opened the door to the evils of anti-Semitism. Some of these dark chapters in human history include, but are certainly not limited to:

1. **1096 AD.** Crusaders massacred Jews in Rhineland (modern-day Germany). This resulted in many Jews committing suicide.

2. **1144 AD.** First accusation against Jews of "blood libel" occurred in England. This was the lying rumor to give an excuse to persecute and steal from the Jews, saying that they were killing Gentiles to use their blood in ceremonies.

3. **1190AD.** Jews were massacred in York, England. The First and Second Crusades had taught the Jews a lesson, so they committed mass suicide for fear of massacre by the soldiers of the Third Crusade. When the crusaders arrived, they murdered all those who had not committed suicide.

4. **1255 AD.** Innocent Jews in Lincoln, England, were convicted of blood libel, resulting in executions and arrests.

5. **1290 AD.** Jews were expelled from England.

These acts of cruelty, genocide, and ethnic cleansing continued throughout Europe's history, culminating where it began—in Germany, with the Holocaust.

One thing we can see is that place in an inverted and perverted sense played a big part in this because what the crusaders prized in all their campaigns was the place that rightfully belonged to the Jews, Palestine, Israel.

We also see displacement on a grand scale with the Jewish diaspora persecuted and exiled from place to place.

# A SUMMARIZED TIMELINE

*T*his is a basic timeline for our selected leaders from the history of the church in its context to place, from a UK perspective, usually expressed through church planting and missions.

Not everyone in the timeline is a classically reformed, Protestant evangelical; some are from the mediaeval times of the Roman church, like Patrick, but they are important to the history of the church in the earth in regard to place and the UK in particular.

I should also say, I've left out some absolute giants of Christian history, from Augustine of Hippo to Jonathan Edwards to John MacArthur. This is a very short list of forty from hundreds:

1. **48 AD.** Paul the Apostle embarks on his first missionary journey.

   **Note:** Between the time of the apostles and Patrick was a time of immense church growth despite state-sanctioned persecution, which ended with the edict of toleration.

2. **53 AD.** Diaspora of Jews, the displacement of Jews from Israel. Sending believing Jews throughout the world at this time meant the gospel spread to many nations.[74]

3. **156 AD.** Polycarp, the student of the Apostle John is martyred.

4. **432 AD.** Patrick the missionary travels to bring the gospel to Ireland.

5. **563 AD.** Columba the missionary brings the gospel to Scotland.

6. **597 AD.** Augustine of Canterbury (not Hippo) brings the gospel to England.

7. **716 AD.** Boniface of Devonshire evangelizes Europe.

8. **731 AD.** Bede of Durham, known as the father of English history, wrote *Ecclesiastical History of the English People*; thus he is worthy of mention in this timeline.

---

[74] E. H. Broadbent, *The Pilgrim Church* (London: Pickering & Inglis LTD, 1931).

9. **1173 AD.** Peter Waldo starts the Waldenses, pre-Reformation evangelical Christians that are still around today.

10. **1380 AD.** John Wycliffe, the morning star of the Reformation, supervises the translation of the Bible into English.

11. **1382 AD.** The Lollard Revival spreads across England by John Wycliffe's followers who travels with his translation for the common people. They were called Lollards, a derogatory term meaning mumbler, because they brought God's Word in the common tongue.

12. **1525 AD.** William Tyndale, the British reformer, translated the Bible into English.

13. **1555 AD.** Hugh Latimer and Thomas Cranmer, both prominent reformers, are martyred by the Crown in England.

14. **1678 AD.** John Bunyan, the Puritan, preacher, and author from Bedford, England, publishes *Pilgrims Progress.*

15. **1722 AD.** Count Zinzendorf and the Moravians begin to send missionaries, the first Protestant church to do so.

16. **1728 AD.** John and Charles Wesley start the Holy Club at Oxford University, which plants the seeds of revivals across England (starting in the fields of Bristol in 1739) and the world, giving rise to the Methodist Church.

17. **1735 AD.** George Whitfield is converted and goes on to be a great instrument of revival here in the UK, but mostly in the United States.

18. **1787 AD.** William Wilberforce fights for the abolition of the slave trade in the British Parliament.

19. **1793 AD.** William Carey from the village of Paulerspury in the heart of England becomes the father of modern Protestant missions through his life's work of sharing the gospel throughout India.

20. **1836 AD.** George Müller opens orphanages in Bristol, England, trusting God for all provisions.

21. **1844 AD.** George Williams founds the YMCA in London.

22. **1846 AD.** The Evangelical Alliance is formed in London.

23. **1854 AD.** Charles Spurgeon, the prince of preachers, starts his ministry in the heart of London at the Metropolitan Tabernacle and, among other endeavors, opens Spurgeon's College in South Norwood, just up the road from our current church building.

24. **1854 AD.** Hudson Taylor begins his mission to China and later forms the China Inland Mission in 1865.

25. **1858 AD.** John Gibson Paton sets out from Glasgow to the New Hebrides.

26. **1860 AD.** Revival breaks out in Jamaica and affects the entire island across denominational boundaries. The timing could not have been better as the enslaved people had recently been liberated. I just had to mention this because I am of Jamaican descent.

27. **1873 AD.** Dwight L. Moody begins his revivals in England. His revivals gave birth to the Keswick revival in 1875 in the lake district, which led to the annual Keswick Convention, which still happens today.

28. **1876 AD.** Mary Slessor (nicknamed the white queen) sails on mission from her native Scotland to Nigeria to work among the Ebo, establishing over fifty churches, starting the Hope Waddell Institute, and establishing the Ebo as one of the most Christian tribes in Africa.

29. **1878 AD.** William and Catharine Booth found the Salvation Army in London. Its impact was immense and can still be felt around the world today.

30. **1883 AD.** Sir William A. Smith starts the Boys Brigade in Scotland. This one is close to my heart because the boys brigade continues throughout the world today, and I am an officer in the 7th London, Croydon Battalion.

31. **1895 AD.** Peter Cameron Scott starts the Africa Inland Mission after his time as a missionary in Asia.

32. **1901 AD.** Amy Wilson Carmichael missions to India from Northern Ireland lead to the creation of the Dohnavur Fellowship.

33. **1904 AD.** Robert Evans is instrumental in the great Welsh revival in a year that also saw an outpouring of the Spirit in Azusa Street.

34. **1931 AD.** C. S. Lewis becomes a Christian in his native England and goes on to become one of the leading apologetic voices for the faith with classic works like *Mere Christianity*.

35. **1945 AD.** John R. W. Stott's ministry begins in London. He later wrote *The Cross of Christ*.

36. **1949 AD.** Billy Graham's ministry begins and impacts the entire world.

37. **1949 AD.** Duncan Campbell is used in the awakening off the coast of Scotland in the New Hebrides.

38. **1973 AD.** Dennis and Anita Greenidge plant a church in West Norwood called Worldwide Mission Fellowship after immigrating to England from Barbados in 1959–1960. This is my church today. The church is now led by their son Dennis Greenidge and daughter Rosemary Taylor.

39. **1979 AD.** The Jesus Film arrives and is used to bring millions to faith.

40. **1980 AD.** John Piper becomes a pastor. He later founds Desiring God and is today one of the most influential and respected Christian authors and teachers, inspiriting new generations to finish the mission. His book *Don't Waste Your Life* is one of the things I read that inspired me to write this book.

# EIGHT PIONEERS OF PLACE
## IN CHURCH HISTORY

*L*ooking at our Christian heritage is really important; we can better see where we are going by looking back at where we have come from and what we have learned along the way. If we are not students of our own history, we are bound to repeat the mistakes of yesterday and learn lessons or fight battles already won. We have a rich and long history; our roots go deep and wide. The church is connected through time and space over two thousand years; to disconnect ourselves by the hubris of "now" and "today" is foolish and dangerous. We neglect our history at our own peril.

I live in the United Kingdom; I always have, and I have no plans to leave, so of all the figures for church history that I could choose, I have chosen those who have had the greatest impact on (and many are from) this place called Britain. These ambassadors of the King have had an impact all over the world.

Here are just eight from the list of forty above. For each I will attempt to summarize their story and lasting impact by mentioning the reach of their pioneering work with regard to place.

It should be noted that I have kept these histories brief, very brief. In the suggested reading section at the end of this book, I'll recommend some resources you can turn to for a more detailed treatment of many of the people and movements listed here.

So join me on a journey down the historical road of faith, mission, and growth in the church as we enjoy a brief review of our "place and faith hall of famers."

# 1. WILLIAM TYNDALE (1525 AD)

*I do marvel greatly, dearly beloved in Christ, that ever any man should repugn or speak against the Scripture to be had in every language, and that of every man. For I thought that no man had been so blind to ask why light should be shewed to them that walk in darkness, where they cannot but stumble, and where to stumble is the danger of eternal damnation; other so despiteful that he would envy any man (I speak not his brother) so necessary a thing; or so Bedlam mad to affirm that good is the natural cause of evil, and darkness to proceed out of light, and that lying should be grounded in truth and verity; and not rather clean contrary, that light destroyeth darkness, and verity reproveth all manner lying.[75]*

—William Tyndale,
from his tract A Pathway into the Holy Scripture,
1532 AD

*T*first learned about William Tyndale (1494–1536) from an excellent video series called "The Indestructible Book" by the late Ken Connolly; I had the video on VHS in the early 2000s and watched it many times. It traces the history of the English Bible, and one of the stars of that story is William Tyndale.

William was born in Gloucester. He studied at Oxford and later Cambridge. He was a towering intellect, speaking seven languages with ability in ancient Hebrew and Greek.

Tyndale became a Protestant reformer after reading a copy of Desiderius Erasmus's Greek New Testament, where he found the teaching that we are saved through faith, not works.

His conviction, which would become his life's work, was that the Bible should be available in the common language. He approached the Bishop of London for funding

---

[75] William Tyndale, "Doctrinal Treatises and Introductions to Different Portions of the Holy Scriptures," ed. Henry Walter, vol. 1, *The Works of William Tyndale* (Cambridge: Cambridge University Press, 1848), 7.

to help make this a reality but was refused. Tyndale had to move to the free Protestant cities of Europe to begin and continue his work.

In 1525 the New Testament in English was ready and smuggled into England. The authorities of King Henry VIII bought up and burned as many as they could, which only served to further finance the project as Tyndale worked on the Old Testament.

William Tyndale, the father of the English Bible, known as "God's Outlaw" because of the years he spent on the run from Rome and the British Crown, was finally captured when a pretend friend named Henry Phillips betrayed him to the guards in Antwerp, where Tyndale was living and carrying out his ministry of writing, translation, teaching, and reaching out to the poor.

He was denounced as a heretic and condemned to be burned alive for his "sin" of translating the Bible into the common tongue and his reformed beliefs regarding salvation and life by faith in Jesus Christ. His final recorded words were "Lord, open the King of England's eyes!"[76]

The lasting impact of his life is that we have God's Word in an easy-to-understand and applicable format. It is from the Word of God in the common tongue that we are able to learn about God, his creation, kingdom, and message. It is with the foundation of the Bible that we are able to approach the call to be place makers before God.

---

[76] Quote's cross reference, Mark Galli and Ted Olsen, "Introduction," *131 Christians Everyone Should Know* (Nashville, TN: Broadman & Holman Publishers, 2000), 350.

# 2 . JOHN WESLEY (1739 AD)

*It is now upwards of forty years since my brother and I were convinced of that important truth, which is the foundation of all real religion, that "by grace we are saved through faith." And as soon as we believed, we spoke; when we saw it ourselves, we immediately began declaring it to others. And, indeed, we could hardly speak of anything else, either in public or private. It shone upon our minds with so strong a light, that it was our constant theme. It was our daily subject, both in verse and prose; and we vehemently defended it against all mankind.*[77]

—*John Wesley,*
*From his thoughts on salvation by faith,*
*1751 AD*

To talk about John Wesley in context, we need to spend some time talking about the Moravians from Germany who had such a profound impact on him.

Nicolaus Ludwig von Zinzendorf, known simply as Count Zinzendorf, was from one of the greatest families in Europe with immense riches and land. He was born into a family with a rich Reformed Christian heritage on May 26, 1700.[78]

The Count grew up surrounded by prayer and Bible reading; added to this was his own encounter with Christ, which caused the roots of his faith to go down deep. He grew to become the leader and protector of a community of Christians he allowed to live on his vast lands in Germany. These were the Moravian Brethren, who trace their roots back to the Waldensians, who themselves trace their roots back directly to the apostles, a line of evangelical Christians set apart from the heresies of Rome from generation to generation.

History records that in 836 AD, the brothers—Cyril and Methodius—from Constantinople (Eastern rather than Western Christians) went to Moravia as missionaries. They created an alphabet for the people and translated a Bible for them

---

[77] John Wesley, *The Works of John Wesley*, 3rd ed., vol. 11 (London: Wesleyan Methodist Book Room, 1872), 492–493.

[78] "The Rich Young Ruler ... Who Said Yes!," *Christian History Magazine-Issue 1: Zinzendorf & the Moravians* (Worcester, PA: Christian History Institute, 1982).

SACRED PLACES • HISTORY

in their own tongue, it is thought that this planted the seeds of the Bible-based and mission-minded community.

The Moravians were also decedents of the followers of John Hus (who himself was influenced by the English believer and translator of the Bible, John Wycliffe), who was a very early reformer from the twelfth century Czech Republic.

In 1732 AD the Moravians sent out the first explicitly Protestant missionaries to the island of Jamaica and the rest of the Caribbean. Jamaica is an island close to my heart; my family is from there, so we have directly benefited from the faithfulness of those first missionaries. The fire of missions ignited the Moravian community as they were sent across the earth. Along the way they meet other Christians and passed on that fire they had of a love for the Scriptures, piety before God, and the yearning to share Christ with those who did not know him.

In 1738 AD, Peter Boehler established the first Moravian church in Britain at Fetter Lane in London.[79] In God's providence, it was this community that God caused John to come into contact with. Prior to this, the Lord had been working in John's life to form him into the formidable leader we remember today.

He was raised in a Puritan family of nineteen siblings by his mother, Susanna. That is a lot of brothers and sisters, although only ten survived infancy. Susanna taught all her children the Bible. His father, Samuel, who was himself a minister was quoted as saying to his sons on his deathbed in 1735, "The inward witness, son, the inward witness—this is the proof, the strongest proof of Christianity."[80]

John's brother Charles had begun the Holy Club in Oxford, which became known as the Methodists. The name was meant to be derogatory because these young men met together to study the Bible and ordered their lives to be disciplined after the Scriptures. John, Charles, and George Whitfield (the famous preacher of the American Great Awakening) were some of the founding members of the Methodist movement.

In the same year as his father's death, John traveled to Georgia for ministry; it was a fruitless, even disastrous, trip. This was God at work. On the way to Georgia, a storm threatened the lives of everyone on the ship. John was terrified, but he observed some Moravians who had the confident peace of God. It stirred his soul to desire

---

[79] F. L. Cross and Elizabeth A. Livingstone, eds., *The Oxford Dictionary of the Christian Church* (Oxford: New York: Oxford University Press, 2005), 1119.
[80] D. Partner, "Wesley, John," ed. J.D. Douglas and Philip W. Comfort, *Who's Who in Christian History* (Wheaton, IL: Tyndale House, 1992), 709.

the real sort of faith that they had, to have the inner witness his father had told him about. In light of all this, John wrote the following:

> I went to America, to convert the Indians; but O! who shall convert me? who, what is he that will deliver me from this evil heart of unbelief? I have a fair summer religion. I can talk well; nay, and believe myself, while no danger is near: But let death look me in the face, and my spirit is troubled. Nor can I say, 'To die is gain!'[81]

John met the Moravian Peter Bohler in London and was instructed by him in the assurance of salvation, pointing him to the works of Luther on Galatians among others. These events, experiences, and desires all culminated in the Moravian gathering at Aldersgate Street where he was truly born again. In his own words:

> In the evening I went very unwillingly to a society in Aldersgate-Street, where one was reading Luther's preface to the Epistle to the Romans. About a quarter before nine, while he was describing the change which God works in the heart through faith in Christ, I felt my heart strangely warmed. I felt I did trust in Christ, Christ alone for salvation: And an assurance was given me, that he had taken away my sins, even mine, and saved me from the law of sin and death.[82]

What followed was quite extraordinary. The foundations to the greatest revival the British Isles have ever seen were laid, and it would be exported from here across the earth. John began to preach in the open air, beginning in the fields of Bristol, and God moved by his Holy Spirit on the people of the land.

The practice of these believers was real and active, soaked in the Bible and prayer. John mentions the following in regard to the life of active believers in the world.

> Beware of sins of omission; lose no opportunity of doing good in any kind.
> Be zealous of good works; willingly omit no work, either of piety or mercy.
> Do all the good you possibly can to the bodies and souls of men. Particularly, 'thou shalt in anywise reprove thy neighbour, and not suffer sin upon him.'
> Be active. Give no place to indolence or sloth; give no occasion to say, "Ye are idle, ye are idle."[83]

---

[81] John Wesley, *The Works of John Wesley*, 3rd ed., vol. 1 (London: Wesleyan Methodist Book Room, 1872), 74.

[82] John Wesley, *The Works of John Wesley*, 3rd ed., vol. 1 (London: Wesleyan Methodist Book Room, 1872), 103.

[83] John Wesley, *The Works of John Wesley*, 3rd ed., vol. 11 (London: Wesleyan Methodist Book Room, 1872), 432.

Though he desired to stay within the Church of England, the reach and success of this movement organically grew out of the C of E and became a denomination in its own right. At his death, John's Methodists numbered 71,668 members in the United Kingdom and 43,265 in the United States, with almost five hundred preachers and missionaries between them.[84]

The impact of John and his associates is still felt in the earth today. In the year 2000, members were reported at 38 million worldwide, today they are estimated at over 75 million.[85]

---

[84] Numbers taken from Mark Galli and Ted Olsen, "Introduction," *131 Christians Everyone Should Know* (Nashville, TN: Broadman & Holman Publishers, 2000), 183.
[85] Numbers from F. L. Cross and Elizabeth A. Livingstone, eds., *The Oxford Dictionary of the Christian Church* (Oxford: New York: Oxford University Press, 2005), 1086.

# 3. WILLIAM WILBERFORCE (1787 AD)

*Great indeed are our opportunities; great also is our responsibility.*[86]
*—William Wilberforce*

William Wilberforce became a household name a few years ago in 2007 after the release of the film *Amazing Grace* by Walden Media for the two-hundred-year anniversary of the abolition of the slave trade, which was his life's work.

He was one of the main instruments used by God to accomplish the end of this awful transatlantic slave trade, which saw my own ancestors sold by their kinsmen and stolen from the coasts of Africa to be sold into slavery in the Caribbean, America, and throughout Europe.

In his early years, he was influenced for a small time by John Newton, the ex-slave trader who became born again and was now a preacher. He also meets George Whitfield. He was from a very rich and privileged family from Hull, so attended Cambridge but was a distracted young man with no lack of funds to feed his temptations.

He had a full conversion at the age of twenty-five. He was part of a group called the Clapham Sect, whose aim was to revive and invigor the upper classes in the way John Wesley had done for the common man.

His Christian faith drove his political ambition as a part of William Pitt's government to seek the abolition of the slave trade among other things regarding morals and social justice. After much resistance politically and poor health in his own life, his faith and endurance paid off when his bill was passed in 1807 AD.

The lessons today are clear: in the Western world, people of African descent are no longer in direct and oppressive slavery, although they may still be dealing with the consequences of over four hundred years in slavery still as well as the whole issue of institutional racism.

---

[86] Elliot Ritzema and Elizabeth Vince, eds., *300 Quotations for Preachers from the Modern Church*, Pastorum Series (Bellingham, WA: Lexham Press, 2013).

The other heritage we have today will be in the fight to end all the other types of slavery like the slavery in the sex trade and the place of the Christian and Christianity in the public square for the good, freedom, and flourishing of all.

# 4 . WILLIAM CAREY (1793 AD)

*As our blessed Lord has required us to pray that his kingdom may come, and his will be done on Earth as it is in Heaven, it becomes us not only to express our desires of that event by words, but to use every lawful method to spread the knowledge of his name. In order to this, it is necessary that we should become, in some measure, acquainted with the religious state of the world; and as this is an object we should be prompted to pursue, not only the gospel of our Redeemer, but even by the feelings of humanity, so an inclination to conscientious activity therein would form one of the strongest proofs that we are the subjects of grace, and partakers of that spirit of universal benevolence and genuine philanthropy, which appear so eminent in the character of God himself . . .* [87]

*—William Carey,*
*from his famous pamphlet "An Enquiry into the Obligations of Christians to use Means for the Conversion of the Heathens,"*
*1792 AD*

William Carey was born in a little village not far from Northampton. He had little to no education, but he was an avid reader. He worked as a shoemaker. Eventually after his conversion, he became pastor and teacher in the Calvinistic arm of the nonconformist (non-Anglican) Baptists in 1786.

William lived in a day of exciting and worrying change in the world; the French and American revolutions were underway, and there was a sense of revival and expectation in the air for believers who were praying for God to reach all peoples of the earth.

In the midst of this, the heart, faith, and even imagination of the young William was captured by the call of the lost in faraway lands who needed to hear the gospel.

In 1792 AD he wrote the pamphlet I quoted above, laying out his vision for global mission. That same year he preached a now famous sermon titled "Expect Great

---

[87] H. Leon McBeth, *A Sourcebook for Baptist Heritage* (Nashville, TN: Broadman & Holman Publishers, 1990), 135.

Things from God; Attempt Great Things for God." Within four months he formed a mission society for the Baptist church.

The following year he set sail for Calcutta, India, with John Thomas. His adventures in that mission are well documented and told visually in the film *A Candle in the Dark*. I was first shown that film by my pastor, Dennis Greenidge, nearly twenty years ago. The fuller account of his suffering and work will inspire you.

He took four years to learn the local language and translated the majority of the Bible into Bengali; he even set up his own press to print the Bible. In 1800, he moved from Bengal to Serampore and worked from there for the next thirty years.

He had set a successful pattern for modern missions and is therefore known as the father of modern missions. He spent his life applying this model throughout India and the rest of Asia as well as training others in the language and methods for effective mission. The pattern Carey established, which is still used today, would start with Bible translation and production, followed by evangelism, church planting, and finally social works like education and medical relief.[88]

The impact today is that missions all over the world are still using this model to spread the good news about the King, his triumph, and kingdom and further expanding the territory and influence of that kingdom to places and people that have never heard.

---

[88] My main source for Carey's life and work is J. D. Douglas, Earle E. Cairns, and James E. Ruark, *The New International Dictionary of the Christian Church* (Grand Rapids: Zondervan Publishing House, 1978), 192.

# AN ESSENTIAL DETOUR:
# CHARLES HADDON
# SPURGEON (1853 AD)

*Submit yourselves to the whole word of God, for it is living and powerful. It will search your inmost soul even to the joints and marrow; habitually let it do so. Never be afraid of your Bibles. If there is a text of Scripture you dare not meet, humble yourself till you can. If your creed and Scripture do not agree, cut your creed to pieces, but make it agree with this book. If there be anything in the church to which you belong which is contrary to the inspired word, leave that church.*[89]

—*C. H. Spurgeon,*
*Sermon at the Metropolitan Tabernacle,*
*1874*

*B*efore I go any further, we need to take a detour. I have not mentioned Charles Spurgeon in my final eight. If I had a final nine or if the importance of my review was on preaching and the impact of the Word aside from mission, he would certainly be included. But it is not; it is particularly concerned with mission.

However, it is impossible for me to talk about the time when George Muller and, later, Hudson Taylor lived without talking about the great Prince of Preachers, whose ministry has had such an impact across the earth and in my own life. So join me as I indulge on a little off-road trip to that effect.

Charles Haddon Spurgeon was born in a place called Kelvedon, Essex, in 1834 AD to a Christian family. His father and grandfather were both congregational ministers, further back down his family line were Quakers and Huguenots. It was while in Colchester, the town where he went to school, that in 1850 he stumbled into an old Methodist church (notice the influence of John Wesley here; it was his work that meant there was a place for Charles to happen upon). After hearing the unknown minister, he was born again.

---

[89] C. H. Spurgeon, *The Metropolitan Tabernacle Pulpit Sermons*, vol. 20 (London: Passmore & Alabaster, 1874), 335.

He was baptized, which was a big thing, considering his congregational background. After his baptism, he became a member and then very quickly a preacher in a Baptist church in Cambridge, due to his obvious gift as a preacher and expositor of the Bible. He even started his own school there too, which is remarkable because he did not have the type of privileged and advanced education that some of our other "place and faith hall of famers" like Tyndale, Wesley, or Wilberforce had.

> How many of you go to chapel, and must confess your own absence of mind while you have bowed your knee in prayer, or uttered a song of praise! My friends, it is one thing to go to church or chapel; it is quite another thing to go to God.[90]

Spurgeon's gift made room for him, and he became famous and in demand in the Baptist communion. He first pastored at Waterbeach in Cambridge; he was then called to London, to a place not far from where I grew up and where my mum still lives in the borough of Southwark, to a flagship Baptist church in New Park Street, which could seat some 1,200 people. The amazing thing about this chapter in Surgeons life is that this all happened in 1854 when he was just twenty years old.

Despite the seating capacity of the chapel, numbers were small when Charles arrived, but that soon changed. His dynamic, Spirit-filled, and Bible-based teaching and preaching with his gifted oratory and wit was used by God to draw thousands to the church within just a few weeks, to the point that the building was no longer fit for purpose.

He preached in other large venues while the Baptists extended the building, but the extension was to no avail because it too almost immediately was too small. A plan was set in motion to build the iconic Metropolitan Tabernacle. So let's just get this into perspective: the flagship building for the Reformed Baptists in London was too small, as were Exeter Hall and Surrey Gardens Music Hall, so one of the largest churches in Victorian England was built to accommodate the congregants who wanted to hear Spurgeon preach.

The Metropolitan Tabernacle could hold six thousand people, a mega-church even by modern standards. This would become the home of this great preacher for thirty-one years from 1861 until his death in 1892. He preached from this place with power and conviction. Theologically he was a Calvinist and would rebuke the two Protestant extremes of either hyper-Calvinism (a warped view of God's role in salvation) or

---

[90] C. H. Spurgeon, *The New Park Street Pulpit Sermons*, vol. 2 (London: Passmore & Alabaster, 1856), 242.

Arminianism (a warped view of man's role in salvation). The effect and quality of his sermons is made clear by the fact they are still in heavy circulation today; I have a copy of his entire collection myself.

The place, the Metropolitan Tabernacle, was more than just a church building or place for preaching; it functioned as an educational and social center for the surrounding community as well. Spurgeon had a very biblical understanding of place and the church's mission in the earth. He went beyond the multifaceted tabernacle to establish a college to train pastors and missionaries in South Norwood in 1856, just up the road from my own church in West Norwood.

Spurgeon and his church were involved in various charitable works. One of the most notable was the orphanage he opened in Stockwell (again, a place where I grew up). When laying the foundation stone for the boys' homes in 1867, he made the point that where true Christians may disagree on a point or two of doctrine, they could unify around the cause of the kingdom to relieve the suffering of the fatherless in Jesus's name. There were eventually four boys' homes and five girls' homes on Clapham Road. The stated vision of these orphanages was "free and gratuitous residence, maintenance, clothing, instruction, and education of destitute, fatherless children.[91]

This shows that the biblical preaching and teaching of the Word and the acting out of the theology of place for social action and outreach are inextricably linked. It was the powerful preaching of Spurgeon that drew the crowds that provided the funds to create a place for these placeless children.

Spurgeon was a man of the Word; he was beholden to God and the Bible, which put him at odds with men and their institutions, fads, and persuasions. This included the rising liberalism of the day in what became known as the downgrade controversy. He was a prolific writer, publishing sermons, a monthly magazine, and advice to upcoming pastors (lectures to my students' volumes, which are excellent), to name just a few.[92]

One of Spurgeon's many sermons was on the importance of place, taken from John 14:2. It is in the public domain, so I have included it in Appendix B. However, here is a quote from it. If you get the time, I really think you should read it in its entirety.

---

[91] Ian F. Shaw, "Caring for Children," *Christian History Magazine—Issue 29: Charles Spurgeon: England's "Prince of Preachers"* (Carol Stream, IL: Christianity Today, 1991).

[92] P. Toon, "Spurgeon, Charles Haddon," J.D. Douglas and Philip W. Comfort, eds., *Who's Who in Christian History* (Wheaton, IL: Tyndale House, 1992), 636.

*I do not profess to be able to explain our Lord's words, but I am going simply to make a few remarks upon them; and, first, I ask you to notice that Heaven is already prepared for Christ's people. Christ has told us that, when he comes in his glory, he will say to those on his right hand, "Come, ye blessed of my Father, inherit the kingdom prepared for you from the foundation of the world." So, there is an inheritance which the Father has already prepared for the people whom he gave to his Son, and this inheritance is reserved for them. But if it was prepared from the foundation of the world, how can it be said to be prepared by Christ? The explanation probably is, that it was prepared in the eternal purpose of the Father,—prepared by wise forethought,—arranged for,—predestinated,—prepared in that sense,—it was provided, in the eternal arrangements of Jehovah, that there should be a suitable place for his people to dwell in for ever. He made the pavilion of the sun, and he gave the stars their appointed positions; would he forget to prepare a place for his people? He gave to angels their places, and even to fallen spirits he has appointed a prison-house; so he would not forget, when he was arranging the entire universe, that a place would be needed for the twice-born, the heirs of grace, the members of the mystical body of Christ Jesus, his brethren who were to be made like unto him. Therefore, in purpose, and plan, and decree, long ere God had laid the foundations of this poor world, and the morning stars had sung together over creation's six days' work accomplished, he had prepared a place for his people; it was not actually prepared, but it was in the purpose and plan of the eternal mind, and therefore might be regarded as already done.*[93]

---

[93] C. H. Spurgeon, *The Metropolitan Tabernacle Pulpit Sermons*, vol. 47 (London: Passmore & Alabaster, 1901), 518.

# 5. GEORGE MÜLLER (1836 AD)

*Here is the great secret of success, my Christian Reader. Work with all your might;*
*but trust not in the least in your work. Pray with all your might for the blessing*
*of God; but work, at the same time, with all diligence, with all patience, with all*
*perseverance. Pray then, and work. Work and pray. And still again pray, and then*
*work. And so on all the days of your life. The result will surely be, abundant blessing.*
*Whether you see much fruit or little fruit; such kind of service will be blessed.* [94]

—George Müller,
*A Narrative of Some of the Lord's Dealings with George Müller,*
1853

first learned about George Müller in another video by Ken Connolly,
although this time it was on DVD. The film is called *Obstacle to Comfort*
and is excellent; I highly recommend it. It is the type of overview that
will give you a real sense of the enormity of his faith and impact.

Müller was born near Halberstadt in Germany in a place called Kroppenstadt to
a Lutheran family who intended him for the ministry, however he lived a reckless
and wicked life as a young man. It was not until 1825, when he attended a Moravian
home fellowship at the age of twenty, that he was born again. The account of his
conversion in his own words is riveting reading. See Appendix C for the full story;
here is a short, moving snippet:

*The kind answer of this dear brother I shall never forget. He said: "Come as often*
*as you please; house and heart are open to you." We sat down and sang a hymn.*
*Then brother Kayser, afterwards a Missionary in Africa in connection with the*
*London Missionary Society, who was then living at Halle, fell on his knees, and*
*asked a blessing on our meeting. This kneeling down made a deep impression*
*upon me; for I had never either seen any one on his knees, nor had I ever prayed*
*myself on my knees… When we walked home, I said to Beta, "All we have seen*
*on our journey to Switzerland, and all our former pleasures, are as nothing*
*in comparison with this evening." Whether I fell on my knees when I returned*
*home, I do not remember; but this I know, that I lay peaceful and happy in my*

---

[94] George Müller, *A Narrative of Some of the Lord's Dealings with George Müller*, vol. 2 (London: J. Nisbet & Co., 1886), 301.

*bed. This shows that the Lord may begin His work in different ways. For I have*
*not the least doubt that on that evening He began a work of grace in me …*[95]

Four years later he would travel to London to minister to the Jews. Unfortunately, this mission work was short lived due to poor health; within two months, he was in Teignmouth in Devon. A variety of events there, including the meeting of his wife, caused him to become acquainted with the Plymouth Brethren.

He became a preacher at the Ebenezer Chapel in Teignmouth, which grew under his leadership from 18 to 227 members in just three years. Müller was a man of great faith; he believed that God would provide for him, so he refused a salary and lived on direct gifts from fellow believers. God honored his faith because he never went without.

In 1832 he moved to Bristol and began ministry with his brother in-law A. N. Groves. Bristol would become the capital of his ministry efforts. It was from here in 1834 that Müller founded the Scriptural Knowledge Institution for Home and Abroad. This was set up to support missions, circulate Bibles, and promote the teaching of biblical principles for faith and life.

It was in 1835 after reading the lifework of A. H. Francke, who set up and ran an orphanage with no financial support just faith in God for provision back in Halle, Germany, (one that Müller had visited while there), that he heard the Spirit's voice call him to his life's work.

He began an orphanage in Bristol, based on the same trusting-God-for-provision model as Francke, rather than asking people for financial support. The results were nothing short of supernatural. He began with just a few children, and at its peak, two thousand boys and girls were given a place to live, fed, and educated across five buildings—five very special places on Ashley Down, not far from Bristol.

George Müller was friends with Charles Spurgeon; they spoke highly of each other.

At his death, over ten thousand orphans had been cared for by his orphanages, while his personal finances stood at just a few hundred pounds.

His lasting impact is that through his testimony of faith and answered prayer, other missions and orphanages have been set up on the same or similar principles all over the world. [96]

---

[95] George Müller, *Autobiography of George Müller: A Million and a Half in Answer to Prayer* (London: J. Nisbet and Co., 1914), 10.

[96] Main Historical Source: N. Hillyer, "Müller, George," J.D. Douglas and Philip W. Comfort, eds., *Who's Who in Christian History* (Wheaton, IL: Tyndale House, 1992), 494.

# 6. JAMES HUDSON TAYLOR (1854 AD)

*It is always helpful to us to fix our attention on the God-ward aspect of Christian work; to realise that the work of God does not mean so much man's work for God, as God's own work through man. Furthermore, in our privileged position of fellow-workers with Him, while fully recognising all the benefits and blessings to be bestowed on a sin-stricken world through the proclamation of the Gospel and spread of the Truth, we should never lose sight of the higher aspect of our work—that of obedience to God, of bringing glory to His Name, of gladdening the heart of our God and Father by living and serving as His beloved children.*[97]

—*John Hudson Taylor,*
*A Retrospect,*
*1906*

My first real exposure to Hudson Taylor was through my pastor, Dennis Greenidge. He pointed us in his direction when we were preparing for a ministry trip to China in 2007. I was blown away by the short story about his life, faith, and accomplishments for the Lord in China.

In 1832 James Hudson Taylor was born to James and Amelia Taylor, Methodists who lived in Barnsley, Yorkshire. There was a link to another pioneer of the past, John Wesley—Hudson's grandparents had received him in their home.

His parents had a particular burden for China and lifted each of their children up to the Lord when they were born, asking that the Lord might use them to reach the souls of China. It would seem God heard their prayer with young Hudson. At the age of five, he exclaimed that he would one day be a missionary to China as his father wanted.

In 1849 Hudson was truly born again at the age of sixteen when he read a tract in his father's study on the finished work of Christ. He records in his own words a pivotal event after his conversion, which would set the course for his entire life:

> *Not many months after my conversion, having a leisure afternoon, I retired to my own chamber to spend it largely in communion with God. Well do I remember*

---

[97] J. Hudson Taylor, *A Retrospect*, 3rd ed. (Toronto: China Inland Mission, n.d.), 1–2.

*that occasion. How in the gladness of my heart I poured out my soul before God; and again and again confessing my grateful love to Him who had done everything for me—who had saved me when I had given up all hope and even desire for salvation—I besought Him to give me some work to do for Him, as an outlet for love and gratitude; some self-denying service, no matter what it might be, however trying or however trivial; something with which He would be pleased, and that I might do for Him who had done so much for me. Well do I remember, as in unreserved consecration I put myself, my life, my friends, my all, upon the altar, the deep solemnity that came over my soul with the assurance that my offering was accepted. The presence of God became unutterably real and blessed; and though but a child under sixteen, I remember stretching myself on the ground, and lying there silent before Him with unspeakable awe and unspeakable joy.*[98]

Taylor felt this call was to China. He began to prepare his life for this calling in many ways; this included his decision, like Müller, to live by pure faith in Jesus without asking anyone for financial support. It also meant he would study medicine so he would have practical services to offer.

Before even going to China, he was able to get a copy of Luke's gospel in Mandarin, which he compared with the English to teach himself the language.

He would give away all his earnings and trust God for his own provision, as a matter of course, he would give to missions already operating in China, deciding to live on oatmeal and rice. Once he even gave away his last coin while ministering to the wife of a man he met while reaching out to the poor in the streets of London. His faith-filled gift saved her life. Later the same day, someone brought him a package with money; this experience solidified the practice that he would keep for his whole life and ministry—to trust God unreservedly.

At the same time as all this, he was studying theology, Greek, and Latin.

He set sail for China in 1853. His journey was fraught with difficulty and disappointment, but his faith remained strong. He learned more of the language and soon adopted a local style of dress to help him reach the people. His great desire was to go inland, the place where few missionaries ventured, and he did so at great personal risk to himself and Joseph Edkins, who accompanied him.

Three years after arriving in China, Hudson began ministry in Ningpo (now pronounced Ningbo), a very important city in the northeast of the Zhejiang province.

---

[98] J. Hudson Taylor, *A Retrospect*, 3rd ed. (Toronto: China Inland Mission, n.d.), 7–8.

Important things happened here, like his marriage to Maria Dyer. He also left the mission society that had sent him because of their debts and so became independent. He took charge of the hospital for a time and had such an impact that many recovered under his care and turned to Christ.

Within another four years in 1860, Hudson had to return to England because of failing health. While he was recovering in London, his passion for the mission did not end; he set himself to prayer and, with the help of F. F. Gough, to revising and improving the New Testament in Mandarin.

It was in this time in London, as more and more missionaries left for China, that Hudson felt a need for an organization dedicated to inland missions, so he established the China Inland Mission as a cross-denominational mission society.

After a prolonged time of prayer, Hudson, his wife, and a new mission party designated to work in each of the ten unevangelized inland provinces and Mongolia set sail for China in 1866. Hudson suffered the loss of a child and his wife to Cholera in 1870. However, the mission extended throughout the interior of China.

Taylor wrote in 1855:

> Can the Christians of England sit still with folded arms while these multitudes are perishing—perishing for lack of knowledge—for lack of that knowledge which England possesses so richly, which has made England what England is, and has made us what we are? What does the MASTER teach us? Is it not that if one sheep out of a hundred be lost, we are to leave the ninety and nine and seek that one? But here the proportions are almost reversed, and we stay at home with the one sheep, and take no heed to the ninety and nine perishing ones! [99]

By 1900 more than half the missionaries in China were from the Inland Mission from multiple denominations. Hudson retired from active service in 1901 and passed away in 1905. [100]

Hudson Taylor's influence again changed the face of missions like Carey had done. Now his method of living with the people and contextualizing the message by dressing like and knowing the customs of the people is a standard part of modern missions. His faith stands as a testament and example to everyone who wants to be used by God for his purposes.

---

[99] J. Hudson Taylor, *China's Spiritual Need and Claims*, 7th ed. (London: Morgan & Scott, 1887), 12.

[100] T. Firak, "Taylor, James Hudson," J.D. Douglas and Philip W. Comfort, eds., *Who's Who in Christian History* (Wheaton, IL: Tyndale House, 1992), 657–659.

# 7. WILLIAM AND CATHERINE BOOTH (1878 AD)

*When I saw those masses of poor people, so many of them evidently without God or hope in the world, and found that they so readily and eagerly listened to me, following from Open-Air Meeting to tent, and accepting, in many instances, my invitation to kneel at the Saviour's feet there and then, my whole heart went out to them. I walked back to our West-End home and said to my wife:*

*"O Kate, I have found my destiny! These are the people for whose Salvation I have been longing all these years. As I passed by the doors of the flaming gin-palaces to-night I seemed to hear a voice sounding in my ears, 'Where can you go and find such heathen as these, and where is there so great a need for your labours?' And there and then in my soul I offered myself and you and the children up to this great work. Those people shall be our people, and they shall have our God for their God."*[101]

—William Booth,
*The Authoritative Life of General William Booth,*
*1912*

The first time I did any real research on William Booth was for a mission awareness day we had a few years ago. The Salvation Army he started has its headquarters on Denmark Hill, just up the road from the house I grew up in at the Oval.

William Booth was born in 1829 in Nottingham, England. His father was a struggling builder, which exposed Booth to hardship. As a child he worked in a pawnbroker, which again gave him early exposure to the desperation of the poor. He attended an Anglican church but was not truly born again until the Lord saved him when he was fifteen. He recalls

*When as a giddy youth of fifteen I was led to attend Wesley Chapel, Nottingham, I cannot recollect that any individual pressed me in the direction of personal*

---

[101] George S. (George Scott) Railton 1849–1913, *The Authoritative Life of General William Booth, Founder of the Salvation Army*, n.d.

*surrender to God. I was wrought upon quite independently of human effort by the Holy Ghost, who created within me a great thirst for a new life.*

*I felt that I wanted, in place of the life of self-indulgence, to which I was yielding myself, a happy, conscious sense that I was pleasing God, living right, and spending all my powers to get others into such a life.*[102]

Meanwhile, Catherine Mumford was born in that same year to a devout Methodist family in Ashbourne, Derbyshire. They moved to London in 1844. In that year she was born again and joined a Methodist church in Brixton, London (my hometown).

She soon left that church and helped to found the Reformers Chapel under the Methodist New Connexion movement. In 1851, she and William met at the church, by this time he was a preacher with the movement. They were married four years later in 1855.

Six years after marriage and William's successful time as a preacher in 1861, they left the New Connexion, partly because of the restriction of having to preach on a circuit and a restriction on street preaching. William wanted to dedicate himself to evangelistic outreach.

In 1865 they founded the outreach ministry in Whitechapel with a very long name, called "Christian Mission for the amelioration of the condition of the destitute and vicious population of the eastern portion of London;" after more than a decade of work among the poor in the city of London the name changed to The Salvation Army.

Booth was the first general of this army, he passed his core principles unto the army, which in a nutshell were twofold: firstly, faith in God's saving grace through the gospel, and secondly, a heart to help relieve the suffering of the poor.

Regimented like a real army, they had uniforms and had orders and regulations to follow. The army's numbers swelled as they went into the slums of London, and soon the entire county, sometimes singing with a band and open air preaching.

Uniquely, male and female offices were treated equally. This ethos saw a brand-new opportunity open up for Catherine, who because of curvature of the spine in earlier life had to spend much time in bed. But she was a voracious reader and felt a call to preach the Word. She was a successful preacher, seeing many come to know the

---

[102] Ibid.

Lord, and she inspired other women in the movement too. One account of eighteen-year-old Rose Clapham saw her and a fellow officer invite miners in Yorkshire to a theatre to hear the gospel. Under this young woman, over seven hundred came to know the Lord that night, with 140 of them becoming the foundation of a new church. All were inspired by the dynamic preaching of Catherine Booth.

William and the army he formed used a range of unconventional methods to reach the poorest in society. They visited pubs and jails, theaters, factories, and other places that could be considered as "un-churchy."

William defined social work in his vision for God's kingdom and the mission of the army as follows:

> *Our Social Operations, as thus defined, are the natural outcome of Salvationism, or, I might say, of Christianity, as instituted, described, proclaimed, and exemplified in the life, teaching, and sacrifice of Jesus Christ.*
>
> *Here I would like to say that Social Work, in the spirit and practice which it has assumed with us, has harmonised with my own personal idea of true religion from the hour I promised obedience to the commands of God.*
>
> *To help the poor, to minister to them in their slums, to sympathise with them in their poverty, afflictions, and irreligion, was the natural outcome of the life that came to my soul through believing in Jesus Christ.[103]*

At the death of the general, thousands turned out to honor the man who had done so much for the poor in the name of Jesus right here in London. They lined the streets, and it was in the national newspapers. Even the royal family and leaders of governments around the world sent their condolences. Here is a letter from our king at the time.

> *I am grieved to hear the sad news of the death of your Father. The nation has lost a great organiser, and the poor a whole-hearted and sincere friend, who devoted his life to helping them in a practical way.*
>
> *Only in the future shall we realise the good wrought by him for his fellow-creatures.*

---

[103] George S. (George Scott) Railton 1849–1913, *The Authoritative Life of General William Booth, Founder of the Salvation Army*, n.d.

*To-day there is universal mourning for him. I join in it, and assure you and your family of my true sympathy in the heavy loss which has befallen you. George R. I.[104]*

Other greetings came in from Queen Alexandra, President Taft, the King of Denmark, and the Lord Mayor of London.

The impact of the Salvation Army is still felt in a real way across the earth today, where the organization continues to serve with a heart toward helping the poor and spreading the gospel.

---

[104] Ibid.

# 8. DENNIS AND ANITA GREENIDGE (1959 AD)

*J*first heard about and came into contact with the life and work of the Greenidge family in 1989, when I first attended the church they planted. I was eleven years old and came from a non-Christian background. I arrived at the start of a new era, one year after Dr. Dennis Greenidge Sr. had passed away and been promoted home to glory.

Dennis and Anita were both saved at a young age in the island of Barbados. Anita was saved as a little child, while Dennis did not come from a Christian family and was not saved until he was in his teenage years.

At just thirteen years old, Anita's faith and pioneering spirit were evident. She began gathering children under a tamarind tree close to her home in Barbados in a place called Britton Hill. That gathering became an outreach ministry for children called a "Good News Club." Amazingly, over sixty years later, the Good News Club is still a thriving ministry at Worldwide Mission Fellowship.

Dennis and Anita were married after they met at an event called a Singspiration, where Anita sang and Dennis preached. They were married within six months of courtship, on January 4, 1957. Within two years, Dennis went ahead of Anita to London, to work on the trains and prepare for her arrival with the children, who were at that point only Esther (Rev. Taylor) and Dennis Jr. (Rev. Greenidge). It was not long before Anita joined him in London (circa 1960).

With limited finances and the racist climate of 1960 London, it was not easy to find a place to live, but the Lord provided a flat in South London and again, just like in her native Barbados, Anita started a good news club for children from all backgrounds, regardless of the color of their skin.

God's hand was on Dennis; he would sometimes struggle in prayer while asleep at night. One night the Lord said, "Holland" to him, showed him a place in the Hague, and told him that there would be a man there named Marspark. Anita challenged him, but he heeded the call of the Spirit and went in faith to the place in Holland that God had revealed to him. Remarkably, when he asked for Marspark, there really was a man by that name who had just begun a work in that place.

It was while on a trip to Kenya, after seeing the situation the people were in out there, that he brought back slides to show believers in London so he could raise awareness and support for the people. This gave birth to a ministry and commitment to sponsor children, which continues today. This mission work to minister to the least would take Dennis to India and Haiti too. Through his efforts, thousands were fed, clothed, and given the opportunity to go to school.

When Anita saw the situation of the people in Haiti, she asked to join Dennis the next time he went out there. The Lord provided for them, and she was able to accompany him not just once, but three times. While out there, she started a feeding program for the children.

Back in London, Anita wanted to show the film footage they had gathered. She went to the school where her children attended, St. Luke's in West Norwood, and asked to speak to the caretaker in order to lease the school dinner hall to show the film. The school dinner hall was called St. Paul's Hall and is the site of our church today over forty years later.

Anita was at first met with resistance, but the caretaker gave her the address of the vicar, warning her an appointment would be needed. In the 2007 film *Going Back to Our Future*, celebrating forty years of ministry, Anita goes on to tell us the fateful moment in her encounter with the vicar when she stepped out in pioneering faith to secure a place for a placeless and oppressed people, so they could better minister to the displaced at home and abroad.

Worldwide Mission Fellowship was then founded in 1973 and is still thriving today. It is my church; it is the place where I came to know the Lord in Sunday school, was baptized, and have been through discipleship, taught and trained for usefulness in God's kingdom. I met my wife, Michelle, there, and now our children attend the same Sunday school and good news club that was started all those years ago under the tamarind tree.

I want to close this section with the words of my own pastor, the son of the late Dr. Dennis Greenidge who bears the same name. While on a ministry trip with him to Jamaica in 2005, I recorded him encouraging the believers in a local church in a place called Rock Place. This is what he said regarding his father:

> *Let me tell you something, I have not forgotten where I'm coming from, and I know when I come back and see, in a place like this, if you see the church my dad went to, not even half the size of this place, yet still we know that in that*

> *place, because he was willing and he was a man of faith, to step out by faith and not look at where he was coming from but where he could go ... fifty-six countries around the world, he raised up churches and raised up people.*

The account of the life of these two pioneers is very special to me. If they had not launched out in faith, there would have been no safe and sacred place for me to come into from the dark and cold of the devil's domain, to hear the truth, experience the joy, feel the warmth, and see the light of God our King, his kingdom, and his people.

Not only that, Mother Greenidge helped to raise my wife as a child. She made her home a safe place in her vocation as a child minder and even brought Michelle with them on ministry trips to Europe. In the providence and grace of God, over twenty years later, the church was preparing to go to a Christian family retreat called Ashburnham Place, and Mother Greenidge reached out to and invited Michelle, who was lost at the time, not walking with the Lord. She came, got saved, and by God's grace, today she is my wife.

So this account, although historical, is deeply personal to me and is why this book is dedicated to Anita "Mother" Greenidge, the woman with a pioneering and persevering faith who secured a place for us for God's glory and our joy.

# SECTION 6

## APPLICATION

# PLACE MAKERS

*I* have two memories of places that had a big impact on my life. One was Poland; the other was Rwanda.

In 2003 I was invited to join our pastor, Dennis Greenidge, on a ministry trip to Poland. While there, we visited one of the darkest places I've ever been to, Auschwitz.

This most infamous death camp was a place desecrated by the systematic genocide of the Jewish peoples of Europe, under the Nazi tyranny of Adolf Hitler's conquest in the Second World War. Other "undesirables" were also killed in the camps.

We went to rooms with shoes stacked in cages to the ceiling, those shoes belonged to many who had been killed. We went in the gas chambers where millions were killed and the ovens where so many were burned to ash. There were piles of watches and gold teeth; it was just unimaginable.

There was a sense of death and despair in the air. The land itself seemed scarred with the atrocities of the past. I left that place under a cloud of heaviness.

The other place, Rwanda, struck me by the present state of the people more than the atrocities of the recent past, which saw almost a million native Tutsi people killed by their Hutu neighbors in eighty days of horror.

Years later, we attended a mission trip with our pastor again, this time in 2009. As a church we sponsored an entire project through Compassion. We went to Rwanda to see these displaced people and offer them hope through child sponsorship, acting as God's place makers in this broken world.

Both these experiences and others in China and Jamaica lead us to the practical implications of this book.

We have come to the final section of this book in terms of our initial thesis regarding the nature and purpose of places under God. Now we look to our identity as place makers and various plans of action, to see our King's kingdom come and his will done in the earth.

Before we delve into the final three areas to help us apply the realities revealed in this book to our faith and practice, it will be useful to get an overall summary regarding the human and, specifically, the believer's position before God in terms of place. For this we turn to the Scriptures and, in particular, the book written by Luke the Physician and companion of Paul the Apostle, which details a speech Paul gave. His words center us around God and his purposes when we consider the earth, mankind, and the purpose of places. An exposition of this passage will serve us well as we seek to apply the theology of place to our life and practice.

> *The God who made the world and everything in it, being Lord of heaven and earth, does not live in Temples made by man, nor is he served by human hands, as though he needed anything, since he himself gives to all mankind life and breath and everything. And he made from one man every nation of mankind to live on all the face of the earth, having determined allotted periods and the boundaries of their dwelling place, that they should seek God, and perhaps feel their way toward him and find him. Yet he is actually not far from each one of us, for "In him we live and move and have our being'; as even some of your own poets have said, "'For we are indeed his offspring.'"*
>
> —Paul the Apostle,
> The book of Acts 17:24–28,
> The Areopagus at Mars Hill, Athens in 51 AD

A good way to begin will be for us to break this passage down into its component parts. A quick summary could be worded as follows:

"God is the creator and sustainer of all life and has *set man's times and places* with the desire that man world worship God as his source and Father."

Here it is in a basic structural sense in fifteen parts. Sometimes the correct structure is seen by working backward from the end of a sentence:

1. God created the world.
2. God created creatures in the world.
3. This God is Lord or owner of all he has created.
4. God is omnipresent so does not live in manmade temples.
5. God is the provider and sustainer of all life.
6. God is self-sufficient; he does not need man.
7. All men share a common origin; we are one race created by God.
8. The nations or people groups have their source in God.
9. Man was created by God with the purpose to live on the created earth.
10. Times are allotted by God.
11. Places are determined by God.
12. God's purpose in allotting times and places is that man would seek his Creator.
13. God is closer than we think; infinite yet imminent.
14. We live before God's face, in his world. He is the sustaining and life-giving source of creation.
15. God the creator is our source; we are created in his image to reflect and represent him as his children.

This passage makes clear to us that God has a purpose for man in the places he has allotted to man. It is in this context with God over all and sustaining all that we explore what it means for us to be not just place dwellers but place makers.

# THE ECOLOGICAL CHALLENGE

*The heavens declare the glory of God, and the sky above proclaims his handiwork. Day to day pours out speech, and night to night reveals knowledge. There is no speech, nor are there words, whose voice is not heard.*

—*Psalm 19:1–3*

We have an ecological (environmental, natural world) challenge before us as believers. We will review this with a biblical worldview in five subsections, looking at:

*God's good creation*—The fact that God made the world has profound implications.

*The destroyers of the earth*—The exploitation of the planet and its people through pollution is a sin that must be dealt with.

*The original mandate*—Keeping the garden.

*Creation's redemption*—How the creation can and will be redeemed.

*Place in the city*—The call to place making in the city.

# 1. GOD'S GOOD CREATION

*T*he Bible begins with the biggest claim in history, that God created everything. The first verse of the Bible in Genesis 1:1 states "In the beginning, God created the heavens and the earth."

Is this true or not? Our presupposition as believers is an absolute, unequivocal yes. You do not have to be a scientist or apologist to confidently affirm this; you just need to be a disciple of Jesus Christ.

We follow Jesus, and he taught that God created everything in accordance with the Genesis account in Matthew 13:35; 25:34; Mark 10:6; 13:19; 16:15; and Luke 11:50.

One example from this list are the words of Jesus in Mark 10:6:

> *But from the beginning of creation, 'God made them male and female.'*

The theological teaching of the Bible found in the rest of the New Testament also makes the Genesis account of creation a clear object of our faith. A great, possibly the best, example of this is Hebrews 11:3, which releases us from the burden of evidence-based belief in creation, instead calling us to make this stand on faith in God and his historical action of creation.

> *By faith we understand that the universe was created by the word of God, so that what is seen was not made out of things that are visible.*

Other Scriptures that explicitly teach us that God is the creator of the entire cosmos are included in Appendix D; the references found there are 53 in total.

Having said that, the evidence for creation is overwhelming. I am no science expert but can point you in the direction of those who are and have used science to explore the created world and discover the evidence of God's design. These are included in the recommended reading area in the creation section and include resources like Ken Ham's *Answers in Genesis*.

Having established the fact that God created the world, we are left with more questions like: What was it made for?

The Scriptures teach us that God as King created the creation to reflect his royal glory. We also learn that he created creatures to inhabit and fill his kingdom, which is the creation itself. His desire is that those creatures would know him intimately and worship him as their King, as he so rightly deserves.

The biblical narrative teaches us that man rebelled against his King, switching his allegiance and worship to the creation instead of the Creator. Paul summarizes our treason against our King well in Romans 1:25:

> Because they exchanged the truth about God for a lie and worshiped and served the creature rather than the Creator, who is blessed forever! Amen.

Does this high treason make the creation inherently evil? The answer is no. God declared at the historical event called the creation week, that all creation was good. Although the creation was subjected to decay as a result of man's sin, it is not inherently evil; after all, it was God's idea, his plan, and he made it. The physical world is not evil; on the contrary, it is good—decaying, but good.

Paul develops our understanding of the current state of creation later in his letter to the church at Rome in chapter 8:19–22:

> For the creation waits with eager longing for the revealing of the sons of God. For the creation was subjected to futility, not willingly, but because of him who subjected it, in hope that the creation itself will be set free from its bondage to corruption and obtain the freedom of the glory of the children of God. For we know that the whole creation has been groaning together in the pains of childbirth until now.

There is no space for a lengthy exposition of this fascinating passage, but there are some basic lessons to learn about the relationship between believers and creation (sub human creation) and the current state of creation. Here are eight guiding thoughts:

1. The suffering of humanity and the surrounding creation are linked through their common origin.

2. This common origin means the judgment passed on man by God by extension affects the creation.

3. The him who subjected creation to corruption was not Adam; it was certainly Adam's fault, but the decisive action of subjecting the earth to corruption was within the remit of the King and Righteous Judge, God.

4. This also points to the link between man, who is a spiritual being created from the material of the earth and the creation itself. This connection is, therefore, on a physical and metaphysical level.

5. Man had dominion over the earth as God's ambassadors or rulers in it (God's image), so when he fell, his domain fell by extension, according to the laws of God's kingdom (creation itself).

6. The particular suffering of Christians in their desire to glorify God in the earth is connected to the creation's yearning to glorify the God by whom and for whom it was made too.

7. God subjected creation to corruption as a mercy, rather than simply obliterating it and starting again, with the hope that one day the corruption could be reversed or stopped.

8. God subjected creation to judgment in hope, not as an end in itself; creation was God's idea, and he wants it redeemed along with the creatures he made from it to inhabit it.

When creation is in its right place, in context to its creator (God) and the creatures that inhabit it or use it (humans or spirit begins), it is good.

The inanimate creation has no will of its own, so in a sense it is amoral, but it does have a purpose, and when that purpose is not perverted, it is good. Creatures impose their will on the creation and, by extension, corrupt the creation.

We are God's children, his image bearers in the earth, the earth that he created, the creation that he seeks to redeem. We need to consider that as we interact with the world around us. It was not made for us to abuse; it was made to be used to the glory of God.

The physical realm will always be a part of God's kingdom; his original idea of a physical realm was a good idea and is still a good idea, so we need to drop the warped way of thinking that causes us to not care for God's earth. He made it, so we should love it,[105] not worship it instead of him but care for it because of him.

Someone may argue that 1 John 2:15–17 teaches that the world is passing away so we should not love it, or that 2 Peter 3:7 teaches that the earth will all burn up one day, so what's the point. I want to demonstrate briefly that both these interpretations are

[105] The physical earth itself, not the evil spiritual world system as referred to in 1 John 2:15–17.

wrong in accordance with the context of the passages themselves, the theological trajectory of the wider text that they are a part of, and how the Bible's big story or narrative is unfolding.

## Translating 2 Peter 3:5–7 and 10–13

For full context, you really should read the whole letter and certainly the whole passage or thought that our two texts have come from, which is 2 Peter 3:1–13.

To begin with, let's read the plain English text of verses 5–7 (emphasis added):

> *For they deliberately overlook this fact, that the heavens existed long ago, and the earth was formed out of water and through water by the word of God, and that by means of these the world that then existed was **deluged with water and perished**. But by the same word the heavens and earth that now exist are **stored up for fire, being kept until the day of judgment** and **destruction of the ungodly**.*

The context here is that there were teachers and critics saying that the Lord had already returned spiritually and that the prophesied coming judgment was trumped up because the world has been the same day after day and age after age since the beginning. Peter is combating these misrepresentations of God, his Word, and the nature of the world. Here are some important observations.

1. **Previous earths?** Some have taken this passage to indulge wild legends about previous Earths with deep histories before the world we live in now. This is not biblical and requires a great deal of overreaching and special pleading to begin to be plausible as well as being a theory based on the gaps rather than the text. It should be noted that other religions do believe that the cosmos goes through cycles of creation and destruction. Christianity does not hold this belief, and it is alien to the text.

2. **Who perished?** This is pointing to the great flood, the great displacement caused by God's great judgment on the world of Noah's day. The earth itself did not perish; the people on the earth perished.

3. **The Word?** The Word of God is central to the passage. Peter is upholding that, despite the apparent delay, the Word of God is the decisive power that created the world in the first place, caused the judgment in Noah's day, sustains the current world, and will bring the future judgment on the world.

4. **What does world mean?** It seems clear from the text that world has a wider meaning than merely the earth itself. This term includes the inhabitants of the world and the general world system of the age. This, by the way, explains the use of the term *world* in 1 John 2:15–17.

5. **Water versus fire:** The compassion is between the water of the first great judgment and the fire of the coming great judgment. The question to be answered is: how are these two to be compared? The only way to answer that is to work historically from the event that has already happened, Noah's flood, with our range of questions:

   a. **Did the water of the flood mean the world was destroyed?** No, because the same earth God created at creation is here now; we are living on it. This is about judgment, not utter destruction.

   b. **Did the waters put an end to the world system of the time?** Yes, many systems and ways of life formed before the flood were fundamentally changed or washed away by the flood.

   c. **Did people perish?** Yes, the waters drowned everyone but the people on the ark.

   d. **Did the ecology of the earth change?** Yes, the seasons, continents, waters, and rain cycles were all affected by the global flood.

   e. **Would it be fair to say that the flood purged the earth?** Yes, albeit temporally. The fire should parallel this and every one of the points above.

   f. **What other comparisons are there with fire and water?** The most obvious to the Christian mind is that of baptism. John the Baptizer baptized with water, while Jesus baptizes with fire. Baptism is a ritual cleansing and symbol of death and resurrection.

   This sheds some light on the passage from a spiritual perspective and begs the question, will the fire of judgment be a blanket burning on a physical level only, or will it have wider and deeper spiritual implications and application in the way that the baptism of fire is the fuller spiritual reality of the physical act of water baptism?

In concluding my thoughts on this part of the passage, I would say that we take the text too far to assume the complete destruction and replacement of this world with a new one. The text instead points to a transformed world and order, which will be transformed by either or both spiritual and physical fire.

Now on to the second passage, which again I have laid out in plain English for our investigation of verses 10–13 (emphasis added):

> *But the day of the Lord will come like a thief, and then* **the heavens will pass away with a roar,** *and the* **heavenly bodies will be burned up and dissolved,** *and the earth and the works that are done on it* **will be exposed.** *Since all* **these things** *are thus to be* **dissolved,** *what sort of people ought you to be in lives of holiness and godliness, waiting for and hastening the coming of the day of God, because of which* **the heavens will be set on fire and dissolved, and the heavenly bodies will melt as they burn!** *But according to his promise we are waiting for* **new heavens** *and a* **new earth** *in which* **righteousness dwells.**

If we do not pause to examine this text carefully, it can seem to say that the earth will be burned up and replaced by a new one. But on more careful inspection at a surface level, that is not what it says at all. Again, let's make some observations and ask some questions:

1. **What will be burned?** Look at the Scripture again; every reference to burning up or being set on fire is in regard to the heavens and the heavenly bodies (sun, moon, etc.), not the earth.

   This holds well with the final vision of the new heaven and earth, which will have no sun or moon because God's light will be more than enough.

2. **Okay, what does the passage say about the earth?** It speaks about the earth being exposed. N. T. Wright points out that the word for burned up in the previous verses is rendered "will be found," or "will be discovered," or "will be disclosed" in some very reliable ancient manuscripts of the New Testament.[106]

3. **Destruction versus judgment.** The passage has the judgment of God as its subject. Redemptive history has taught us that God's judgment has a

---

[106] Tom Wright, *Early Christian Letters for Everyone: James, Peter, John and Judah,* For Everyone Bible Study Guides (London; Louisville, KY: SPCK; Westminster John Knox Press, 2011), 119.

purpose, to bring glory to his name for his righteousness, justice, mercy, and grace.

We do not see a God who simply casts away or utterly destroys; he did not do this with Israel, will not do this with the redeemed, and will not do it with the good earth he created. With all these objects of his affection he will bring restoration and even regeneration or transformation, but utter destruction is not on his agenda.

4.  **Replaced versus renewed and restored.** God is not in the habit of replacing that which he has set his affection on. This is true of his people (both Israel and the church), and it is true of the earth he made.

    What we see happening in the text is the regeneration of the earth, much like the regeneration of a sinner; it will receive a baptism of fire and of the Spirit of God, the same Spirit that brooded over the original birth of the earth will be active in its re-birth.

    This also dovetails with the passage from Hebrews; God is not hoping for the destruction but the freedom and restoration of the earth, and the hope is not so much God's as it is creation's hope.

5.  **Okay, so what is the new earth?** Well it is new, but in the sense of re-new. In a way, the earth will go through a final and great re-placement after the final displacement of the judgment or cleansing by fire. The creation, earth in particular, will go through a death, resurrection, and glorification of its own.

I have been very brief; discussing the reality of the coming judgment and the new heaven and earth would take its own book.

You may not agree with my emphasis or interpretation of the passage, and that is okay. It should still suffice to say that there is enough evidence here to conclude that God has a plan for the earth and he made it in the first instance. Therefore, as beneficiaries of the earth and God's grace, we have a mandate to care for the Earth that God made and loves.

## Translating 1 John 2:15–17

*Do not love the world or the things in the world. If anyone loves the world, the love of the Father is not in him. For all that is in the world—the desires*

*of the flesh and the desires of the eyes and pride of life—is not from the Father*
*but is from the world. And the world is passing away along with its desires,*
*but whoever does the will of God abides forever.*

*—1 John 2:15–17*

The world spoken of here is quite clearly not he physical cosmos but operates in the physical world. The world here is the world system and the sin it incubates and fosters.

We do not store up treasure on this earth, as Jesus taught us in Matthew 6:19–21. We store up treasure in the world to come. These are tangible treasures, more fully material and physical than the things of the current world because they are not subject to decay but have the full reality of "things," not abstract notions or ideals.

The reality is that the world to come, the earth to come, will be more fully physical in some glorified way than the current state, free from corruption. In fact, it will be in reverse, being renewed daily in the life and strain of the resurrection, which began the new creation and itself reverses the effects of the fall.

The earth has not yet been glorified in its own resurrection as it were, so everything in the world as we know it is passing away, subject to decay and part of an order and age that is coming to an end. However, that is no excuse to sin against the earth.

My point here is: drop the mentality that the earth does not matter because judgment is coming. It really does matter what we do and how we take care of the earth, as the next point explains.

# 2. THE DESTROYERS
## OF THE EARTH

*W*e are free as Christians to choose from a number of interpretations on how the end will be; this freedom is partly allowed because it is a time we have not yet seen, and the Scriptures around it are often of a seemingly mystical nature.

The classical options include amillennialism, postmillennialism, classical premillennialism, and dispensational premillennialism. As their names suggest, they are different ways of seeing the "Millennial" or one-thousand-year reign of Jesus on the earth at the end of the age.

I covered this on the last week of the Hold and Advance course, which looks at the area of apologetics using the essential or core Christian doctrines as a basis from which to build out our presuppositional stand. Here is one of the summaries I provided as a statement on how all the views have at least some benefit to all believers.

In my opinion, the most biblical of all models is the classic premillennial view; however, the following are lessons we can learn from the other perspectives:

- **Amillennial**—It is true that the kingdom of God is here in a spiritual sense now and that Christ reigns through and in the hearts of his people.

- **Postmillennial**—We should seek to establish the Lord's kingdom through missionary, evangelical, social, and political work.

- **Dispensational Premillennial**—Always be prepared for the Lord's return.

- **Classic Premillennial**—Be prepared to endure suffering and tribulation prior to the Lord's actual return to rule and reign as King.

However, whichever camp we fall into, our eschatology should not make us abusers of the earth who just don't care because it's all going to burn.

Consider the following verse from Revelation 11:18 (emphasis added).

*The nations raged, but your wrath came, and the time for the dead to be judged, and for rewarding your servants, the prophets and saints, and those who fear your name, both small and great, and **for destroying the destroyers of the earth**."*

God's wrath or anger has come to destroy the destroyers of the earth. It would seem deliberate and careless treatment of the earth is a sin that makes him angry; after all, he made it and always intended that it would be used to cause humans and all other creatures in the physical realm to thrive, to the pleasure, glory, and fame of his name.

Those who willfully destroy the planet are like insurrectionists setting fire to the property of the King, which when he returns from putting his enemies under his feet at war, he will judge them severely for. He loves his kingdom, and his kingdom is a reflection of him, so polluting and sinning against the creation is to sin against him by extension.

I must add a caveat to this by making it clear that we are not pantheists who believe that nature is God. No, we believe that nature was created and therefore reflects its creator and King, God.

Consider for yourself what the Bible has to say about God's relationship to his creation in these selected passages:

*Deuteronomy 10:14: Behold, to the LORD your God belong heaven and the heaven of heavens, the earth with all that is in it.*

*Psalm 24:1–2: The earth is the Lord's and the fullness thereof, the world and those who dwell therein, for he has founded it upon the seas and established it upon the rivers.*

*Psalm 89:11: The heavens are yours; the earth also is yours; the world and all that is in it, you have founded them.*

No long commentary is required; the Scripture is clear. God and creation are distinct from each other, and the creation has a creator, God. This God is the Lord, or King, owner and ruler of creation.

# 3. THE ORIGINAL MANDATE

So far we have seen that God's creation is good, that it will be renewed, and that he will judge those who destroy it.

So if destroying the earth is a sin, the cultivating, nurturing, and preserving of it is not a sin but a good and godly thing.

The very first mandate given to man, even before his first command to not eat from the tree, was to keep the garden in Genesis 2:15 (emphasis added):

> The Lord God took the man and put him in the garden of Eden to **work it** and **keep it**.

Work is not a result of the fall; fruitless and agonizing work is a result of the fall. Work was there in the perfect state of Eden and will be there in the eternal glories of the new heaven and earth. What is it that you suppose we will rule over or judge or do for eternity in the kingdom of God? (For example, see Matthew 25:21.)

Only after the creation of woman do we see the mandate of dominion to accompany the mandate to work in Genesis 1:28, which serves as a summary for the expanded narrative concerning the creation of humans in chapter 2:

> And God blessed them. And God said to them, "Be fruitful and multiply and fill the earth and subdue it, and have dominion over the fish of the sea and over the birds of the heavens and over every living thing that moves on the earth."

So we are to have dominion over the earth, but in a kingdom sense, we are to serve and work in the earth to ensure it best reflects God's glory and enables us to reflect his glory as the King of the kingdom we have been given a charge and authority in.

Jesus taught what it really means to have dominion; it's not about lording it over others, abusing, or exploiting the thing we have dominion over.

His kingdom is one of ruling servants. The hallmark of its citizens, like their King, is humble majesty. Note Jesus's words in Mark 10:43–45:

> But it shall not be so among you. But whoever would be great among you must be your servant, and whoever would be first among you must be slave of all.

*For even the Son of Man came not to be served but to serve, and to give his life as a ransom for many."*

So let's fulfill the original mandate to work for the benefit of the earth to the glory of the King of this kingdom of creation by serving.

You may ask how we can do that practically today or in the near future. Here are some ideas that we can all consider as his servants.

## Christian environmentalism?

One way is to be concerned about the environment but from the perspective of the biblical worldview. Steer clear of the politically motivated eco movements, which seek to oppress the advancement of the third world while ignoring data from scientists that do not agree with the status quo.[107]

There are two historical case studies that can help us in this regard. One would be the agricultural system of the Franciscan monks; the other would be the kibbutz systems of the Jews.

I'm not going to do a historical review or in-depth study of either of these; it suffices to say that they are or were communal, agricultural projects that were environmentally friendly while adding to the welfare of the people they served or who were a part of the community or those surrounding it.

This is something that leaders in the evangelical world need to start to consider. How can we in a communal and Christ-centered sense, honor God as good stewards of his creation and honor our mandate as his vice regents on the Earth to tend, nurture, and protect "the garden"?

We are called just like Adam to be place makers, so don't spiritualize this and lose its essence. We should be making a mark in the earth in regard to the environment from a distinctly Christian perspective.

I do not want to prescribe the details of how a faith community might express this; I think it is best that the Holy Spirit would take the ignition this book should spark and cause God's people individually and corporately in every place to reaffirm and fulfill mankind's original mandate to the glory of God and for the joy of all peoples.

---

[107] See the documentary *Great Global Warming Swindle* by Martin Durkin 2007.

# 4. CREATION'S REDEMPTION

*T*he Bible's narrative is going in a particular direction. We see the end of the story best in the book of Revelation. One of the passages regarding this is Revelation 21:5, in which the enthroned Jesus states (emphasis added):

> And he who was seated on the throne said, "Behold, I am **making all things new**." Also he said, "Write this down, for these words are trustworthy and true."

This is further evidence that the creation is in for a major overhaul, not destruction and recreation, rather recreation through renewal, restoration, and glorification.

Is there something to make of the fact that Jesus uses the present tense rather than future or past tense by using the word *making* rather than *made* or *will make*?

I believe the word choice is deliberate to indicate that the making all things new is already underway, now.

God seeks to renew the creation on one level through his children, although the ultimate renewal or refreshing of the earth will come at the end.

Again the question stands for us as place makers: how can we work as an extension of Jesus's ministry to make all things new? How can you redeem the fallen creation?

For example, I remember our church working with other Christians from our area to restore a local park that had fallen into dangerous squalor. With some gardening and a fresh lick of paint, it had an impact on the lives of those in the area.

We close this section by looking at one area where we can work on behalf of Jesus to make all things new.

*M*ost people on the earth live in urban areas. Urban life in the cities of the world can be really fast paced, crowded, and impersonal.

Christianity has always been an urban movement. Even in the end, our ultimate destination is the greatest city, New Jerusalem.

What we need is "sacred space" in the city. I know I'm using the term space instead of place in this instance, but there is a good reason for that. It is appropriate to say this because cities can be so crowded and busy that space itself is rare but a necessary element of city life.

The challenge for the church is how do we, with a realigned theology of place, create sacred space in the city so that people can enter and encounter the God of that place?

One way to do this is to open our church buildings in the working week so the weary souls of the city have a place to retreat to. But it should not just be a place of peace or rest, it needs to above all be a place filled with God's presence, a place of revelation, where people can come to know God.

As place makers, carriers of God in the earth, harbingers of his presence, heralds of his kingdom, and servants of all, we have a mandate to make sacred places in the city.

This is not just a mandate for the church building; it extends to outreach programs like a Christian café or bookshop and extends further to the clubs we may run for children. It even extends into our own space, our homes.

A revived emphasis on hospitality will serve well to ignite our hearts to be the place makers the earth so desperately needs and the kingdom of God so urgently demands.

Set up an embassy for God through your life and ministry today. Sacred places are made by his decree and presence, you can decree his word and bring his presence because he dwells in you and fills the corporate gathering and worship of his people.

Consider this passage regarding the hospitality we should provide according to Jesus, recorded in Luke 14:12–14:

*He said also to the man who had invited him, "When you give a dinner or a banquet, do not invite your friends or your brothers or your relatives or rich neighbors, lest they also invite you in return and you be repaid. But when you give a feast, invite the poor, the crippled, the lame, the blind, and you will be blessed, because they cannot repay you. For you will be repaid at the resurrection of the just."*

Other Scriptures regarding Christian hospitality will also help feed our hearts and minds in regard to being the place makers we have been called to be.

*1 Peter 4:9: Show hospitality to one another without grumbling.*

*Romans 12:13: Contribute to the needs of the saints and seek to show hospitality.*

*3 John 8: Therefore we ought to support people like these, that we may be fellow workers for the truth.*

*Revelation 3:20: Behold, I stand at the door and knock. If anyone hears my voice and opens the door, I will come in to him and eat with him, and he with me.*

*Luke 15:1–2: Now the tax collectors and sinners were all drawing near to hear him. And the Pharisees and the scribes grumbled, saying, "This man receives sinners and eats with them."*

# THE ANTHROPOLOGICAL CHALLENGE

*... he made from one man every nation of mankind to live on all the face of the earth ...*

—*Acts 17:26*

We have a call beyond the places to the people in those places; this is our anthropological (the study of mankind) challenge. The world is filled with displaced peoples that we have been called to minister to.

Again we will briefly look at five subsections:

**Be informed**—We need to be students of the human condition in ourselves and the wider world.

**Prayer**—This is our most important tool in fulfilling our call to humanity.

**Mission**—Missionary work today and living lives on mission.

**Planting**—The necessity of church planting throughout the earth.

**Justice**—Pursuing social and political justice in Jesus's name.

# 1 . BE INFORMED

This is a short and practical call to all believers. We need to keep ourselves informed about the needs of the people across the earth so we can better pray, provide for, and minister to them.

Paul mentioned to the believers at Corinth, in 2 Corinthians 1:8, that he did not want them to be uninformed:

> For we do not want you to be unaware, brothers, of the affliction we experienced in Asia. For we were so utterly burdened beyond our strength that we despaired of life itself.

There are multiple agencies and ministries (secular and Christian) that can keep us abreast of the needs in the world and especially with regard to the reach of the gospel of the kingdom, including some I will list in the recommended resources section.

I want to take a moment here to promote one of the most important ministries in the earth today. I'm talking about the Joshua Project, a ministry from the kingdom-focused Frontier Ventures founded by the late Dr. Ralph D. Winter.

The Joshua Project works to keep the information regarding the various people groups of the earth up to date, with particular regard to the unreached and unengaged peoples in terms of the gospel of the kingdom and the King's great commission to make disciples of every nation (another word for people group).

It is reasonable to say that every people group must be reached, so it is crucial that our information regarding these people is up to date, so we can best mobilize ourselves to reach them with the word of the good news.

The Joshua Project explains their purpose on their website as follows:

> Joshua Project is a research initiative seeking to highlight the ethnic people groups of the world with the fewest followers of Christ. Accurate, updated ethnic people group information is critical for understanding and completing

> *the Great Commission. Revelation 5:9 and 7:9–10 show that there will be some from every tribe, tongue, nation and people before the Throne.[108]*

You can visit the about page (https://joshuaproject.net/about/details) to read the rest of their vision and strategy, which is really great and absolutely needed.

The current overall statistics at the time of writing this book were as follows:

Of the 9,817 people groups comprising approximately 7,290,985,000 individuals, 4,054 people groups comprising approximately 3,076,658,000 individuals are essentially unengaged or unreached with the gospel.

So let's make a commitment to stay informed about the needs and use that information to take action as God's place makers in the earth.

This information is part of the fuel for our prayers as we seek to complete our mission to bring the news of the King and his kingdom to all mankind without distinction.

---

[108] "Joshua Project," accessed March 27, 2016, https://joshuaproject.net/about/details.

# 2 . PRAY

*O*ur most important and sometimes underrated tool in fulfilling our anthropological challenge is prayer.

We are people of prayer, and even our gatherings should be marked by prayer. Jesus affirmed that his Father's house, the temple in Jerusalem, was meant to be a house of prayer for all nations (people groups).

Jesus spent his entire life praying and took time to teach us how to pray, so let's not neglect it.

The information we receive should fuel our prayers, but more importantly the Scriptures should fuel our prayer. I have always been taught by my own pastor, Dennis Greenidge, that the best way to pray is to pray God's own words, found in the Bible, back to him.

Our God answers prayer, as Jesus encourages us in Matthew 21:22, "And whatever you ask in prayer, you will receive, if you have faith." So ignite your faith and pray about your call to be a place maker, the needs of the world, and the completion of the King's commission.

One of the things that the focus on prayer highlights is the supernatural nature of the battle we are engaged in.

God has set the boundaries of man but has also set the boundaries, limits, and territory of the fallen elohim, commonly referred to as principalities, powers, and demons.

In the following passage from Deuteronomy 32:8, we can see that God divided the peoples of the earth not just along geographical lines but along spiritual authority lines too.

The term *sons of God* is used of the created divine beings we call angels, whether elect or fallen.

> *When the Most High gave to the nations their inheritance, when he divided mankind, he fixed the borders of the peoples according to the number of the sons of God.*

We need the Holy Spirit to guide us along with the information we gather so we can pray strategically and bind the strong powers over a particular place or people, so they can be free to receive the news and associated benefits of the King's kingdom.

Jesus said we should bind the strong man before the place he occupies can be taken in Matthew 12:28–29:

> *But if it is by the Spirit of God that I cast out demons, then the kingdom of God has come upon you. Or how can someone enter a strong man's house and plunder his goods, unless he first binds the strong man? Then indeed he may plunder his house.*

The prophet Daniel experienced this when he prayed for the children of Israel in the captivity of Babylon. The answer to his prayer was delayed; Gabriel explains the delay was due to a spiritual battle with fallen spiritual princes who presided over the territory he came to pass through in Daniel 10:13:

> *The prince of the kingdom of Persia withstood me twenty-one days, but Michael, one of the chief princes, came to help me, for I was left there with the kings of Persia.*

Paul warns us that our war is not in the physical realm, but the spiritual in Ephesians 6:12:

> *For we do not wrestle against flesh and blood, but against the rulers, against the authorities, against the cosmic powers over this present darkness, against the spiritual forces of evil in the heavenly places.*

This is something we are all called to and can do today, first personally but also corporately when we come together to the place of prayer.

Just praying in a place can bring a sense of God's presence and go toward making that place sacred.

Many reading this book already pray; I want to encourage you to pray with the importance of place and our mission to humanity (the anthropological challenge) in mind.

[236]

# 3 . MISSION

*T*he next step in tackling the anthropological challenge is mission. Missionary work is needed to reach mankind with the liberating good news that the King has come and will return to reign as King of the earth. The evil one has been defeated and his reign is over, this disposed wicked king will one day be cast out of the kingdom once and for all.

This is not new; the church has been engaged in mission work since we received the great commission from our conquering King; this book affirms what we have done, are doing, and will do in fulfilling the great, holy charge to make disciples of all people groups.

We need to ensure we are doing our part in the mission; if we cannot go, then we should sponsor missionaries, or missions. A practical way to do this is through a dedicated Christian mission organization like Compassion child sponsorship or Operation Mobilization.

A distinctive of missions is that we go to where the people are, to the place they live, and in that place we share the gospel, so that place is transformed in the context of its own culture and people.

Another distinctive is that we seek to build disciples who can themselves maintain and grow the influence of the kingdom by making disciples too, so that the kingdom becomes indigenous to the people.

Missions should transform the place and people it is aimed at. One of the important aspects of the Bible's narrative is God conquering all other false gods. This is connected to place in a remarkable way, which is why mission is the frontline of the war. The King is advancing his kingdom through his presence via his people and his message.

The places and peoples of earth are, in a spiritual sense, under the dominion of spirit beings the Bible calls the sons of God. God's mission is to dispossess each of these by invading their territory and setting up his kingdom as opposed to theirs.

If we take the place or territory, then we can capture the allegiance of the people, which is what relationship with the Lord, discipleship, and love is really all about. It's not merely a sentimental abstract or affection, it is all about allegiance and territory; it always has been and always will be.

Missions exist because worship or allegiance to God does not exist in some territory or place, with the people of that place. Instead their allegiance or worship is aligned to false gods, powered by fallen spirit beings known as demons.

As Paul encourages us in Romans 10, how can they know unless we go, and how can we go unless we are sent? Determine to play your part in seeing the mission finished today.

Finishing the mission is not only about the unreached people groups of the earth, it's also about everyday Christianity with those around us in our local areas and especially in our own families.

As a father, one of the most important missions I have is to ensure my children are raised to know the Lord and pledge their allegiance to him as their King.

Disciplining our own families is a unique and wonderful privilege that we should not squander. After all, Jesus did tell his disciples to start at home before reaching out to the ends of the earth. The two should not be juxtaposed against each other. Discipleship, evangelism, and mission should be pursued on all possible levels: with family, locally, nationally, and abroad.

That being said, we should live our lives on mission. You don't need to be called a missionary to live on mission, ready to give a reason for the hope you have in the King and his kingdom.

At the same time, I don't want to take away from the importance of the call to be an actual missionary to an unreached people; more of us need to answer the call. Just be sure you have truly been called to that particular vocation. If you have, then go with the faith and grace God has supplied.

For those like me, you may not be called as a missionary at this point in your life, but we can still be involved with the battle on the front lines through financial support and prayer support.

Another way that we, the non-fulltime missionaries, can help is through giving time to a short-term mission or two. For the long-term missionaries, this can serve as the surge in boots on the ground needed in the same way reserves help an embattled platoon in the heart of war.

# 4. PLANTING

*In him you also are being built together into a dwelling place for God by the Spirit.*

*Ephesians 2:22*

No, I'm not talking about planting flowers or trees; there is something far more important that needs to be planted—churches!

Church planting should be the aim of missions. This is place making at its pinnacle, on this side of the fullness of the kingdom. The church is still the best solution. They should not be dead and formal buildings but actual sacred places filled with the presence of God through the gathering of the people of God.

Staying with the wartime image for missions. What do we do when we take the hill, the stronghold, the mountain or town? We should build a stronghold of our own and stick a flag in the ground and build a fort and claim the land for our King and assimilate it into his advancing kingdom. In other words, we should plant a church.

Jesus said of the church that the gates of hell would not prevail against it, so planting a church in newly taken ground only strengthens our foothold and position. The enemy will not stop fighting, but having our own stronghold and barracks for training new soldiers will aid in the advancement and establishment of the kingdom in this new area.

With reference to answering the anthropological challenge, we should seek to allow these churches to be built out of the culture of the place rather than importing our own culture too heavily.

We should also seek to raise up leaders from among the people. In the same way God incarnated himself to relate to us in the most remarkable and relevant way, so should we seek to be incarnational in our place making.

If Dennis and Anita had not planted a church in West Norwood, London, I may never have met the Lord, let alone written the book you are reading now.

So speak to God about church planting today. Are you called to do this? If you are, then do it. If not, then how can you support it as the aim of a local, national, or global mission?

Again, we should not allow our eschatology, whatever particular flavor it is, to stunt our appetite for planting new churches and, in doing so, taking new territory.

There is a lesson to be learned from history here. Churches were often built on the site of old so-called sacred places of the pagans to say that a new God was in town and was taking over the site, thus defeating the old god of the place. A new King had arrived and conquered the old king. This practice tells us we once had a better sense of place and the importance of territory and allegiance.

This same principle was applied to the pagan holidays too, although that was ill-advised in my opinion because we disconnected ourselves from our own distinctly Jewish times and feasts, which have their fullness in Christ, but that is a subject for another book.

This should also give us pause, when we consider the reversal of this principle, when the Church of England and others are now giving sites over to Islam, which in a sense is a victory for the god of that religious and ideological kingdom.

We should regain the wartime command and conquer mentality in the church, let's go take some ground, overturning the false gods and all they represent and establish another outpost for the kingdom of our King, Jesus.

# 5. JUSTICE

isplaced people are everywhere. The best hope for them is the kingdom, the message about the kingdom, and all it entails, and most importantly the King himself. In practical terms, we, the church, are the solution as ambassadors of the King and his kingdom.

People are displaced for all sorts of reasons, including:

- **Wars**—like the one happening in Syria now can cause people to become asylum seekers and refugees.
- **Economic difficulty**—this can affect anyone at any time and can lead to depression with the sense of displacement it brings and can ultimately lead to homelessness.
- **Natural disasters**—like earthquakes and tsunami's.
- **Diaspora**—this term simply means a scattered people. It is the term used for Jews who do not live in Israel but is also used for other people groups. My own people group of African slave descendants in the West are classed as a diaspora too.

We have a mandate to reach out to these people so they can find their place, identity, and relative safety in the grace of our King, God, and his kingdom.

It is part of our DNA as God's place makers to pursue justice. What use is a place that is not safe and conducive to the flourishing of its occupants?

We pursue justice on various levels, including social justice for the marginalized and forgotten as well as political justice against unjust laws.

Another area to consider in regard to justice will be our stance regarding Israel and those who unfairly boycott and misrepresent Israel with the driving desire to make them a placeless, scattered people again at best and no people at all at worst.

Justice and worship go hand in hand. We are encouraged to minister to widows and the fatherless, which in a way represents all those who are oppressed and without defense or have no real sense of place in this life.

Justice matters, so pursue it in the way you shop, the way you vote, the things you advocate for and provide support to.

# THE BELIEVER'S RESPONSE

Well here we are, the final chapter, it's time for our response. How should we then live in light of all we have learned?

Here are five things we need to consider as we respond to God our King and the ecological and anthropological challenges before us in light of the theology of place:

**Worship**—Our first and most important response to God our King is to worship him.

**Study**—We need to study the word and the world around us to fuel everything, including our thinking, prayer, work, and living.

**Pray**—We respond directly to God through prayer; nothing makes more difference in the earth than our prayers.

**Work**—The task of being a place maker, including personal evangelism in its many forms.

**Sojourner Living**—place dwellers, makers, and sojourners. Our call to sojourner living.

# 1 . WORSHIP

*T*his goes against our pragmatic culture, which just wants to go and get the work done, but it is the heart of our lives as believers.

> *To the King of the ages, immortal, invisible, the only God, be honor and glory forever and ever. Amen. (1 Timothy 1:17)*

As we consider all we have seen in our survey of the centrality of place in God's purpose and mission, we should respond in awe of him and sing to him in praise of his great name.

> *... to the only God, our Savior, through Jesus Christ our Lord, be glory, majesty, dominion, and authority, before all time and now and forever. Amen. (Jude 25)*

Does that ride you the wrong way? Are you thinking—really? If that is the case, then you may have a heart problem between yourself and God.

When we consider the sacrifice he made on the cross, the kingdom he has made us a part of, and the victory he has won as our King, we really should glorify and worship him in love, gratitude, praise, and awe.

> *For from him and through him and to him are all things. To him be glory forever. Amen. (Romans 11:36)*

When we consider that he has set the boundaries of all men that they might seek him and be saved, we should worship him.

When we consider his faithfulness to his promises to Israel and to the body of Christ, we should praise him.

> *... to the praise of his glorious grace, with which he has blessed us in the Beloved. (Ephesians 1:6).*

When we consider the fact that he is the one who decided to create a place called earth and to create a people called Man and decided to deliver humans from the dark one and his kingdom, we should bless his name.

> *For by him all things were created, in heaven and on earth, visible and invisible, whether thrones or dominions or rulers or authorities—all things were created through him and for him. (Colossians 1:16)*

When we understand that he now lives inside us, by God the Holy Spirit, we should cry out to him in thankfulness!

> *For you did not receive the spirit of slavery to fall back into fear, but you have received the Spirit of adoption as sons, by whom we cry, "Abba! Father!" The Spirit himself bears witness with our spirit that we are children of God. (Romans 8:15–16)*

When we consider the grace the King has shown to us sinners by electing us in his holy love, before he even made the world, we should stand in awe of him.

Make this your response today, have focused times of private and corporate praise and worship, and live a life of worship.

Consider Psalm 100:

> *Make a joyful noise to the LORD, all the earth! Serve the LORD with gladness! Come into his presence with singing! Know that the LORD, he is God! It is he who made us, and we are his; we are his people, and the sheep of his pasture. Enter his gates with thanksgiving, and his courts with praise! Give thanks to him; bless his name! For the LORD is good; his steadfast love endures forever, and his faithfulness to all generations.*

# 2 . STUDY

We need to be students of the word, the truth, and the rule by which we dwell in the places allotted to us. We also need to be students of our world, the place in which we dwell. These two disciplines will make us effective place makers.

I cannot commend the study of God's Word to you enough. The Bible is God's revelation of himself and his kingdom to us for our benefit and his glory. C. H. Spurgeon makes the point well in a sermon delivered here in London over a hundred years ago. It is even more relevant now in the days of audio Bibles, Bible apps, and short devotionals:

> ... *what poor reading some of you give to your Bibles. I do not want to say anything which is too severe because it is not strictly true - let your own consciences speak, but still, I make bold to enquire, - Do not many of you read the Bible in a very hurried way - just a little bit, and off you go? Do you not soon forget what you have read, and lose what little effect it seemed to have? How few of you are resolved to get at its soul, its juice, its life, its essence, and to drink in its meaning. Well, if you do not do that, I tell you again your reading is miserable reading, dead reading, unprofitable reading; it is not reading at all, the name would be misapplied. May the blessed Spirit give you repentance touching this thing.*[109]

A light reading of the Scriptures will be of little to no use; read it slowly, then stop and reflect on what you have read, then maybe make some notes about what you have read. If you want to go further with a passage then do that, look at what others have said about the passage, dig into the original languages if you have the tools.

Bible reading and study should be a joy-filled, happy experience. Please don't get me wrong—it can be a crushing, soul-searching, tear-filled event, but the desire to run to the Scriptures and search out its obvious and less obvious treasures and nutrients should come from the happiness fostered from the relationship of holy love shared with the Father.

---

[109] C. H. Spurgeon, *The Metropolitan Tabernacle Pulpit Sermons*, vol. 25 (London: Passmore & Alabaster, 1879), 631.

Make the Bible the lens, filter, and guide for everything. It is the framework through which we relate to the entire creation, and it is from it—not philosophy, sociology, psychology, ecology, or anthropology—that we get our sense, calling, and theology of place. It must come from the Bible or it is not a thing at all.

The Bible is the objective truth by which all other ideas, worldviews, opinions, and philosophies can be measured to ascertain their validity. It is not the Bible that is on trial; you and your ideas are on trial. In the same way, if I went to see a masterpiece at the National Gallery, my opinion about the masterpiece means noting. I cannot judge it; it is already a masterpiece. It judges me.

So in response to all we have learned, look at your Bible again, this time look for place, look for placement, displacement, and re-placement. Now look for the King and his kingdom with his desire to dwell in the midst of his people. Look for God's holy love, glory, sovereignty, and narrative. See Jesus and his work at the center of it all.

Let what you read and study fuel your entire life in faith and practice, and once you have done that, do it all again.

Consider the words of the ultimate Apostle and Teacher, Jesus, regarding God's written Word, the Bible, in Matthew 5:18:

> For truly, I say to you, until heaven and earth pass away, not an iota, not a dot, will pass from the Law until all is accomplished.

Consider the words of the Apostle Paul regarding God's written Word, the Bible, in 2 Timothy 3:16–17:

> All Scripture is breathed out by God and profitable for teaching, for reproof, for correction, and for training in righteousness, that the man of God may be complete, equipped for every good work.

Consider the words of the Apostle Peter regarding God's written Word, the Bible, in 2 Peter 1:19–21:

> And we have the prophetic word more fully confirmed, to which you will do well to pay attention as to a lamp shining in a dark place, until the day dawns and the morning star rises in your hearts, knowing this first of all, that no prophecy of Scripture comes from someone's own interpretation. For no

*prophecy was ever produced by the will of man, but men spoke from God as they were carried along by the Holy Spirit.*

Consider the words of the Apostle John regarding God's written Word, the Bible, in 1 John 1:1–4:

> *That which was from the beginning, which we have heard, which we have seen with our eyes, which we looked upon and have touched with our hands, concerning the word of life—the life was made manifest, and we have seen it, and testify to it and proclaim to you the eternal life, which was with the Father and was made manifest to us—that which we have seen and heard we proclaim also to you, so that you too may have fellowship with us; and indeed our fellowship is with the Father and with his Son Jesus Christ. And we are writing these things so that our joy may be complete.*

What do these, the four most highly esteemed teachers the world has ever seen, teach us about the Bible, and how should the lesson they teach affect the way we study the Bible?

Jesus's statement that the word will not pass away until it is all fulfilled points us to the sureness and inability of the word to fail with regard to God's decrees recorded in it. God's promises and truth are a sure and firm foundation on which we can and should trust, to build a place to dwell in, on multiple levels.

Paul teaches us that the Bible's origin is divine; he uses the term God breathed. We learn from him that the Bible's ultimate author is God; this is commonly known as the doctrine of inspiration. If God wrote it and inspired the very words, that means it is unlike any other book and is full of inherent power because of the origin of the words.

Paul goes on to tell us how the word can be used practically. It can and should be used to train us up as God's place makers. It corrects us when we think or go in the wrong direction. The results of the reading, studying, and application of the Bible is that we will be ready, equipped, and fueled up for the good work God has for us to do.

Peter points us to the illumination of the Scriptures. The Bible is like a lamp in a dark place, it exposes the world for what it really is and is the shining light on the path to God's city. It is by the light of the Scriptures that we get to work, building places to the glory of God.

He also highlights the universality and completeness of Scripture. It is immature and dangerous to cut ourselves off from our elders in the faith and from the rich almost two-thousand-year history we have as the church when interpreting the Scriptures because the Bible is not so much a private self-help book as it is a public declaration of truth for all to see.

We can unify around the truth that the Bible so openly declares to all who will hear and to those who will persist in rebellion and stubborn treason against the King of the book.

Finally, Peter elaborates on Paul's point by saying explicitly that the Holy Spirit is the one who used men over the years to write the Scriptures, maintaining their own langue, nuances, and culture but all the while being used as willing vessels for God, to make his self-exposure and declarations of truth.

All that being said, we can have even more trust in the Bible as the very word of God, written by men who were inspired by Spirit (God, the Holy Spirit).

Last of all is John, who confirms the historicity of the Bible. It is not a book of fables and fictional stories. These are factual, eye-witness accounts that are part of a larger plan and narrative but all the while rooted in the firm ground of actual creation and redemption history in the places and people of the physical world.

He calls Jesus and, by extension, the words of Jesus the "Word of Life." The Bible is alive, God's word lives, it breathes and speaks NOW, today, into the lives of the living and calling the dead to life by the power of God, the Spirit.

He ends by reminding us the Word is not something to be kept privately but proclaimed publicly, and last of all, but by no means least, he centers the Word around the person who is at the center of human history, God's story and the theology of place, Jesus the Christ, the Son of the Living God, The Word of God.

Our study of, well, everything should spring from our study of God, which we do by studying his word, the Bible.

Make a plan to dig into the Scriptures today; this may just mean waking up an hour earlier than usual so you have time to read, reflect, and note what you learn each morning.

We close this section with the words of Hebrews 4:12:

> For the word of God is living and active, sharper than any two-edged sword, piercing to the division of soul and of spirit, of joints and of marrow, and discerning the thoughts and intentions of the heart.

# 3 . PRAY

*I*t is right that prayer comes after the Word because without it we would not know what to pray or even who to pray to.

Prayer came up before, and yes, it is here again, but in a different context. The fact it has come up again shows you just how important prayer is to our response as Christians.

The kingdom taking over every other kingdom in every other place, the whole battle of territory and allegiance, all hinges on the prayers and declarations of God's government on the earth, his people, his image bearers, his human council, and the church.

So pray about everything you have read and been challenged by or enlightened about in this book and ask God to help you make a full and faithful response to it.

Use prayer in every way possible to:

*Wage a good warfare* against the spiritual opponents who occupy the places of the earth that belong to God.

*Make request to God* in regard to expanding his kingdom in the earth through your place-making activities as a believer and those of the church.

*Commune with God*, the King, who wants to live with you and all his people.

Paul encourages us to take on the whole armor of God as we use prayer and the Word of God in our fight with the usurping spirits of the kingdom of darkness, which are struggling against the light of God's kingdom, but they cannot resist the light. Darkness, after all, is only the absence of light; the very presence of light means darkness cannot abide.

In your payers, be encouraged by the following Scriptures because Jesus, our King, has all authority and has given us the power of his name, otherwise known as the power of attorney (a person appointed to act for another in business or legal matters)

SACRED PLACES • APPLICATION

to speak on his behalf on the earth, just like God intended for Adam when he named God's creations on God's behalf.[110]

The following Scripture reminds us of the authority we have in Christ:

## The authority of Christ advocated by believers

*The light shines in the darkness, and the darkness has not overcome it. (John 1:5)*

*And Jesus came and said to them, "All authority in heaven and on earth has been given to me. (Matthew 28:18)*

*He is the image of the invisible God, the firstborn of all creation. For by him all things were created, in heaven and on earth, visible and invisible, whether thrones or dominions or rulers or authorities—all things were created through him and for him. And he is before all things, and in him all things hold together. And he is the head of the body, the church. He is the beginning, the firstborn from the dead, that in everything he might be preeminent. For in him all the fullness of God was pleased to dwell, and through him to reconcile to himself all things, whether on earth or in heaven, making peace by the blood of his cross. (Colossians 1:15–20)*

*… and what is the immeasurable greatness of his power toward us who believe, according to the working of his great might that he worked in Christ when he raised him from the dead and seated him at his right hand in the heavenly places, far above all rule and authority and power and dominion, and above every name that is named, not only in this age but also in the one to come. And he put all things under his feet and gave him as head over all things to the church, which is his body, the fullness of him who fills all in all. (Ephesians 1:19–23)*

*"Ask, and it will be given to you; seek, and you will find; knock, and it will be opened to you. For everyone who asks receives, and the one who seeks finds, and to the one who knocks it will be opened. Or which one of you, if his son asks him for bread, will give him a stone? Or if he asks for a fish, will give him a serpent? If you then, who are evil, know how to give good gifts to your*

---

[110] See Genesis 2:19.

*children, how much more will your Father who is in heaven give good things to those who ask him! (Matthew 7:7–11)*

*... so that through the church the manifold wisdom of God might now be made known to the rulers and authorities in the heavenly places. This was according to the eternal purpose that he has realized in Christ Jesus our Lord, in whom we have boldness and access with confidence through our faith in him. (Ephesians 3:10–12)*

*Finally, be strong in the Lord and in the strength of his might. Put on the whole armor of God, that you may be able to stand against the schemes of the devil. For we do not wrestle against flesh and blood, but against the rulers, against the authorities, against the cosmic powers over this present darkness, against the spiritual forces of evil in the heavenly places. Therefore take up the whole armor of God, that you may be able to withstand in the evil day, and having done all, to stand firm. Stand therefore, having fastened on the belt of truth, and having put on the breastplate of righteousness, and, as shoes for your feet, having put on the readiness given by the gospel of peace. In all circumstances take up the shield of faith, with which you can extinguish all the flaming darts of the evil one; and take the helmet of salvation, and the sword of the Spirit, which is the word of God, praying at all times in the Spirit, with all prayer and supplication. To that end keep alert with all perseverance, making supplication for all the saints. (Ephesians 6:10–18)*

Now with the power and perspective of these Scripture, pray with the authority of one of God's ambassadors in the earth for his kingdom and glory.

# 4 . WORK

ur response is not all in the spiritual or mental realm with worship, study, and prayer, all of that is essential and forms the roots of a fruitful life, but the tree and fruit are very much in the here and now.

There is work for us to do as the place makers God has called us to be, in answering the ecological and anthropological challenges.

As members of the body of Christ, we have work to do in God's house, to make it a place of safety, prayer, and the refuge of God where the displaced can come and find a home with us in Christ.

There are many ways that you can serve in your local church. Don't just be a Christian consumer, be a producer. How can you serve in the body of Christ as we are built up together into a place where God's presence comes to abide and where the lost can run to like a lighthouse in the dark?

We need to keep the ship running, keep the guns cleaned for the battle and the beds clean for the patients. So enlist, stop sitting on the sidelines as a constantly consuming critic or famished non-consuming critic, take your pick. You need to stop the impotent habit of pulling the church and God's people down. Drop your excuses, repent, and get in the game, fill your stomach, clean your gun, and get on the field, take ground for the kingdom and be the place maker, the place taker you have been called to be.

Paul encourages us not to compare ourselves to each other or force others to be like us or operate only in the gifts we affirm and like. He teaches clearly that as a body we have many members, and each can be used by God in different ways. This diversity and multifaceted nature of the church, when utilized and given the opportunity to flourish, will and has caused us to be a force to be reckoned with in the earth.

We can adapt to anything, we can answer anything, we are the church, the embassy of heaven on the earth, God's own government extending his kingdom by divine commission.

Paul mentions a few things about this specifically in 1 Corinthians 12:4–6, teaching us:

*Now there are varieties of gifts, but the same Spirit; and there are varieties of service, but the same Lord; and there are varieties of activities, but it is the same God who empowers them all in everyone.*

Paul goes on to expand this summary argument for the rest of the chapter by comparing various gifts and then comparing various body parts, and exposing the folly of saying we should all have the same gift or of exalting particular gifts while neglecting others. Take time to read the entire chapter slowly you will see what I mean.

It is also important to read chapter 13 because working without God's holy love means the work is pointless, lacking in impact and worth. What follows is some selective commentary from my notes on our daily Bible reading written for Worldwide Mission Fellowship © 2014. It focuses on 1 Corinthians 10–15.

## Use freedom to serve others

*"All things are lawful," but not all things are helpful. "All things are lawful," but not all things build up. Let no one seek his own good, but the good of his neighbor.*

—*1 Corinthians 10:23–24*

The Corinthians were very much concerned with their rights and their freedom to do what they wanted to do and what pleased them. Paul reverses this and explains to them and to us that the freedom and rights we have in Christ are not for our own benefit but so that we can become servants of all (Mark 9:35), purposefully building up fellow believers.

Paul bases this thinking on the teaching and example given to us by Jesus in His sacrificial suffering and death on the cross. Let us lay down our rights, freedom, and lives to serve and build others.

## Will this bring glory to God?

*So, whether you eat or drink, or whatever you do, do all to the glory of God.*

—*1 Corinthians 10:31*

Paul was dealing with a new question in the church about eating meat that had been used in pagan sacrifice, this seemed like a grey area to the Corinthians, which is why they asked the questions and contended over the issue.

Paul gives us a great test for assessing all the things we are not sure about. We can ask ourselves this question: Will this bring glory to God? We need to ensure that this is the overarching motivation in our hearts for everything that we do. We cannot compartmentalize our life so that a part of it brings glory to God and the rest is for our own pleasure—our entire life should bring glory to God.

## Will this lead to salvation?

> ... just as I try to please everyone in everything I do, not seeking my own advantage, but that of many, that they may be saved.
>
> —1 Corinthians 10:33

Another guiding principle for our thinking and behavior is the desire to see others saved.

## God created order for men and women

> But I want you to understand that the head of every man is Christ, the head of a wife is her husband, and the head of Christ is God.
>
> —1 Corinthians 11:3

This first half of 1 Corinthians 11 is a part of the New Testament that is the subject of much debate among biblical scholars. One thing we can certainly see in the issues dealt with before and after this section is that Paul is concerned with proper Christian conduct within the church.

The point Paul is driving home is that there is order, rank, and authority in God's created order and even in the relationship between the Father and the Son. This should be reflected in creation and most clearly in the church.

A pressing point for Paul was to address the Corinthians' tendency to allow male and female distinctions to become blurred (under the influence of the secular world around them at the time). We have the same issues in today's culture, which is trying to make sexuality and creation roles so androgynous, so as to lose the distinction altogether.

We must uphold the image of God within the church; men must dress and act as men and women as women, not in competition with each other but complementing one another.

# God's purpose in division

*... for there must be factions among you in order that those who are genuine among you may be recognized.*

*—1 Corinthians 11:19*

The divisions in the Corinthian church were sometimes along social lines and betrayed the message of the gospel, by giving preference to the rich. Paul summarizes this activity as unbiblical and points to the divisions as a tool that God would use to weed out the church and to distinguish between those who were genuine and those still governed by the flesh.

In church history, division in the church has given rise to the firmer definition of our doctrines, creed, and confessions, just like germs in a body give rise to antibodies, making the body stronger.

# Self-examination

*Let a person examine himself, then, and so eat of the bread and drink of the cup.*

*—1 Corinthians 11:28*

We are reminded of this at every Lord's Supper and must take the command seriously; we really need to examine our hearts toward God and our fellow believers, and if we have not been walking as we ought to, then we should refrain from taking the Lord's Supper until we have made things right. Self-examination should be a daily Christian discipline.

# A variety of gifts

*Now there are varieties of gifts, but the same Spirit; and there are varieties of service, but the same Lord; and there are varieties of activities, but it is the same God who empowers them all in everyone.*

*—1 Corinthians 12:4–6*

This is such a wonderful passage; God has given a diverse variety of gifts to the church through the members of the church. We do not all have the same gift; all our gifts and callings are different. Another amazing thing about this passage is that the entire Trinity is involved in the distribution of the varied gifts to the church. The Spirit, The Lord Jesus, and God the Father.

## Gifted to serve others

*To each is given the manifestation of the Spirit for the common good.*
*—1 Corinthians 12:7*

Our gifts are not for us but for the common good of our fellow believers. We are not supposed to use our gifts to build ourselves up or for our own advantage, but to lovingly serve the body of Christ.

## Not everyone gets the same gifts

*... to another the working of miracles, to another prophecy, to another the ability to distinguish between spirits, to another various kinds of tongues, to another the interpretation of tongues.*
*—1 Corinthians 12:10*

Tongues, and the interpretation of tongues, is a gift of the Spirit given to some rather than to all believers.

Some today say that a believer does not have the Holy Spirit unless they speak in tongues, but this is a mistake, as speaking in tongues is one of the list of possible gifts given to individuals, alongside prophecy, healing, words of wisdom, etc.

As the final verse states, we cannot decide or dictate which gifts we are given, the Holy Spirit apportions to each person individually, according to His own will.

## Build others up

*Now I want you all to speak in tongues, but even more to prophesy. The one who prophesies is greater than the one who speaks in tongues, unless someone interprets, so that the church may be built up.*
*—1 Corinthians 14:5*

Paul's main point in this section is to encourage the Corinthians who were fond of using the gift of tongues (the miraculous ability to speak unlearned human and angelic languages), to see the greater worth in prophesying (bringing a message from God under the direction of the Holy Spirit to the body of believers that is intelligible), as this builds up the body, which is one of his main points in the letter as a whole.

For the immature believer it seemed that the gift of tongues was one of the things leading to pride and a false sense of maturity. We should use our gifts to build up our fellow believers. Prophesying provides insight, warning, correction, and encouragement ... tongues will do this too, only with interpretation.

## Guidelines for public ministry

*Nevertheless, in church I would rather speak five words with my mind in order to instruct others, than ten thousand words in a tongue. Brothers, do not be children in your thinking. Be infants in evil, but in your thinking be mature.*
—*1 Corinthians 14:19–20*

Paul made clear that he spoke in tongues more than everyone in the Corinthian church, but it seems he did this speaking in tongues "more than them all" in private.

Paul makes his point even clearer by saying that he would rather speak just five words that were intelligible while in the public assembly of the church, than ten thousand words in tongues that are not intelligible (without interpretation). So the point is made again that we should seek to build one another up; this should be the motivation behind the pursuit of and use of the gifts in the church.

God made our minds, not the devil. God wants our minds to be engaged and used for Him and His glory. In light of this, Paul calls the church to clear and mature thinking. As Christians, we need to engage in the discipline of thinking, meditating on God's Word and using our God-given intellectual faculties to build up and encourage one another in the Lord.

## Harmony, peace, and order

*For God is not a God of confusion but of peace. As in all the churches of the saints ...*
—*1 Corinthians 14:33*

This is the main point for Paul; he was dealing with a very unruly church in Corinth where there was a lack of order in the service, with tongues and prophecies being said over each other, which resulted in no one benefiting, as everyone tried to say their piece. James 3:16–17 paints a picture of the problems in the church at Corinth.

Instead of this, our worship should reflect the nature of our God. Mayhem and confusion are not characteristics of God (but these were the traits of the false gods).

God is not the author or cause of confusion in the church, the charge for this lies at our own feet, so we must abandon all self-centered behavior.

God desires harmony, peace, and order in His church, for the mutual benefit of its members and for His glory, so let us reflect Him in our worship.

## We don't need questions to prophesy

> ... the women should keep silent in the churches. For they are not permitted to speak, but should be in submission, as the Law also says. If there is anything they desire to learn, let them ask their husbands at home. For it is shameful for a woman to speak in church.
>
> —1 Corinthians 14:34–35

Understanding the background to the problems in the church at Corinth will help us to put these statements from Paul into their proper context. In the Greek tradition, prophecy like the ones coming from the Oracle at Delphi, required questions being asked to prompt the prophetic utterance. It is likely that some married Corinthian women in the church, who were likely prophetesses themselves and involved in the weighing of prophesies, were influenced by their surrounding culture and asked questions as part of the service.

Paul wanted to make the point that unlike the Oracle at Delphi and other forms of prophecy from the ancient world, prophecy in the church did not require priming questions; instead it was completely dependent on the inspiration and direction of the Holy Spirit. Paul addresses these women in this context, suggesting that they ask questions at home and not to disrupt the service, therefore the theme of order within the service remains.

## First importance, the gospel

> For I delivered to you as of first importance what I also received: that Christ died for our sins in accordance with the Scriptures, that he was buried, that he was raised on the third day in accordance with the Scriptures ...
>
> —1 Corinthians 15:3–4

Paul made it clear that the thing of first or greatest importance is the gospel message, which he summarizes here.

# Evangelism

One work we all need to do in some way is evangelism.

C. H. Spurgeon put it like this:

> *It is a very material point in salvation to be saved from hardness of heart and carelessness about others. Do you want to go to Heaven alone? I fear you will never go there. Have you no wish for others to be saved? Then you are not saved yourself. Be sure of that.*[111]

This is the personal work of evangelism, of spreading the good news of the kingdom and all that Jesus has actually done to defeat the enemy and save us. Tell someone today.

A great resource to help teach you a biblical way to share the gospel is *The Way of the Master* by Ray Comfort and Kirk Cameron from Living Waters.

Worldwide Mission Fellowship also has its own resource to help you in the personal work of evangelism in media form called "The Gospel, what is it and how does it affect you."

These and other links are listed in the suggested reading section.

Finally, Jesus encourages us to work while it is day in John 9:4:

> *We must work the works of him who sent me while it is day; night is coming, when no one can work.*

So work today. Be the place maker God has called you to be.

---

[111] C. H. Spurgeon, *The Metropolitan Tabernacle Pulpit Sermons*, vol. 34 (London: Passmore & Alabaster, 1888), 222.

# 5. SOJOURNER LIVING

*S*o far we have looked at our response in terms of our affections and feelings in the section on worship, our minds and will in the section on study, spiritually in the section on prayer, and practically or physically in the last section on work.

This final section, which brings the book to an end, looks at life, our lives, and how we live them in light of the theology of place.

One of the first things we need to grapple with is the Bible's description of believers as pilgrims, exiles, sojourners, and strangers in the earth. That seems to drive against the grain of the theology of place; let's see what the Scripture actually says in Hebrews 11:13–16 (emphasis and expansion of the term exiles added)

> *These all died in faith, not having received the things promised, but having seen them and greeted them from afar, and having acknowledged that they were* **strangers and exiles (pilgrims, sojourners, foreigners)** *on the earth. For people who speak thus make it clear that they are seeking a homeland. If they had been thinking of that land from which they had gone out, they would have had opportunity to return. But as it is, they desire a better country, that is, a heavenly one. Therefore God is not ashamed to be called their God, for he has prepared for them a city.*

This is not against the theology of place; in fact, it upholds it. This is why this final section in our last chapter on the believer's response is called "sojourner living."

Like the saints of old spoken about in Hebrews 11, we live in this life as exiles or pilgrims—and, in a way, strangers—to this world. But what does this mean? Let's have a quick word study of both terms to help us understand and apply this.

## Quick word study: strangers

The word used for *stranger* is *xenos*. As an adjective, this word means strange or foreign as it denotes the one with the properties of that adjective as either strangers or aliens.[112]

---

[112] H. Bietenhard, "Ξένος," ed. Lothar Coenen, Erich Beyreuther, and Hans Bietenhard, *New International Dictionary of New Testament Theology* (Grand Rapids, MI: Zondervan Publishing House, 1986), 686.

The Bible sense lexicon describes the functional use of the word in this case as a person who "comes from a foreign country who does not owe allegiance to your country; frequently of someone who does not speak one's native tongue."[113]

## Quick word study: exile

The word used for *exile* is *parepidēmos*, which as an adjective means staying for a while in a strange place; as a noun, it speaks of the one who does this, which can be translated as a stranger, resident alien, exile, or sojourner.[114]

The Bible sense lexicon describes the functional use of the word in this context as "a person who comes from a foreign country into a city or land to reside there with the natives temporarily."[115]

With the help of our word definitions and with the wider context in which we find these words in the passage and the Bible as a whole narrative, we can describe ourselves in context to place as the following:

> *We are a particular and peculiar people, the called out ones who are by the King's choice and adoption, sons of a better place, living in this place as ambassadors and heirs of the place our King has prepared for us and by his decree sent us out from as his messengers in this place, which itself will one day be the better place we long for. (C. J. Scott, 2016)*

The earth is the Lord's, so in a sense, we are sojourners because the land belongs to him, not us, as he tells the children of Israel in Leviticus 25:23:

> *"The land shall not be sold in perpetuity, for the land is mine. For you are strangers and sojourners with me."*

Jesus also taught us that we are sojourners in this world. When speaking to his disciples, he said in John 15:19:

> *If you were of the world, the world would love you as its own; but because you are not of the world, but I chose you out of the world, therefore the world hates you.*

---

[113] Faithlife Corporation, Logos Bible Software Bible Sense Lexicon, 2016.

[114] H. Bietenhard, "Παρεπίδημος," ed. Lothar Coenen, Erich Beyreuther, and Hans Bietenhard, *New International Dictionary of New Testament Theology* (Grand Rapids, MI: Zondervan Publishing House, 1986), 690.

[115] Faithlife Corporation, Logos Bible Software Bible Sense Lexicon, 2016.

Later in his prayer to the Father for believers before his crucifixion, he prayed the following in John 17:14–16:

> *I have given them your word, and the world has hated them because they are not of the world, just as I am not of the world. I do not ask that you take them out of the world, but that you keep them from the evil one. They are not of the world, just as I am not of the world.*

With our identity established as citizens of God's kingdom over and above any mortal kingdom or state we find ourselves in, how should we then live as sojourners on the earth?

The Apostle Peter sums it up best in 1 Peter 2:11:

> *Beloved, I urge you as sojourners and exiles to abstain from the passions of the flesh, which wage war against your soul.*

The passions of the flesh point to the desires we have in this life that lead us into temptation and result in sin, decay, and death.

So we are called to live holy lives in this life; that is what it means to live as a sojourner. Remember holy or sacred just means to be set apart, and we are the called-out, collected, and connected people, the church.

We live our lives "Coram Deo," which means before the face of God. If this is true, and if his Spirit lives inside us, tabernacle-ing with us, and he sees and knows everything we do and is omnipresent, then we need to live accordingly.

The Scriptures admonish and encourage us to live holy lives. There are so many Scriptures that speak to us about the way we should live holy lives here on earth as sojourners. These include but are not limited to:

## Paul's Teaching

Romans 8:13; 12:1, 19; 13:14; 1 Corinthians 10:14; Galatians 5:16–17, 24; Ephesians 2:19; Philippians 3:3; Colossians 4:5–6; Titus 2:11–14

## James's Teaching

James 4:1

## Peter's Teaching

1 Peter 1:17–18; 4:2, 12; 2 Peter 3:14, 17

## Citizens of heaven

If we are sojourners of one place, then we cannot be sojourners in another place at the same time. With the better place, heaven in all its forms, we are citizens, while we are sojourners in the world. If not, our citizenship is the other way around. Consider Paul's words in Ephesians 2:19:

> So then you are no longer strangers and aliens, but you are fellow citizens with the saints and members of the household of God ...

If we are citizens of heaven, then our lives in this world should not be about storing up riches and prosperity in this place. This is why the prosperity gospel, which has been incubated and grown into popular theology through the so-called Word of Faith movement, is so wrong and dangerous.

The prosperity gospel inverts the theology of place and makes it all about riches and prosperity itself, as if our citizenship was here, as though we are not aliens and strangers in this world.

The prosperity gospel is wrong. We should live lives of contentment and soberness, not of materialism, drunk with the wine of ambition and sensual pleasures.

John Piper calls this (contentment and soberness) wartime living, and I like that term. We live like we are at war because we are, not as if we are already in heaven, because we are not. We long for it and will go to the prepared place, but while we are here, we must live as sojourners, ambassadors of the King and his kingdom, advancing his kingdom not in the ways of the kingdom of darkness but in the ways of his kingdom, which are righteous, peace, and joy in the Holy Ghost. See Romans 14:17.

So how should we live? Paul gives a great example 2 Corinthians 12:15 that also serves as a blast against the warped position of the prosperity gospel:

> I will most gladly spend and be spent for your souls. If I love you more, am I to be loved less?

Even for those of us who are not fooled by the folly of the prosperity gospel can be helped in our focus as we live out our lives as disciples of Jesus Christ by remembering that this world's system really is passing away, giving way to God's kingdom, as Paul mentions in 1 Corinthians 7:31:

*… and those who deal with the world as though they had no dealings with it.*
*For the present form of this world is passing away.*

We may not be fooled by the prosperity gospel and may be aware that the things of this world are passing away so are not easily trapped or shackled by them. But even we need to remember that the very use of our time is important. How are you using your time? Are you pursuing a sojourner's life with a wartime mentality? Again, Paul encourages us in Ephesians 5:16 to make "the best use of the time, because the days are evil."

For all of us, we should turn our hearts toward the King's return with joy and expectation, not fear and doubt. This will help the trajectory of our lives run toward God's glory and fame, while we spread as his place makers in the earth. We agree with the call at the end of Revelation 22:20: "He who testifies to these things says, 'Surely I am coming soon.' Amen. Come, Lord Jesus!"

## Counter culture

A major part of sojourner living is living counterculturally, making a difference in the world in which we live. The following is taken from the final part of the Total Truth course I wrote for Worldwide Mission Fellowship.

As Christians, we have the truth; the nature of the truth is total, affecting all of life. In light of this, how do we live in this world? Do we ride along with the cultural tide, the spirit of the age, keeping in step with conventional wisdom, the status quo, acceptable relativistic political correctness and cultural indifference? God forbid. We are called to live as *witnesses to the truth* just like Jesus. We are called to live countercultural lives.

**Poverty:** There is poverty across the earth today. It is the clear call of God's people throughout Scripture to minister to the needs of the poor. The truth of Scripture points us to a reason for poverty and an answer to poverty.

**Abortion:** The biblical revelation of truth, of reality as it really is, sees humans as creatures, designed in God's own image and endowed with worth, purpose, and dignity. Abortion is another name for murder; infanticide (the killing of babies) should never be condoned, whether inside or outside the womb. We must respond in love.

**Orphans and Widows:** Naturalism would see orphans and widows as a burden to society and the progress of humankind. Our stand as Christians is contrary to the culture. God is Father to the fatherless and Husband to the widows. As God's people, we are called to minister to and provide for the least of these.

**Sex Slavery:** This is a very inconvenient truth; it is not the sort of thing we like to think about in our sophisticated, detached, and relatively comfortable lives, but we are called to face this evil and answer it decisively and practically as God's representatives. These precious girls, women, and even boys need our help in Jesus's name.

**Marriage:** This has been under attack in various ways. Most recently the challenge of the LGBT sexual revolution and the so-called redefinition of marriage needs to be answered by the true church of Jesus Christ. We need to address other attacks on marriage, including divorce, the avoidance of commitment, the downplaying of its importance, etc.

**Sexual Morality:** Our culture has become highly sexualized; this is related to the last two points. Pornography, adultery, sex outside of marriage, homosexuality, and pedophilia all need to be addressed with the liberating truth of God and his Word. God's good plan for sex, men, and women must be recovered.

**Ethnicity:** We have recently seen the issue of racism coming to the surface in America and even here in the UK. The other worldviews are woefully inadequate for dealing with racism and, in fact, often give rise to it. The Bible's view of humankind and people groups is the only answer to heal the divisions fostered by the devil's lies today.

**Religious Liberty:** The Bible upholds the religious liberty of all peoples, even those who do not believe as we do have the right to practice their beliefs in freedom and safety. Across the Islamic and Communist worlds in particular, Christians are persecuted and killed for their faith. We are called to advocate for the church and address this injustice. In the West they want to shut us and our faith in the upper room with God, excluding us from the public lower room, but we will not be silent. It is for freedom that Christ set us free.

**Unreached People Groups:** The gospel is true, total, and ultimate truth, it is the means, the only means by which humanity can be saved in a full sense. The end of the story when all the earth is filled with the knowledge of the glory of the Lord (Hab. 2:14) cannot come until the gospel is heard by every people group, so we need to press forward in the missionary, disciple making, church planting work of the church until Jesus, the King, returns.

These nine countercultural areas are based on the chapters of David Platt's book called *Counter Culture*. He also has a website which can be found at <u>counterculturebook.com/get-involved</u> which contains a directory to help you reach out for each area including sex trafficking, poverty, and unreached people groups.

## The victory now and then

Finally, in closing I want to encourage us that the kingdom is advancing all the time and will soon be here in fullness. The kingdom truly is now and not yet. When it comes in fullness, we will see the union of heaven and earth through the New Jerusalem, the ultimate place, here on earth.

> *Beloved, I am writing you no new commandment, but an old commandment that you had from the beginning. The old commandment is the word that you have heard. At the same time, it is a new commandment that I am writing to you, which is true in him and in you, because the darkness is passing away and the true light is already shining. (1 John 2:7–8)*

The true light of God's kingdom is already shining, so let's cry out for revival as we seek to spread God's kingdom as his place makers, carrying his presence and decreeing his word and gospel to the glory and fame of his name.

## Praise be to our God and King

> *Then the seventh angel blew his trumpet, and there were loud voices in heaven, saying, "The kingdom of the world has become the kingdom of our Lord and of his Christ, and he shall reign forever and ever." (Revelation 11:15)*

We pray that this day will come quickly for God' glory and pleasure and our eternal joy with our King, in his presence, in that place he has prepared for us.

The city of God our King, the New Jerusalem, heaven on earth. The ultimate place!

And at the end of it all is the King in all his glory, in the sacred place.

> *When all things are subjected to him, then the Son himself will also be subjected to him who put all things in subjection under him, that God may be all in all.*
> —*1 Corinthians 15:28*

# SECTION 7

## STUDY

# REFERENCES AND SOURCES

*... they received the word with all eagerness, examining the Scriptures daily to see if these things were so.*

*—Acts 17:11*

B e like the Bereans and take this study further to see for yourself if it's true.

This section includes some suggested additional reading, a number of appendixes that you may find useful, and a bibliography of references and source materials. I hope you find it useful in your own study and practice.

C. J. Scott, 2016

## God's incommunicable attributes

**1. Infinitude**—Psalm 147:5, Job 11:7
God has no limits (cannot be measured).

**2. Unity**—Deuteronomy 6:4, John 17:3
God is one in number and nature.

**3. Spirituality**—Exodus 33:20, John 4:24
God is an invisible Spirit. Personal, living, self-conscious, and self-determining.

**4. Independence**—Exodus 3:14, John 5:26
God is self-existent, self-reliant, and self-sustaining.

**5. Immutability**—Malachi 3:6, James 1:17
God does not change; he is constant and faithful.

**6. Eternal**—Deuteronomy 33:27, 1 Timothy 1:17
God had no beginning (aseity). He is timeless and transcendent over time.

**7. Omnipresence**—Jeremiah 23:23–24, Psalm 139:6–12
God is everywhere, ever present, transcendent over space.

**8. Incomprehensibility**—Romans 11:33, 1 Corinthians 13:12
God is beyond full human comprehension.

**9. Transcendent**—Isaiah 55:8–9, 1 Timothy 6:16

God is above all, in quality of (uncreated) being and ways.

# God's communicable attributes

## Intellectual Attributes

**1. Omniscience**—Psalm 139:1–5, 1 John 3:20

God knows everything, now!

**2. Wisdom**—Psalm 104:24, 1 Corinthians 1:24

God uses His knowledge in the best possible way.

**3. Veracity**—2 Timothy 2:13, 1 John 1:5

God is truthful and faithful.

## Moral attributes

**4. Goodness**—Psalm 119:68, Psalm 34:8

God is kindhearted, gracious, good-natured, and benevolent in intention (A. W. Tozer, 2003).

**5. Love**—1 John 4:7–21, John 17:24

God's desire and concern for personal relationship in Himself and with His creatures.

**6. Holiness**—Leviticus 11:44–45, 1 Peter 1:14–15

God's moral purity and excellence.

## Volitional (choice or will) attributes

**7. Sovereignty**—Ephesians 1:11, 1 Timothy 6:15

God's total authority over all He has made.

**8. Omnipotent**—Genesis 18:14, Revelation 4:8

God is almighty or all powerful.

**9. Beauty**—Zechariah 9:17, Revelation 21:23

The sum of God's attributes and glory.

# APPENDIX B: A PREPARED PLACE FOR A PREPARED PEOPLE BY CHARLES SPURGEON

*"I go to prepare a place for you."*—*John 14:2.*

*"Giving thanks unto the Father, which hath made us meet to be partakers of the inheritance of the saints in light."*—*Colossians 1:12.*

Y real text is not in the Bible; it is one of those Christian proverbs, which are not inspired in words, but the spirit of which is inspired, "Heaven is a prepared place for a prepared people." You have often heard that sentence; it is familiar in your mouths as household words, and well it may be.

Yet I shall have two texts from the Scriptures; the first will be our Saviour's words to his disciples, "I go to prepare a place for you," from which we learn that "Heaven is a prepared place;" and the second will be Paul's words to the Colossians, "Giving thanks unto the Father, which hath made us meet to be partakers of the inheritance of the saints in light," from which we learn that there is a prepared people, a people made meet to be partakers of the inheritance which Christ has gone to prepare for them.

I. I am not going to have any further preface, but I will begin at once to speak upon THE PREPARATION OR HEAVEN: "I go to prepare a place for you."

It is many months since I began to turn this sentence over; I think I might truly say that, for several years, I have thought of it, and thought of it again, and thought of it

[272]

yet again,—that our Lord Jesus Christ, before returning to heaven, should say to his disciples, "I go to prepare a place for you." Is there any difficulty about this passage? Yes, it is very difficult to explain; indeed, I do not think that we really can know here all that Christ meant when he uttered these words. A father said to his children, when the summer sun had waxed hot, "I shall go to the seaside to-day, to prepare a place for you." His little child asked, "What does father mean when he says that he will prepare a place for us?" And his mother answered, "My child, I cannot tell you all that your father means, but you will see when you get there; and, now, it must be enough for you that, although you do not know what father will have to do at the seaside in preparing a place for you, he knows what he is going to do." And, dear friends, there is this consolation for us that, even if we can hardly guess what it is that Christ can find to do to prepare heaven for us, he knows what is wanted, and he knows how to do it; and that is infinitely better than our knowing, because, even if we knew what was needed, we could not do it. But, with Christ, to know and to do are two things that run parallel.

He knows that there are certain preparations to be made, he knows what those preparations must be, and he is equal to the task of making them; he has not gone upon an errand which he cannot fulfil; and when we get to heaven, we shall know— perhaps it may take us a long while to find it all out,—but we shall know and discover throughout eternity what he meant when he said, "I go to prepare a place for you."

I do not profess to be able to explain our Lord's words, but I am going simply to make a few remarks upon them; and, first, I ask you to notice that *heaven is already prepared for Christ's people.* Christ has told us that, when he comes in his glory, he will say to those on his right hand, "Come, ye blessed of my Father, inherit the kingdom prepared for you from the foundation of the world." So, there is an inheritance which the Father has already prepared for the people whom he gave to his Son, and this inheritance is reserved for them. But if it was prepared from the foundation of the world, how can it be said to be prepared by Christ? The explanation probably is, that it was prepared in the eternal purpose of the Father,—prepared by wise forethought,—arranged for,— predestinated,—prepared in that sense,—it was provided, in the eternal arrangements of Jehovah, that there should be a suitable place for his people to dwell in for ever. He made the pavilion of the sun, and he gave the stars their appointed positions; would he forget to prepare a place for his people? He gave to angels their places, and even to fallen spirits he has appointed a prison-house; so he would not forget, when he was arranging the entire universe, that a place would be needed for the twice-born, the heirs of grace, the members of the mystical body of Christ Jesus, his brethren who were to be made like unto him. Therefore, in purpose, and plan, and decree, long ere God had laid the foundations of this poor world, and the morning stars had sung

[273]

together over creation's six days' work accomplished, he had prepared a place for his people; it was not actually prepared, but it was in the purpose and plan of the eternal mind, and therefore might be regarded as already done.

Our Lord Jesus Christ has gone to heaven, he says, that he may prepare a place for his servants, and we may be helped to form some idea of what he means by this expression if we just think a little about it. And, first, I am sure *that must be a very great and glorious place which needs Christ to prepare it*. If we do not know all that he means, we can get at least this much out of his declaration. He spake this world into being. It was not; but he said, "Be," and it was at once made. Then he spake it into order, into light, into life, into beauty. He had but to speak, and what he willed was done. But now that he is preparing a place for his people, he has gone to heaven on purpose to do it. He used to stand still here on earth, and work miracles; but this was a miracle that he could not perform while he was here. He had to go back to his home above in order to prepare a place for his people. What sort of place, then, must it be that needs Christ himself to prepare it? He might have said, "Angels, garnish a mansion for my beloved." He might have spoken to the firstborn sons of light, and said, "Pile a temple of jewels for my chosen." But, no, he leaves not the work to them; but he says, "I go to prepare a place for you."

Brethren, *he will do it well, for he knows all about us*. He knows what will give us the most happiness,—and what will best develop all our spiritual faculties for ever. He loves us, too, so well that, as the preparing is left to him, I know that he will prepare us nothing second-rate, nothing that could possibly be excelled. We shall have the best of the best, and much of it; we shall have all that even his great heart can give us. Nothing will be stinted; for, as he is preparing it, it will be a right royal and divine preparation. If, when the prodigal came back to his father, there was the preparation of the fatted calf, and the music and dancing, and the gold ring and the best robe, what will be the preparation when we do not come home as prodigals, but as the bride prepared for her husband, or as the beloved children, without spot, or wrinkle, or any such thing, coming home to the Father who shall see his own image in us, and rejoice over us with singing? It is a grand place that Christ prepares, I wot, for never was there another such a lordly host as he is. It is a mansion of delights, I ween, that he prepares, for never was there another architect with thought so magnificent as his, and never were other hands so skilled at quarrying living stones, and putting them one upon another, as his hands have ever been. This thought ought to cheer us much; it must be something very wonderful that Christ prepares as a fit place for his people.

And methinks I may add to this, that *it must be something very sweet when it is prepared*. If you go to a friend's house, and just fall in with the ordinary proceedings of the family, you are very comfortable, and you are glad not to disarrange anything; but if, when you arrive, you see that everything has been done on an extra scale to prepare for your coming, you feel still more grateful. It has often happened to an honoured guest that he could not help observing that he was not being treated as his friends lived every day of the week, and all the year round. That guest-chamber had evidently been newly furnished, and everything that was possible had been thought of to do him honour. If you were treated thus as a guest, there was pleasure for you in the fact that so much had been prepared for you. Did your husband ever take you to a new house, and point out to you how he had purchased everything that he thought would please you? Had that little room been furnished specially for you, and did he anticipate your tastes, provide this little thing and that that he knew you would like? Well, it was not merely that you enjoyed the things themselves, but they all seemed to you so much sweeter because they had been prepared for you by your beloved. And when you get to heaven, you will be astonished to see this and that and the other joy, that was prepared for you, because Christ thought of you, and provided just what you would most appreciate. You will be no stranger there, beloved; you will say, "There has been here a hand that helped me when I was in distress; there has been here, I know, an eye that saw me when I was wandering far from God; there has been, in this place, a heart that cared for me,—that selfsame heart that loved me, and that bled for me down below upon the cross. It is my Saviour who has prepared this place for me."

I do not know whether I can convey to you all my thoughts upon this theme, but it does seem to me so pleasant to think that we are going to a place where we shall not be the first travellers through the country; but where *a Pioneer has gone before us*,—the best of pioneers, who went before us with this one object in his mind, that he might get all ready, and prepare the place for us. Methinks, brethren, that those who will be there before us will say, when we arrive there, "We are glad you have come, for everything has been prepared for you." It would be an eternal sorrow in heaven if the saints should miss their way, and perish, as some croakingly tell us; for, then, what about the preparations for their reception? They would all have been made in vain;—harps prepared, which no fingers would ever play, and crowns which no heads would ever wear. I do not believe it; I have never dreamed that such a thing could happen. I feel certain that he, who prepared the place for the people, will prepare the people for the place; and that, if he gets all ready for them, he means to bring them home that they may enjoy the things which he hath laid up for them that love him.

I know that I am not explaining the preparation of heaven, yet I hope I am drawing some comfortable thoughts out of the subject. If Christ is preparing heaven, then it will be what our Scotch friends call "a bonny place;" and if it be prepared for us, when we get there, it will exactly fit us, it will be the very heaven we wanted,—a better heaven than we ever dreamed of,—a better heaven than we ever pictured even when our imagination took its loftiest flights,—the heaven of God, and yet a heaven exactly suited to such happy creatures as we then shall be.

Now, however, let us try to come a little closer to the subject, and attempt to explain our Lord's words. Jesus Christ has gone to prepare a place for his people; does not this refer, if we keep it to its strict meaning, to *the ultimate place of God's people*? You see, Christ mentions a place, not a state; and he speaks of going to it, and coming back from it: "I go to prepare a place for you. And if I go and prepare a place for you, I will come again, and receive you unto myself." Christ is speaking of himself in his full manhood, without any figurative meaning to his words. He meant that he was going, with all his human nature on him, away from this world; and that he was going to prepare a place for us, intending to come again, with all that glorified human nature about him, to receive us unto himself. This does not mean his spiritual coming in death; nor any kind of spiritual coming, as to its first meaning, at any rate. I am persuaded that the clear run of the words involves our Lord's coming, in his second advent, when he will come to receive, not you or me as individuals who, one by one, will enter into rest, but to receive his whole Church into the place which he shall then have prepared for her. After the resurrection, you must remember, we shall need a place to live in,—a literal, material place of abode, for this body of ours will be alive as well as our spirit, and it will need a world to live in, a new heaven and a new earth.

I am not going to enter into any speculations about the matter, but it seems to me clear enough, in this text, that Christ is preparing a place somewhere—not for disembodied spirits, for they are already before the throne of God perfectly blest,—but for the entire manhood of his people, when spirit, soul, and body shall be again united, and the complete man shall receive the adoption, to wit, the redemption of the body, and the whole manhood of every believer shall be perfected in the glory of Christ. I do not know what better world, in many respects, there could be than this, so far as material nature is concerned; it is so full of the beauty and loveliness that God pours upon it on every side; it is a wonderful world,—

> "Where every prospect pleases,
> And only man is vile;"—

but I could not reconcile myself to the idea that this world would be heaven. No; my thoughts rise far above the loftiest hills, the most flowery meads, the rolling ocean, and the flowing rivers. Earth has not space enough to be our heaven. She has too narrow a bound, and she is too coarse a thing, bright gem though she is, for perfected manhood to possess throughout eternity. It will do well enough for the thousand years of glory, if it shall literally be that we shall reign with Christ upon it during the millennial age; but it is a drossy thing, and if it ever is to be the scene of the new heavens and the new earth, it must first pass through the fire. The very smell of sin is upon it; and God will not use this globe as a vessel unto honour until he has purified it with fire as once he did with water; and then, mayhap, it may serve for this higher purpose; but I scarcely think it will. Even now, Jesus is preparing, and has gone away on purpose to prepare, a place for us; and he will come again, "with the voice of the archangel, and with the trump of God," and he will catch his people away, and will bear them to the eternal home where their felicity shall know no end. That is what I suppose to be the meaning of our Lord's words.

"But," perhaps you say to me, "what do you mean by what you have been saying?" I reply,—I do not know to the full; I can but dimly guess at the meaning of what my Lord has said,—that he is doing something so glorious for all his people that, perhaps, if I did know it, I might not be allowed to tell you; for there are some things which, when a man knows them, it is not lawful for him to utter. Did not Paul see a great deal when he was caught up into Paradise? Yet he has told us very little about it; for there was a finger laid upon his lip, that bade him know it for himself, but not to tell it to others. "Eye hath not seen, nor ear heard, neither have entered into the heart of man, the things which God hath prepared for them that love him;" and though he has "revealed them unto us by his Spirit," even the Spirit who searcheth the deep things of God, yet is it not possible for us to tell all that has been revealed to us.

It strikes me that there is some little light to be obtained concerning this preparation of heaven by Christ, if I leave the direct and literal meaning of the words, and think of the future state as a whole rather than in detail. Do you not think, dear friends, that *our Lord Jesus Christ prepares heaven for his people by going there?* I mean this. Supposing you were to be lifted up to a state which was looked upon as heavenly, but that Jesus was not there, it would be no heaven to you. But wherever I may go, when I do go, if Jesus is already there, I do not care where it is. Wherever he is, shall be my heaven; for, as I said in the reading, that is our very first and last thought about heaven, to be with Christ where he is. To be with Christ is far better than to be anywhere else. Well, then, the first thing that Christ had to do, in order to prepare heaven for his people, was to go to heaven, for that made it heaven. Then were heaven's lamps kindled; then did heaven's heralds ring out their supernal melodies; then did the whole of the New Jerusalem seem to be ablaze with a glory brighter than the sun, for "the Lamb is the light thereof." When he comes there, then all is bliss. Do you not see, beloved, that he has prepared heaven by going there? His being there will make it heaven for you, so you need not begin asking what else there will be in heaven. There will be all manner of rare delights to spiritual men, but the chief of them all will be that Jesus is there. As Rowland Hill used to sing, so may you and I comfort ourselves with this thought,—

> *"And this I do find,—we two are so joined—*
> *He'll not be in glory, and leave me behind."*

If I may but be where he is, that shall be heaven to me.

But another reflection is this,—that *our Lord Jesus Christ has prepared heaven for his people by the merit of his atonement.* Thus hath he opened the kingdom of heaven to all believers. He rent the veil, and made a way into the holiest of all for all who trust him; but, in addition to that, he perfumed heaven with the fragrance of his sacrifice. If heaven be the place of the Godhead, as we know it is, we could not have stood there without the Mediator. If heaven be the throne of the great King, we could not have stood there without the cloud of perfumed incense from Christ's meritorious death and righteousness ever rising up before that throne. But, now, heaven is a safe place for the saints to enter. Now may they tread that sea of glass, like as of fire; and know that it is glass, and that no fire from it will consume them. Now will they be able to come up near to God, and not be afraid. I quote again a passage that often leaps to my lips,—a text of Scripture which is often shamefully misused: "Who among us shall dwell with the devouring fire? who among us shall dwell with everlasting burnings?" Why, none of us could so dwell unless Christ had changed us by his grace; but now we may do so. What is the Scriptural answer to those questions, "Who among us shall dwell with the devouring fire? who among us shall dwell with everlasting burnings?" What saith the Scripture? Listen: "He that walketh righteously, and speaketh uprightly; he that despiseth the gain of oppressions, that shaketh his hands from holding of bribes, that stoppeth his ears from hearing of blood, and shutteth his eyes from seeing evil; he shall dwell on high: his place of defence shall be the munitions of rocks: bread shall be given him; his waters shall be sure. Thine eyes shall see the King in his beauty: they shall behold the land that is very far off." This is the man who shall dwell there. With God, who is a consuming fire, we, like the holy children in the burning, fiery furnace, shall find it safe to dwell, and find it bliss to dwell, because Christ is there. But there would have been no heaven, in the presence of God, for any man that lives, after sin had once come into the world, if Jesus had not gone there as the high priest of old went up to the blazing throne whereon the shekinah shone, and sprinkled it with blood out of the basin, and then waved the censer to and fro till the thick smoke hid the cherubim, and, for a while resting, spake with God. Even so, has Christ gone within the veil, and sprinkled his own atoning blood upon his Father's throne, and then waved aloft the censer full of the incense of his mercy; and now it is safe for us to have access with boldness to the throne of glory as well as to the throne of grace. Thus hath he prepared a place for us.

Another meaning, I think, is allowable, namely, that *Christ has prepared heaven for us by appearing there in his glory*. I said that his very presence made heaven, but now I add that his glory there makes heaven yet more glorious. How does Christ describe the heavenly state? "Father, I will that they also, whom thou hast given me, be with me where I am; that they may behold my glory." It will be their bliss, then, to see his glory; but there would have been no glory for them to see if he had not gone there in his glory. But, now, his presence there, in all his majesty and splendour, makes heaven still more glorious. Oh, how I long to see him in his glory! Long to see him, did I say? I would part with all the joys of time and sense to gaze upon him seated upon his throne. Oh! what will it be to see him? You have seen how painters have failed when they have tried to depict him. The bravest artist may well tremble, and the brightest colours fade, when anyone tries to paint him even in his humiliation. There is no other face so marred as his face was; but what will it be in heaven when it is marred no more? No tear in his eye! No spittle running down his cheeks! No giving of his face to them that pluck out the hair; but, oh, the glory of manhood perfected, and allied with Deity! "The King in his beauty!" Why, methinks, to see him but for a minute, if we never saw him again, might furnish us with an eternity of bliss; but we shall gaze upon him, in his glory, day without night, never fainting, or flagging, or tiring, but delighting for ever to behold him smile, for evermore to call him ours, and to see him still before us. He has gone to heaven, then, in his glory; and, surely, that is preparing a place for us!

Besides that, we cannot tell what arrangements had to be made, in order to prepare a place of eternal blessedness for the Lord's redeemed. Certain it is that, in the economy of the universe, everything has its place. Men have discovered, as you know, what they call evolution. They think that one thing grows out of another, because, long before they were born, everybody with half an eye could see that one thing fitted into another; and as one step rises above another step by a beautiful gradation, so do the created things of God. Not that they grow out of each other any more than the stones of a staircase grow out of one another; they rise above each other, but they were so made from the first by the skill and wisdom of God. That a dewdrop should be precisely of the size and shape that it is, is necessary to the perfection of the universe. That there should be insects born in such a month to fertilize the flowers that bloom in that month, and others to suck the sweetness of those flowers, is all necessary. God has arranged everything, from the little to the great, with perfect skill. There is a place for everything with God, and everything in its place. It was a question where to put man. He had a place once. When God created this world, he made a pyramid, and set man upon the very top of it, giving him dominion over all the works of his hands; but then man fell. Now, it is more difficult to restore than it is at first to place. Often and often, you must have found that, when a thing has gone awry, it has cost you more trouble to set it right than if it had to be made *de novo*. Where, then, was the place for man to be? O matchless love, O sacred wisdom, that provided that man's place should be where Christ's place was and is! Lo, he who came down from heaven, and who also was in heaven, has gone back to heaven. He carried manhood with him; and, in so doing, one with him his Church has found her place. His union to the Godhead has found a place for his Church at the right hand of God, even the Father, where Christ sitteth; and all is as it should be.

As I have already told you, I do not know much about this matter; but I should not wonder if there has been going on, ever since Christ went up to heaven, a putting things straight,—getting this race of creatures into its proper place, and that other race, and the other race; so that, when we get to heaven, nobody will say, "You have got my place." Not even Gabriel will say to me, "Why, what business have you here? You have got my place." No, no; you shall have a place of your own, beloved; and all the members of Christ's Church shall find a place prepared which no one else shall be able to claim, for nobody shall be dispossessed or put out of his rightful position.

It struck me, as I turned this subject over in my mind, that *our Lord Jesus Christ knew that there was a place to be prepared for each one of his people*. It may be—I cannot tell,—that, in some part of the society of heaven, one spirit will be happier than it might have been in another part. You know that, even though you love all the brethren, you cannot help feeling most at home with some of them. Our blessed Lord and Master had no sinful favouritism, yet he did love twelve men better than all the rest of his disciples; and out of the twelve he loved three, whom he introduced into mysteries from which he excluded the other nine; and even out of the three, there was one, you know, who was "that disciple whom Jesus loved." Now, everybody here has his likings; I do not know if we shall carry anything of that spirit to heaven. If we do, Christ has so prepared a place for us that you shall be nearest, in your position and occupation, to those who would contribute most to your happiness. You shall be where you can most honour God, and most enjoy God. You would be glad enough to be anywhere,—would you not?—with the very least of the saints in heaven if there be any degrees of glory among their thrones, or at his feet, so long as you might see Christ's face. But, depend upon it, if there be any association—any more intimate connection—between some saints than among others, Jesus Christ will so beautifully arrange it that we shall all be in the happiest places. If you were to give a dinner-party, and you had a number of friends there, you would like to pick the seats for them. You would say, "Now, there is So-and-so, I know that he would like to sit next to So-and-so;" and you would try so to arrange it. Well, in that grand wedding feast above, our Saviour has so prepared a place for us that he will find us each the right position. I was talking, this afternoon, with one whom I very dearly love, and she said to me, "I hope my place in heaven will not be far off yours:" and I replied, "Well, I trust so, too; but we are not married or given in marriage there." Such ties and such relationships must end, as far as they are after the flesh; but we know that there have been bonds of spirit that may still continue. I sometimes think that, if I could have any choice as to those I should live near in heaven, I should like to live in the region of such queer folk as Rowland Hill and John Berridge. I think I should get on best with them, for we could talk together of the way wherein God led us; and of how he brought souls to Christ by us, though some said that we were a deal too merry when we were down below, and that the people laughed when they listened to us, and some spoke as if that were a great sin. We will make them laugh up yonder, I warrant you; as we tell again the wonders of redeeming love, and of the grace of God, their mouths shall be filled with laughter, and their tongues with singing; and then,—

> *"Loudest of the crowd I'll sing.*
> *While heaven's resounding mansions ring*
> *With shouts of sovereign grace;"*

and I expect each of you, who love the Lord, will say the same.

I have no time for the other part of the sermon. You must come again to hear about THE PREPARED PEOPLE. But let me just say this to you,—The place is prepared, are *you* prepared for it? Dost thou believe on the Lord Jesus Christ? If so, your preparation has begun. Dost thou love the Lord, and love his people? If so, thy preparation is going on. Dost thou hate sin, and dost thou pant after holiness? If so, thy preparation is progressing. Art thou nothing at all, and is Jesus Christ thine All-in-all? Then thou art almost ready; and may the Lord keep thee in that condition; and before long, swing up the gates of pearl, and let thee in to the prepared place! May the Lord bring us all safely there, for Jesus' sake! Amen.[116]

C. H. Spurgeon
May 25th, 1879

---

[116] C. H. Spurgeon, *The Metropolitan Tabernacle Pulpit Sermons*, 1901, 47, 517–526.

# APPENDIX C: THE CONVERSION ACCOUNT OF GEORGE MÜLLER IN HIS OWN WORDS

The time was now come when God would have mercy upon me. His love had been set upon such a wretch as I was before the world was made. His love had sent His Son to bear punishment on account of my sins, and to fulfil the law which I had broken times without number. And now at a time when I was as careless about Him as ever, He sent His Spirit into my heart. I had no Bible, and had not read in it for years. I went to church but seldom; but, from custom, I took the Lord's supper twice a year. I had never heard the gospel preached up to the beginning of November, 1825. I had never met with a person who told me that he meant, by the help of God, to live according to the Holy Scriptures. In short, I had not the least idea that there were any persons really different from myself, except in degree.

One Saturday afternoon, about the middle of November, 1825, I had taken a walk with my friend Beta. On our return he said to me that he was in the habit of going on Saturday evenings to the house of a Christian, where there was a meeting. On further enquiry he told me that they read the Bible, sang, prayed, and read a printed sermon. No sooner had I heard this, than it was to me as if I had found something after which I had been seeking all my life long. I immediately wished to go with my friend, who was not at once willing to take me; for knowing me as a gay young man, he thought I should not like this meeting. At last, however, he said he would call for me. I would here mention that, Beta seems to have had conviction of sin, and probably also a degree of acquaintance with the Lord, when about fifteen years old. Afterwards, being in a cold and worldly state, he joined me in that sinful journey to Switzerland. On his return, however, being extremely miserable, and convinced of his guilt, he made a full confession of his sin to his father; and, whilst with him, sought the acquaintance of a Christian brother, named Richter. This Dr. Richter gave him, on his return to the University, a letter of introduction to a believing tradesman, of the name of Wagner. It was this brother in whose house the meeting was held.

We went together in the evening. As I did not know the manners of believers, and the joy they have in seeing poor sinners even in any measure caring about the things of God, I made an apology for coming. The kind answer of this dear brother I shall never forget. He said: "Come as often as you please; house and heart are open to you." We sat down and sang a hymn. Then brother Kayser, afterwards a Missionary in Africa in connection with the London Missionary Society, who was then living at Halle, fell on his knees, and asked a blessing on our meeting. This kneeling down made a deep impression upon me; for I had never either seen any one on his knees, nor had I ever prayed myself on my knees. He then read a chapter and a printed sermon; for no regular meetings for expounding the Scriptures were allowed in Prussia, except an ordained clergyman was present. At the close we sang another hymn, and then the master of the house prayed. Whilst he prayed, my feeling was something like this: I could not pray as well, though I am much more learned than this illiterate man. The whole made a deep impression on me. I was happy; though if I had been asked why I was happy, I could not have clearly explained it.

When we walked home, I said to Beta, "All we have seen on our journey to Switzerland, and all our former pleasures, are as nothing in comparison with this evening." Whether I fell on my knees when I returned home, I do not remember; but this I know, that I lay peaceful and happy in my bed. This shows that the Lord may begin His work in different ways. For I have not the least doubt that on that evening He began a work of grace in me, though I obtained joy without any deep sorrow of heart, and with scarcely any knowledge. That evening was the turning point in my life. The next day, and Monday, and once or twice besides, I went again to the house of this brother, where I read the Scriptures with him and another brother; for it was too long for me to wait till Saturday came again.

Now my life became very different, though all sins were not given up at once. My wicked companions were given up; the going to taverns was entirely discontinued;

the habitual practice of telling falsehoods was no longer indulged in, but still a few times after this I spoke an untruth. At the time when this change took place, I was engaged in translating a novel out of French into German for the press, in order to obtain the means of gratifying my desire to see Paris. This plan about the journey was now given up, though I had not light enough to give up the work in which I was engaged, but finished it. The Lord, however, most remarkably put various obstacles in the way and did not allow me to sell the manuscript. At last, seeing that *the whole* was wrong, I determined never to sell it, and was enabled to abide by this determination. The manuscript was burnt.

I now no longer lived habitually in sin, though I was still often overcome, and sometimes even by open sins, though far less frequently than before, and not without sorrow of heart. I read the Scriptures, prayed often, loved the brethren, went to church from right motives, and stood on the side of Christ, though laughed at by my fellow students.

What all the exhortations and precepts of my father and others could not effect; what all my own resolutions could not bring about, even to renounce a life of sin and profligacy; I was enabled to do, constrained by the love of Jesus. The individual who desires to have his sins forgiven, must seek for it through the blood of Jesus. The individual who desires to get power over sin, must likewise seek it through the blood of Jesus.[117]

George Müller
1825

---

[117] George Müller, *Autobiography of George Müller: A Million and a Half in Answer to Prayer* (London: J. Nisbet and Co., 1914), 9–10.

# APPENDIX D: GOD AS THE CREATOR IN 53 EXPLICIT SCRIPTURES

## The Torah

### Genesis 1:1

In the beginning, God created the Heavens and the Earth.

### Genesis 1:27

So God created man in his own image, in the image of God he created him; male and female he created them.

### Genesis 14:19

And he blessed him and said, "Blessed be Abram by God Most High, Possessor of Heaven and Earth;

### Exodus 20:11

For in six days the LORD made Heaven and Earth, the sea, and all that is in them, and rested on the seventh day. Therefore the LORD blessed the Sabbath day and made it holy.

# The Histories

## 2 kings 19:15

And Hezekiah prayed before the LORD and said: "O LORD, the God of Israel, enthroned above the cherubim, you are the God, you alone, of all the kingdoms of the Earth; you have made Heaven and Earth.

## 1 Chronicles 16:26

For all the gods of the peoples are worthless idols, but the LORD made the Heavens.

## Nehemiah 9:6

"You are the LORD, you alone. You have made Heaven, the Heaven of Heavens, with all their host, the Earth and all that is on it, the seas and all that is in them; and you preserve all of them; and the host of Heaven worships you.

# The Poetry

## Job 9:8

who alone stretched out the Heavens and trampled the waves of the sea;

## Job 37:18

Can you, like him, spread out the skies, hard as a cast metal mirror?

## Job 38:4–7

4 "Where were you when I laid the foundation of the Earth? Tell me, if you have understanding. 5 Who determined its measurements—surely you know! Or who stretched the line upon it? 6 On what were its bases sunk, or who laid its cornerstone, 7 when the morning stars sang together and all the sons of God shouted for joy?

## Psalm 8:3

When I look at your Heavens, the work of your fingers, the moon and the stars, which you have set in place,

## Psalm 33:6

By the word of the LORD the Heavens were made, and by the breath of his mouth all their host.

## Psalm 89:11

The Heavens are yours; the Earth also is yours; the world and all that is in it, you have founded them.

## Psalm 90:2

Before the mountains were brought forth, or ever you had formed the Earth and the world, from everlasting to everlasting you are God.

## Psalm 96:5

For all the gods of the peoples are worthless idols, but the LORD made the Heavens.

## Psalm 102:25

Of old you laid the foundation of the Earth, and the Heavens are the work of your hands.

## Psalm 104:2

covering yourself with light as with a garment, stretching out the Heavens like a tent.

## Psalm 115:15

May you be blessed by the LORD, who made Heaven and Earth!

## Psalm 121:2

My help comes from the LORD, who made Heaven and Earth.

## Psalm 136:5–6

5 to him who by understanding made the Heavens, for his steadfast love endures forever; 6 to him who spread out the Earth above the waters, for his steadfast love endures forever;

## Psalm 146:6

who made Heaven and Earth, the sea, and all that is in them, who keeps faith forever;

## Proverbs 3:19

The LORD by wisdom founded the Earth; by understanding he established the Heavens;

## Proverbs 8:23

Ages ago I was set up, at the first, before the beginning of the Earth.

# The Prophets

## Isaiah 37:16

"O LORD of hosts, God of Israel, enthroned above the cherubim, you are the God, you alone, of all the kingdoms of the Earth; you have made Heaven and Earth.

## Isaiah 40:12–14

12 Who has measured the waters in the hollow of his hand and marked off the Heavens with a span, enclosed the dust of the Earth in a measure and weighed the mountains in scales and the hills in a balance? 13 Who has measured the Spirit of the LORD, or what man shows him his counsel? 14 Whom did he consult, and who made him understand? Who taught him the path of justice, and taught him knowledge, and showed him the way of understanding?

## Isaiah 40:21–22

21 Do you not know? Do you not hear? Has it not been told you from the beginning? Have you not understood from the foundations of the Earth? 22 It is he who sits above the circle of the Earth, and its inhabitants are like grasshoppers; who stretches out the Heavens like a curtain, and spreads them like a tent to dwell in;

## Isaiah 40:28

Have you not known? Have you not heard? The LORD is the everlasting God, the Creator of the ends of the Earth. He does not faint or grow weary; his understanding is unsearchable.

## Isaiah 42:5

Thus says God, the LORD, who created the Heavens and stretched them out, who spread out the Earth and what comes from it, who gives breath to the people on it and spirit to those who walk in it:

## Isaiah 43:7

everyone who is called by my name, whom I created for my glory, whom I formed and made."

## Isaiah 44:24

Thus says the LORD, your Redeemer, who formed you from the womb: "I am the LORD, who made all things, who alone stretched out the Heavens, who spread out the Earth by myself,

## Isaiah 45:12

I made the Earth and created man on it; it was my hands that stretched out the Heavens, and I commanded all their host.

## Isaiah 45:18

For thus says the LORD, who created the Heavens (he is God!), who formed the Earth and made it (he established it; he did not create it empty, he formed it to be inhabited!): "I am the LORD, and there is no other.

## Isaiah 51:13

and have forgotten the LORD, your Maker, who stretched out the Heavens and laid the foundations of the Earth, and you fear continually all the day because of the wrath of the oppressor, when he sets himself to destroy? And where is the wrath of the oppressor?

## Jeremiah 10:12–16

12 It is he who made the Earth by his power, who established the world by his wisdom, and by his understanding stretched out the Heavens. 13 When he utters his voice, there is a tumult of waters in the Heavens, and he makes the mist rise from the ends of the Earth. He makes lightning for the rain, and he brings forth the wind from his storehouses. 14 Every man is stupid and without knowledge; every goldsmith is put to shame by his idols, for his images are false, and there is no breath

in them. 15 They are worthless, a work of delusion; at the time of their punishment they shall perish. 16 Not like these is he who is the portion of Jacob, for he is the one who formed all things, and Israel is the tribe of his inheritance; the LORD of hosts is his name.

## Jeremiah 27:5

"It is I who by my great power and my outstretched arm have made the Earth, with the men and animals that are on the Earth, and I give it to whomever it seems right to me.

## Jeremiah 32:17

'Ah, Lord GOD! It is you who have made the Heavens and the Earth by your great power and by your outstretched arm! Nothing is too hard for you.

## Jeremiah 51:15

"It is he who made the Earth by his power, who established the world by his wisdom, and by his understanding stretched out the Heavens.

## Amos 4:13

For behold, he who forms the mountains and creates the wind, and declares to man what is his thought, who makes the morning darkness, and treads on the heights of the Earth— the LORD, the God of hosts, is his name!

# The Gospels

## John 1:1–3

1 In the beginning was the Word, and the Word was with God, and the Word was God. 2 He was in the beginning with God. 3 All things were made through him, and without him was not any thing made that was made.

# The Histories II

## Acts 4:24

And when they heard it, they lifted their voices together to God and said, "Sovereign Lord, who made the Heaven and the Earth and the sea and everything in them,

## Acts 14:15

"Men, why are you doing these things? We also are men, of like nature with you, and we bring you good news, that you should turn from these vain things to a living God, who made the Heaven and the Earth and the sea and all that is in them.

## Acts 17:24

The God who made the world and everything in it, being Lord of Heaven and Earth, does not live in Temples made by man,

# The Theology

## Romans 1:20

For his invisible attributes, namely, his eternal power and divine nature, have been clearly perceived, ever since the creation of the world, in the things that have been made. So they are without excuse.

## Romans 1:25

because they exchanged the truth about God for a lie and worshiped and served the creature rather than the Creator, who is blessed forever! Amen.

## 1 Corinthians 11:9

Neither was man created for woman, but woman for man.

## Ephesians 3:9

and to bring to light for everyone what is the plan of the mystery hidden for ages in God who created all things,

## Colossians 1:16–17

16 For by him all things were created, in Heaven and on Earth, visible and invisible, whether thrones or dominions or rulers or authorities—all things were created through him and for him. 17 And he is before all things, and in him all things hold together.

## Hebrews 1:2–3

2 but in these last days he has spoken to us by his Son, whom he appointed the heir of all things, through whom also he created the world. 3 He is the radiance of the glory of God and the exact imprint of his nature, and he upholds the universe by the word of his power. After making purification for sins, he sat down at the right hand of the Majesty on high,

## Hebrews 1:8–10

8 But of the Son he says, "Your throne, O God, is forever and ever, the scepter of uprightness is the scepter of your kingdom. 9 You have loved righteousness and hated wickedness; therefore God, your God, has anointed you with the oil of gladness beyond your companions." 10 And, "You, Lord, laid the foundation of the Earth in the beginning, and the Heavens are the work of your hands;

## Hebrews 3:4

(For every house is built by someone, but the builder of all things is God.)

## Hebrews 11:3

By faith we understand that the universe was created by the word of God, so that what is seen was not made out of things that are visible.

# The Apocalypse

## Revelation 4:11

"Worthy are you, our Lord and God, to receive glory and honor and power, for you created all things, and by your will they existed and were created."

## Revelation 10:6

and swore by him who lives forever and ever, who created Heaven and what is in it, the Earth and what is in it, and the sea and what is in it, that there would be no more delay,

# SUGGESTED READING
# AND LINKS

I have found the following resources very useful and commend them to you for your own study. These sites, books, works, and the related authors are in general agreement with our beliefs and positions. Notwithstanding, there may be elements of their teaching we do not completely agree with (but this is unlikely).

## Creation

### Answers in Genesis

This is an excellent ministry and resource focusing on the biblical account of creation as described in the Bible. Ken Ham and others use biblical apologetics and scientific research to defend the Bible from the very first verse. They have extensive free and paid resources, so check them out today.
Web link: https://answersingenesis.org

### The Institute for Creation Research

This is very similar to Answers in Genesis; they also have great free and paid resources. Their contributors include experts like Dr. Jason Lisle.
Web link: http://www.icr.org

## Day One

This is a UK-based ministry. They have a number of excellent books and other resources defending a biblical understanding of creation versus evolution. Many of their books are included in the list of books on creation below.
Web link: https://www.dayone.co.uk

## Various books

R. C. Sproul, *Not a Chance: The Myth of Chance in Modern Science and Cosmology*, electronic ed. (Grand Rapids: Baker Books, 2000).

David K. Dewolf, John G. West, Casey Luskin, and Jonathan Witt, *Traipsing into Evolution: Intelligent Design and the Kitzmiller v. Dover Decision* (Seattle, WA: Center for Science & Culture, 2006).

John MacArthur, *The Battle for the Beginning: The Bible on Creation and the Fall of Adam* (Nashville, TN: W Pub. Group, 2001).

Norman L. Geisler, *Knowing the Truth about Creation: How It Happened and What It Means for Us, Knowing the Truth* (Ann Arbor, MI: Servant Publications, 1989).

R. J. M. Gurney, *Six Day Creation: Does It Matter What You Believe?* (Leominster, UK: Day One Publications, 2007).

Colin Garner, *Creation & Evolution: Why It Matters What You Believe* (Leominster: Day One, 2008).

Ian McNaughton and Paul Taylor, *Darwin and Darwinism 150 Years Later: Biblical Faith and the Christian Worldview* (Leominster: DayOne, 2009).

Philip Snow, *The Design and Origin of Birds* (Leominster, UK: Day One Publications, 2005).

J. H. John Peet, *Does the Bible Require a Belief in "Special Creation"?* (Leominster: DayOne, 2013).

Peter Williams, *From Eden to Egypt: Exploring the Genesis Themes* (Epsom, Surrey: Day One Publishers, 2001).

Dominic Statham, *Evolution: Good Science? Exposing the Ideological Nature of Darwin's Theory* (Leominster: DayOne, 2009).

Andy McIntosh, *Genesis for Today: The Relevance of the Creation/Evolution Debate to Today's Society*, 3rd ed. (Leominster, UK: Day One, 2006).

Edgar C. Powell, *On Giants' Shoulders: Studies in Christian Apologetics* (Epsom, UK: Day One Publications, 1999).

Stuart Burgess, *Hallmarks of Design: Evidence of Purposeful Design and Beauty in Nature*, Rev. ed. (Leominster, UK: Day One Publications, 2002).

Stuart Burgess, *In God's Image: The Divine Origin of Humans* (Leominster: Day One, 2008).

David Harding Pastor, *An Interview with C H Spurgeon: C H Spurgeon on Creation and Evolution* (Leominster, UK: Day One Publications, 2006).

Mark Haville, *Life's Story: The One That Hasn't Been Told* (Leominster, UK: Day One Publications, 2004).

Stuart Burgess, *The Origin of Man: The Image of an Ape or the Image of God?* (Leominster, UK: Day One Publications, 2004).

Stuart Burgess, *He Made the Stars Also: What the Bible Says about the Stars* (Epsom: Day One Publications, 2001).

Peter Jones, *True or False? Thinking Correctly about New Spirituality* (Leominster, UK: Day One Publications, 2007).

Paul Taylor, *Truth, Lies and Science Education* (Leominster, UK: Day One Publications, 2007).

A. J. Monty White, *What about Origins?* (Leominster: Day One, 2010).

# Theology

## Desiring God

Desiring God is the ministry of John Piper. It's an excellent resource for theology in general and more specifically for Christian Hedonism, which states that God is most glorified in us when we are most satisfied in him. John's books have had a profound impact on my life and theology; these include:

John Piper, *Desiring God* (Sisters, OR: Multnomah Publishers, 2003).

John Piper, *Don't Waste Your Life* (Wheaton, IL: Crossway Books, 2003).

John Piper, *Alive to Wonder: Celebrating the Influence of C. S. Lewis* (Minneapolis, MN: Desiring God, 2013).

John Piper, *Bloodlines: Race, Cross, and the Christian* (Wheaton, IL: Crossway, 2011).

John Piper, *Fifty Reasons Why Jesus Came to Die* (Wheaton, IL: Crossway Books, 2006).

John Piper, *Finally Alive: What Happens When We Are Born Again* (Fearn, Ross-shire, Scotland: Christian Focus Publications Ltd., 2009).

John Piper and David Mathis, Eds., *Finish the Mission: Bringing the Gospel to the Unreached and Unengaged* (Wheaton, IL: Crossway, 2012).

John Piper, *Future Grace* (Sisters, OR: Multnomah Publishers, 1995).

John Piper, *God Is the Gospel: Meditations on God's Love as the Gift of Himself* (Wheaton, IL: Crossway Books, 2005).

John Piper, *A Godward Life: Savoring the Supremacy of God in All Life* (Sisters, OR: Multnomah Publishers, 1997).

John Piper, *A Holy Ambition: To Preach Where Christ Has Not Been Named* (Minneapolis, MN: Desiring God, 2011).

John Piper, *Jesus: The Only Way to God* (Grand Rapids, MI: Baker, 2010).

John Piper, *Let the Nations Be Glad! The Supremacy of God in Missions* (Grand Rapids, MI: Baker, 2010).

John Piper, *The Pleasures of God: Meditations on God's Delight in Being God*, Rev. and expanded (Sisters, OR: Multnomah Publishers, 2000).

John Piper, *Risk Is Right: Better to Lose Your Life than to Waste It* (Wheaton, IL: Crossway, 2013).

John Piper, *Seeing and Savoring Jesus Christ* (Wheaton, IL: Crossway Books, 2004).

John Piper, *Tulip* (Wheaton, IL: Crossway, 2009).

John Piper, *What Jesus Demands from the World* (Wheaton, IL: Crossway Books, 2006).

Web Link: http://www.desiringgod.org/

# Ligonier

This is the ministry of Bible teacher R. C. Sproul, a truly excellent Bible teacher who has impacted my own study. Some of his notable books in my experience include:

R. C. Sproul, *The Crucial Questions Series (23 Vols), First edition* (Orlando, FL; Sanford, FL: Reformation Trust; Ligonier Ministries, 2014), 18.

Various Authors, *Tabletalk Magazine, 1989 2016 (300 | Vols)*

R. C. Sproul, *Everyone's a Theologian: An Introduction to Systematic Theology* (Orlando, FL: Reformation Trust, 2014).

R. C. Sproul, *Essential Truths of the Christian Faith* (Wheaton, IL: Tyndale House, 1992).

R. C. Sproul, *Defending Your Faith: An Introduction to Apologetics* (Wheaton, IL: Crossway, 2003).

Thabiti Anyabwile, Alistair Begg, D. A. Carson, Sinclair B. Ferguson, W. Robert Godfrey, Steven J. Lawson, R. C. Sproul, R. C. Sproul Jr., and Derek W. H. Thomas, *Holy, Holy, Holy: Proclaiming the Perfections of God* (Lake Mary, FL: Reformation Trust Publishing, 2010).

Web Link: http://www.ligonier.org/

# The Gospel Coalition

A great resource from a large coalition of evangelical, reformed leaders led by Don Carson and Tim Keller. Notable books in this category include:

D. A. Carson, *The Difficult Doctrine of the Love of God* (Wheaton, IL: Crossway Books, 2000).

T. Desmond Alexander and Brian S. Rosner, Eds., *New dictionary of biblical theology*, 2000.

D. A. Carson, *The Gagging of God: Christianity Confronts Pluralism*, 15th ed. (Grand Rapids, MI: Zondervan, 2011).

Web Link: https://www.thegospelcoalition.org/

## Grace to You

This is a very good verse-by-verse exposition of the entire New Testament from John MacArthur. Notable books include:

John F. MacArthur Jr., *God in the Manger: The Miraculous Birth of Christ* (Nashville, TN: W Pub. Group, 2001).

John F. MacArthur Jr., *The God Who Loves* (Nashville: Thomas Nelson Publishers, 1996).

John F. MacArthur Jr., *Ashamed of the Gospel: When the Church Becomes like the World* (Wheaton, IL: Crossway Books, 1993).

John F. MacArthur Jr., *The Truth War: Fighting for Certainty in an Age of Deception* (Nashville, TN: Thomas Nelson Publishers, 2007).

John MacArthur Jr., *Saved without a Doubt*, MacArthur Study Series (Wheaton, IL: Victor Books, 1992).

John F. MacArthur Jr., *Alone with God*, MacArthur Study Series (Wheaton, IL: Victor Books, 1995).

John F. MacArthur Jr., *Twelve Ordinary Men: How the Master Shaped His Disciples for Greatness, and What He Wants to Do with You* (Nashville, TN: W Pub. Group, 2002).

John MacArthur, *The Fulfilled Family: God's Design for Your Family* (Nashville, TN: T. Nelson Publishers, 2005).

Web Link: http://www.gty.org/

## Tom Wright and others

N. T. Wright's books have been insightful and useful for me as well as a number of other books that are not necessarily part of an overall ministry resource. Here are a few notable ones regarding theology:

Kevin J. Vanhoozer, Craig G. Bartholomew, Daniel J. Treier, and N. T. Wright, Eds., *Dictionary for theological interpretation of the Bible*, 2005.

N. T. Wright, *The New Testament and the People of God*, Christian Origins and the Question of God (London: Society for Promoting Christian Knowledge, 1992).

N. T. Wright, *Evil and the Justice of God* (London: Society for Promoting Christian Knowledge, 2006).

N. T. Wright, *For All the Saints? Remembering the Christian Departed* (London: Society for Promoting Christian Knowledge, 2003).

Tom Wright, *Early Christian Letters for Everyone: James, Peter, John and Judah*, For Everyone Bible Study Guides (London; Louisville, KY: SPCK; Westminster John Knox Press, 2011).

Rose Publishing and Norman L. Geisler, *Essential Doctrine Made Easy* (Torrance, CA: Rose Publishing, 2007).

Rose Publishing, *Four Views of the End Times* (Torrance, CA: Rose Publishing, 2010).

Doug Powell, *Holman QuickSource Guide to Christian Apologetics* (Nashville, TN: Holman Reference, 2006).

## Systematic and Biblical Theologies

There are many systematic theologies; the list below is limited to those I've actually used.

Millard J. Erickson, *Christian Theology*, 3rd ed. (Grand Rapids, MI: Baker Academic, 2013).

Wayne A. Grudem, *Systematic Theology: An Introduction to Biblical Doctrine* (Leicester, England; Grand Rapids, MI: Inter-Varsity Press; Zondervan Pub. House, 2004).

J. I. Packer, *Concise Theology: A Guide to Historic Christian Beliefs* (Wheaton, IL: Tyndale House, 1993).

Michael S. Heiser, *The Unseen Realm: Recovering the Supernatural Worldview of the Bible*, 1st ed. (Bellingham, WA: Lexham Press, 2015).

Carl F. H. Henry, *God, Revelation, and Authority* (Wheaton, IL: Crossway Books, 1999).

Michael F. Bird, *Evangelical Theology: A Biblical and Systematic Introduction* (Grand Rapids, MI: Zondervan, 2013).

Charles Caldwell Ryrie, *Basic Theology: A Popular Systematic Guide to Understanding Biblical Truth* (Chicago, IL: Moody Press, 1999).

L. Berkhof, *Systematic Theology* (Grand Rapids, MI: Wm. B. Eerdmans publishing co., 1938).

Geerhardus Vos, *Reformed Dogmatics*, ed. Richard B. Gaffin (Bellingham, WA: Lexham Press, 2012–2014), 1–3.

Francis J. Hall, *The Being and Attributes of God*, Dogmatic Theology (New York: Longmans, Green, and Co., 1909).

Mark Driscoll and Gerry Breshears, *Doctrine: What Christians Should Believe* (Wheaton, IL: Crossway, 2010).

Joseph Pohle and Arthur Preuss, *God: His Knowability, Essence, and Attributes, A Dogmatic Treatise*, Dogmatic Theology (St. Louis, MO: B. Herder, 1911).

Elizabeth L. Vander Meulen and Barbara D. Malda, *His Names Are Wonderful: Getting to Know God through His Hebrew Names* (Baltimore, MD: Messianic Jewish Publishers, 2005).

# The Bible

## The Bible Project

The Bible project really has some excellent videos; they are short and easy to digest. They specialize in the central themes of the Bible and Bible book overviews. Web Link: https://www.jointheBibleproject.com/

## Faithlife Study Bible

This is a really good free study bible available to anyone with a computer or mobile device from Faithlife, the creators of Logos Bible Software. Web Link: https://faithlifeBible.com/

## Various books

Adele Berlin, Marc Zvi Brettler, and Michael Fishbane, Eds., *The Jewish Study Bible* (New York: Oxford University Press, 2004).

Crossway Bibles, *The ESV Study Bible* (Wheaton, IL: Crossway Bibles, 2008).

D. A. Carson, Ed., *NIV Zondervan Study Bible: Built on the Truth of Scripture and Centered on the Gospel Message* (Grand Rapids, MI: Zondervan, 2015).

Bryan Chapell and Dane Ortlund, Eds., *Gospel Transformation Bible: English Standard Version* (Wheaton, IL: Crossway, 2013).

D. A. Carson, *The King James Version Debate: A Plea for Realism* (Grand Rapids, MI: Baker Book House, 1979).

Wayne Grudem, C. John Collins, Vern S. Poythress, Leland Ryken, Bruce Winter, and J. I. Packer, *Translating Truth* (Wheaton, IL: Crossway, 2005).

# The Gospel

## The Way of the Master

The way of the Master is a TV series and video-based training program by Ray Comfort and Kirk Cameron from Living Waters. It teaches an excellent time-tested method for sharing the good news of the King's victory, kingdom, and offer of salvation to all.

Web Link: http://www.wayofthemaster.com/ also see Living Waters website here for additional resources and even feature films and documentaries by Ray Comfort http://www.livingwaters.com.

## The Gospel

My own church produced a media presentation about the gospel. It is available for free from our website and also comes in DVD format, which includes additional free resources.
Web Link: https://vimeo.com/channels/wwmfgospel

## Various books

Ray Comfort, *The Evidence Bible: Irrefutable Evidence for the Thinking Mind, Notes*, ed. Kirk Cameron, The Way of the Master Evidence Bible (Orlando, FL: Bridge-Logos, 2003).

Ray Comfort, *Scientific Facts in the Bible: 100 Reasons to Believe the Bible Is Supernatural in Origin* (Alachua, FL: Bridge-Logos, 2001).

Ray Comfort and Kirk Cameron, *The Way of the Master: How to Share Your Faith Simply, Effectively, Biblically ... The Way Jesus Did* (Alachua, FL: Bridge-Logos, 2006).

Kirk Cameron and Ray Comfort, *The School of Biblical Evangelism: 101 Lessons: How to Share Your Faith Simply, Effectively, Biblically—the Way Jesus Did* (Gainesville, FL: Bridge-Logos Publishers, 2004).

# Israel

## The Ezra Foundation

The producers of CHOSEN, a film about Christian Advocacy for Israel.
Web Link: http://www.theezrafoundation.com/

## Khouse

The ministry of Chuck Missler, often dealing with Israel and the Middle East.
Web Link: http://www.khouse.org

## Israel Today

A Christian-based news agency focused on Israel.
Web Link: http://www.israeltoday.co.il/

## Various books

David H. Stern, *Restoring the Jewishness of the Gospel*, 1st ed. (Jerusalem, Israel; Gaithersburg, MD: Jewish New Testament Publications; Distributed by Union of Messianic Jewish Congregations, 1988).

# Church

The following three ministries all report on and support persecuted Christians around the world.

## Open Doors

Web Link: http://www.opendoorsuk.org/

## Christian Solidarity Worldwide

Web Link: http://www.csw.org.uk/home.htm

## Barnabus Fund

Web Link: https://barnabasfund.org/

## Various books

Mark Galli and Ted Olsen, *131 Christians everyone should know*, 2000.

J. D. Douglas, Philip Wesley Comfort, and Donald Mitchell, *Who's Who in Christian history*, 1992.

Sharon Rusten with E. Michael, *The Complete Book of When & Where in the Bible and throughout History* (Wheaton, IL: Tyndale House Publishers, Inc., 2005).

*Christian History Magazine-Issue 1: Zinzendorf & the Moravians* (1982).

## Mission

### The Joshua Project

The Joshua Project was mentioned in the book. It is a ministry dedicated to finishing the mission of bringing the gospel to the unreached people groups of the earth and reports on the progress of the Great Commission in these areas.

Web Link: http://joshuaproject.net/index.php

## Apologetics

In Apologetics, consider the works of Ravi Zacharias, J Warner Wallace, and Lee Strobel.

### CARM

A website with questions and answers about Christianity.
Web Link: https://carm.org/

### Got Questions

A similar website to CARM.
Web Link: http://www.gotquestions.org/

### Various books

Doug Powell, *Holman QuickSource Guide to Christian Apologetics* (Nashville, TN: Holman Reference, 2006).

Got Questions Ministries, *Got Questions? Bible Questions Answered* (Bellingham, WA: Logos Bible Software, 2002–2013).

Dan Story, *Christianity on the Offense: Responding to the Beliefs and Assumptions of Spiritual Seekers* (Grand Rapids, MI: Kregel Publications, 1998).

Josh McDowell, *Josh McDowell's Handbook on Apologetics*, electronic ed. (Nashville, TN: Thomas Nelson, 1997).

Ted Cabal, Chad Owen Brand, E. Ray Clendenen, Paul Copan, J. P. Moreland, and Doug Powell, *The Apologetics Study Bible: Real Questions, Straight Answers, Stronger Faith* (Nashville, TN: Holman Bible Publishers, 2007).

# Worldview

## The Briefing

Excellent analysis of the current news from a biblical worldview with Albert Mohler
Web Link: http://www.albertmohler.com/

## Prager University

Excellent short video courses online
Web Link: https://www.prageru.com/

## Various books

C. Stephen Evans, *Pocket dictionary of apologetics & philosophy of religion*, 2002.

Douglas Groothuis, *Christian Apologetics: A Comprehensive Case for Biblical Faith* (Downers Grove, IL; Nottingham, England: IVP Academic; Apollos, 2011).

Greg Laurie, *Worldview: Learning to Think and Live Biblically* (Dana Point, CA: Kerygma Publishing—Allen David Books, 2012).

Francis A. Schaeffer, *The Complete Works of Francis A. Schaeffer: A Christian Worldview* (Westchester, IL: Crossway Books, 1982).

James P. Eckman, *The Truth about Worldviews: A Biblical Understanding of Worldview Alternatives* (Wheaton, IL: Crossway Books, 2004).

Michael W. Goheen and Craig G. Bartholomew, *Living at the Crossroads: An Introduction to Christian Worldview* (Grand Rapids, MI: Baker Academic, 2008).

Patricia A. Ennis, Clyde P. Greer Jr., Grant Horner, John A. Hughes, Taylor B. Jones, John F. MacArthur Jr., R. W. Mackey II, Richard Mayhue, Brian K. Morley, Paul T. Plew, Stuart W. Scott, John P. Stead, John D. Street, and Mark A. Tatlock, *Think Biblically! Recovering a Christian Worldview* (Wheaton, IL: Crossway, 2003).

# BIBLIOGRAPHY

## Images

Images sourced from various contributors on the Pexels® and Unsplash® platforms and are used under the Creative Commons Zero (CC0) license. This means the pictures are completely free to be used for any legal purpose.

Images not from Pexels® or Unsplash® are also used under the Creative Commons Zero (CC0) license or are in the public domain.

## Sources used

All sources can be found in footnotes throughout the book.

## Software

This book would not have been possible without the tools and resources made available through Logos Bible Software from the Faithlife Corporation.

# THANKS AND ACKNOWLEDGMENTS

*And let the peace of Christ rule in your hearts, to which indeed you were called in one body. And be thankful.*

—*Colossians 3:15*

*I* want to begin by thanking God for his holy love. Thank you, Lord, for all the mercy and grace you have shown to me throughout my life, for the many blessings that are simply innumerable. Thank you for choosing me and saving me.

Jesus, thank you for coming to save us, living for us, dying for us, rising for us, ascending for us, and promising that you will come back for us. Thank you for making our salvation sure. You are our King.

Holy Spirit, thank you for giving us the Bible, for making me alive in Christ, for the church, and for the gifts you bestow. Thank you for your daily guidance. Thank you for the fruit of you living in and through me and for helping me grow in Christ and sanctification. Thank you especially for the strength and wisdom you have provided to write this book.

*I thank my God in all my remembrance of you ... (Philippians 1:3)*

I want to thank my wife, Michelle—for all the support you have shown for this project and for just being a blessing to me by putting up with me for ten years and counting.

Thanks to Hope and Josh—for jumping all over me while I was writing on the sofa ... really helpful, guys, seriously, I love you both.

I want to thank Pastor Dennis—for all your support, teaching, training, and discipleship over the years. I would not be who I am today without your example to look up to and learn from, so thank you for not compromising the truth and for loving God and his Word. Also, thank you for giving me your blessing to write this book and helping me to develop as a teacher by giving me opportunities to use that gift and calling.

Thank you, Rev. Taylor. You have been a constant encouragement and inspiration to me. Like Pastor Dennis, thank you for the example and service of your life for us. I want to take a moment to thank you for taking time to read through the early manuscript of this book and for the support you have been to my teaching ministry by asking me to conduct Bible study courses for our church; some of the content of those courses has even been included in this book.

I want to especially thank Sarah Greenidge—after I shared with the church about starting to write this book in March 2015, your immediate encouraging email and desire to take this further with a film were a real blessing to me. Thank you for also reading an earlier copy of the book and providing valuable feedback about using personal stories and hooks.

Michael Hosannah—thanks for being a real friend and brother and especially for your prayers for this project. Thank you for the graphics and typography work you produced for me too for the cover mock-up.

Amara Sesay—thanks for your friendship and encouragement, especially for always asking, "How's the book going?"

Thank you to my mum, Dawn Williams, for all your love and prayers. Thanks to my sister, Cheryl Clarke, and my brothers, Clyde Khani and Chris Scott, and your families for all your support. I especially want to thank Clyde for being the first person to read through the early copy of the book and for the encouragement you shared after reading it.

To my youngest brother, Christian Scott—I'm praying that one day soon you will be well.

To Dad, Glen Scott—I'm praying that one day your eyes will be opened to know the Lord too.

Thanks to all my brothers and sisters at our home church, Worldwide Mission Fellowship, for your prayers, fellowship, encouragement, and service.

I want to especially thank my official copy editor and line editor, Paige Duke, who did an excellent job trimming the text, fixing my many punctuation, reference and structural errors. This book would not be what it is without her expertise and dedication. Thank you, Paige.

I also want to thank the team at Westbow Press, a division of Zondervan and Thomas Nelson for all their efforts to help me get this volume published.

Thanks to friends and family who have supported this project in so many ways. Thank you to all those who have proofread the manuscript and given feedback and reviews. I appreciate you all.

> *We give thanks to God always for all of you, constantly mentioning you in our prayers, remembering before our God and Father your work of faith and labor of love and steadfastness of hope in our Lord Jesus Christ. (1 Thessalonians 1:2–3)*

# ABOUT THE AUTHOR

C. J. Scott is an ordained Minister at Worldwide Mission Fellowship (WWMF) in London. He has worked in ministry at WWMF for over 17 years, involved in media ministry, youth work, evangelism, missions and outreach. However, he's area of expertise is in biblical teaching and training for the body of Christ, springing from a God given gift, his passion for the truth of God's word and experience as a technical consultant and trainer in the business world.

He writes for Worldwide Mission Fellowship at wwmf.org, blogs at placemakers. blog and is the founder and main writer for Humble Majesty at humblemajesty.com. He is the author and producer of the widely-distributed media tract "The Gospel" and has written and delivered numinous courses for WWMF including "Hold and Advance" and "Total Truth".

He lives in the south of England with his wife Michelle and their two children, Hope and Joshua.

Printed in the United States
By Bookmasters

Printed in the United States
By Bookmasters